Collaborative Innovation

With the development of an aging society and the increased importance of emergency risk management in recent years, a large number of medical care challenges—advancing medical treatments, care and support, pharmacological treatments, greater health awareness, emergency treatments, telemedical treatment and care, the introduction of electronic charts and rising costs—are emerging as social issues throughout the whole world. Hospitals and other medical institutions must develop and maintain superior management to achieve systems that can provide better medical care, welfare and health while enabling "support innovation." Key medical care, welfare and health industries play a crucial role in this, but also of importance are the management innovation models that enable "collaborative innovation" by closely linking diverse fields such as ICT, energy, electric equipment, machinery and transport.

Looking across different industries, *Collaborative Innovation* offers new knowledge and insights on the extraordinary value and increasing necessity of collaboration across different organizations in improving the health and lives of people. It breaks new ground with its research theme of building "health support ecosystems," which focus on protecting people through collaborative innovation. This book opens up new, wide-ranging interdisciplinary academic research domains that combine the humanities with science across various areas, including general business administration, economics, information technology, medical informatics and drug information science.

Mitsuru Kodama is Professor of Innovation and Technology Management at the College of Commerce and the Graduate School of Business Administration at Nihon University.

Routledge Studies in Innovation, Organization and Technology

For a full list of titles in this series, please visit www.routledge.com

Collaborative Innovation

Developing Health Support Ecosystems

Edited by
Mitsuru Kodama

LONDON AND NEW YORK

First published 2015
by Routledge

2 Park Square, Milton Park, Abingdon, Oxfordshire OX14 4RN
711 Third Avenue, New York, NY 10017

*Routledge is an imprint of the Taylor & Francis Group,
an informa business*

First issued in paperback 2018

Library of Congress Cataloging-in-Publication Data
Collaborative innovation : developing health support ecosystems /
    edited by Mitsuru Kodama.
        pages cm
    Includes bibliographical references and index.
    1. Medical care—Technological innovations.   2. Medical technology—
Management.   3. Medical technology—Economic aspects.   I. Kodama,
Mitsuru, 1957–
    R855.3.C65 2015
    610.285—dc23   2015007356

ISBN: 978-1-138-78999-9 (hbk)
ISBN: 978-1-138-61692-9 (pbk)

Typeset in Sabon
by ApexCoVantage, LLC

Contents

PART I
Review of Previous Studies and a New Theoretical Framework

PART II
In-Depth Case Studies

PART III
Results and Discussion

Tables

Figures

Acknowledgements

I would like to express my sincerest gratitude for the guidance and support I have received in writing this book.

Firstly, I would like to thank all the people who gave their time in interviews and who sent the materials I received to present the case studies described in this book.

I would like to extend my gratitude to NTT DOCOMO Chief Strategic Advisor (former President and CEO) Ryuji Yamada, President and CEO Kaoru Kato, Senior Executive Vice President Kazuhiro Yoshizawa and Executive Vice President Hiroyasu Asami for the financial support I received for this research. I would also like to express my gratitude for the Nihon University Multidisciplinary Research Grant (2013–2014) and the University's College of Commerce.

I and Toshiro Takahashi (one of the contributors) would also like to express our gratitude to Dr. Graham D. Sher, Chief Executive Officer, Canadian Blood Services.

Lastly, I would like to express my deepest thanks to Ms. Laura Stearns, Publisher, and Mr. David Varley, Commissioning Editor, and Ms. Manjula Raman, Ms. Lauren-Marie Verity, and Ms. Jabari LeGendre, Editorial Assistants of Routledge, for all of their support and efforts.

Mitsuru Kodama

Preface

In recent years, with continued ageing of populations and increased needs for emergency risk management, societies around the world must deal with a wide range of healthcare issues such more sophisticated and advanced healthcare, nursing support, pharmaceutical treatments, health awareness campaigns, healthcare in emergencies and disasters, remote healthcare, remote nursing, the implementation of electronic medical records, increased healthcare costs and so forth. In addition, societies, in particular their hospitals, must urgently develop and maintain better business in their healthcare institutions to achieve social systems that can provide superior medical, welfare and healthcare services to provide protection to people. Moreover in recent years, to achieve these health support innovations focused on protecting people, not only is it critical for the medical, welfare and healthcare industries play the central roles in their respective fields, but it is also important to create management innovation models to organically link up a wide range of fields such as the ICT, energy, electrical equipment, machine and distribution industries through collaborative innovation.

Different technologies including ICT have been merged to create new product and technological developments and achieve business models and innovations based on new rules that span dissimilar industries. Behind these developments lies the economic and societal phenomenon of "convergence"—a phenomenon that has brought a new layer of complexity to the older, simpler style of competition between organizations, companies and industries.

For organizations and companies, not only does convergence encourage linking between a variety of specializations and enterprises within a corporation and its subsidiaries or group companies, but it also rapidly accelerates strategic alliances and M&As between organizations, companies and industries including customers, and has triggered massive transformations in existing organizational and corporate boundaries. Thus, there is increasing importance on collaborative innovation as corporate management innovation models by linking between dissimilar business types that enable transcendence of business beyond the more simplistic competition between businesses in competitive marketplaces.

This book extracts a theoretical framework for business models for the successful configuration of health support ecosystems through collaborative innovation, and presents research and managerial implications, as well as new practical implications for industry.

The first objective of this book is to present the new concept of health support ecosystems as social and economic platforms to achieve health support innovations focused on protecting people, and study these both theoretically and empirically. The second objective of this book is to present a new management innovation model related to the collaborative innovation indispensable to building health support ecosystems, and analyze both theoretically and empirically the mechanisms and processes of collaborative innovation across different global industries that drives health support innovations in the medical, healthcare and welfare fields.

As well as research questions, this book is significant for its presentation of academic and practical implications merging social sciences, medicine, informatics and ICT shared deeply by researchers in different backgrounds (in particular management studies, ICT, medicine, medical informatics, pharmacy) in terms of the dissimilar fields of business and a management, medical informatics and ICT etc. In addition, these health support ecosystems are of major significance scholastically because they pioneer new academic research territory that fuses the humanities and science. Thus, this also means this work is a case of "convergence" in the academic world.

CIRCUMSTANCES LEADING TO THE WRITING OF THIS BOOK

In promoting collaborative innovation through convergence, not only do companies require closed innovation that integrates wide-ranging knowledge across different organizations and specialties within themselves, but also in recent years has seen increased importance on management that can globally configure knowledge networks connecting leading organizations and partner companies. Therefore, the most challenging issues facing corporations (organizations) are the execution of "open innovation" (Chesbrough, 2003) and "hybrid innovation" (Kodama, 2011) that integrate knowledge scattered across the world with the knowledge within companies (or within organizations).

For example, while medical institutions such as hospitals aim for greater efficiency in business, they also must question how to innovate management of their organizations to substantively improve customer services. In other words this does not just mean driving business improvements and managerial transformations to achieve higher quality medical services, but also points to the importance of innovations that enable sustained learning and growth further into the future. While hospitals must share knowledge within themselves—skills and know-how held by organizations and individuals—there is also great importance on configuring superior management innovation models through collaborative innovation between medical institutions such as hospitals, medical equipment and pharmaceutical manufacturers and ICT companies.

Management innovation models enabled by collaborative innovation lead to the development of new treatment methods, improvements to a wide range of healthcare supports, and better quality healthcare and customer service. An important factor in organizational learning and growth to achieve health support innovations for future growth is the acquisition of corporate or organizational "strategic innovation capability" (discussed in detail in this book) needed to achieve strategic objectives and targets in the financial, customer and business processes perspectives of balanced score card (BSC).

However, academic research has not clarified many of the aspects of the management innovation model in terms of micro strategic processes or organizational mechanisms to handle this collaborative innovation.

All global industries (not only medical, nursing, welfare, and pharmaceuticals, but also all other high-tech industries such as ICT) are faced with a wide range of practical questions such as: How does an organization or company achieve a health support innovation working with its customers as stakeholders? How should a company set its corporate and industrial boundaries in convergence environments, and how should these boundaries be changed dynamically to achieve health support innovations as new business territories? What strategic and organizational action should companies take on these dynamically changing corporate boundaries? What form should a comprehensive management innovation model including the leadership and management required for these processes take for?

From the theoretical and practical research undertaken in the global field (North America, Europe, Asia), the authors of this book derived diverse empirical data and a new theoretical framework for management innovation models made possible through collaborative innovation as an important factor in the achievement of health support innovations to configure health support ecosystems triggered by convergence within companies (organizations), between companies (organizations) and between industries.

Based on the research findings of the authors of this book, researchers operating in different fields of specialty, this book opens up the new research theme of the construction of health support ecosystems through health support innovations that focus on protecting human beings.

Mitsuru Kodama

REFERENCES

Chesbrough, H. (2003). *Open Innovation*. Boston, MA: Harvard Business School Press.
Kodama, M. (2011). *Interactive Business Communities-Accelerating Corporate Innovation through Boundary Networks*. UK: Gower Publishing.

Part I

Review of Previous Studies and a New Theoretical Framework

1 Health Support Ecosystems and Innovation Management

Mitsuru Kodama

Integrating knowledge between different areas of specialization has become a major challenge in the field of innovation and technology management (e.g., Curran and Leker, 2011; Kodama, 2011a). Furthermore, technological convergence between different specializations has become a major factor in bringing about radical innovation (e.g., Kodama, 2007a). New business models and markets are being formed with fusions of mixed specializations, creating new areas such as e-business, microelectronics, mechatronics and nano-biotechnology (e.g., Kodama, 2007a, 2011b). While simultaneously spawning new industries through radical and breakthrough innovations, technological convergence has been linked to the destruction of corporate and organizational capability, the traditional lifelines of corporate growth, as well as the destruction of existing technologies and industries (e.g., Christensen, 1997).

Knowledge integration has become crucial for successful new innovations across different areas of specialization (Klein, 1990; Kodama, 2005, 2009a, 2011a; Lei, 2000; Porter, Roessner, Cohen, and Perreault, 2006). As a new innovation, technological convergence can be thought of as occurring through the knowledge convergence process, in which specialist knowledge is brought together and overlaid (e.g., Hacklin, Marxt, and Fahrni, 2009; Kodama, 2014; Rafols and Meyer, 2010) at a level spanning different areas of expertise (Kodama, 2014). Thus, as a prerequisite, technological convergence entails bringing together knowledge that formally belongs to separate areas of technical specialization—integrating knowledge across dissimilar technical specialties is needed to bring about technological convergence.

This chapter describes how convergence has accelerated collaborative innovation between people, organizations, companies and industries, and has brought about new business ecosystems. The chapter identifies the 'creativity view' and the 'dialectic view'—important factors accelerating collaborative innovation—as 'boundary conceptions' held by stakeholders. Then, the chapter describes the new concept of a "health support ecosystem" through a number of empirical case studies done to date, illustrating the formation of innovation communities that engage in collaborative innovation in the remote healthcare and healthcare information businesses.

1.1 CONVERGENCE ACCELERATING COLLABORATIVE INNOVATION

Convergence is a technical and industrial phenomenon that lies behind the recent advances in information and communication technology (ICT) and the accompanying creation of new business models[1]. According to existing research, technological convergence has been described as the mixing of technical knowledge across clearly definable areas of specialization, in the context of ICT particularly (Duysters and Hagedoorn, 1998; Lee, Olson, and Trimi, 2012; Pennings and Puranam, 2001; Rosenberg, 1976). Technological convergence has caused traditional knowledge in various industries and specializations to become obsolete, and has driven incremental and radical innovation through learning and innovation activities in groups and organizations—not just through the activities of individuals themselves (e.g., Kodama, 2011b). Furthermore, convergence between dissimilar technological elements has driven the formation of company and organization networks, and mergers and acquisitions through strategic alliances formed between different corporations, and between different business classes and industries (e.g., Hacklin, 2008; Harianto and Penning, 1994; Kodama, 2009a, 2009b)[2].

Thus, as an innovation process, convergence has led to new insights and implications for knowledge creation theory (Nonaka and Takeuchi, 1995) and innovation management (e.g., Borés, Saurina, and Torres, 2003; de Boer, van den Bosch, and Volberda, 1999; Goktan and Miles, 2011; Harianto and Pennings, 1994; Kodama, 1992; Patel and Pavitt, 1994; Pennings and Puranam, 2001; Prahalad and Krishnan, 2008; von Hippel, 1994). As seen in the ICT industry, causing technological convergence across entire industries (D'Aveni, Dagnino, and Smith, 2010; Hacklin, Marxt, and Fahrni, 2010; Kodama, 2014; Zhang and Li, 2010) also causes the formation of business ecosystems in new business environments and markets in which many companies are involved (e.g., Ghoshal and Bartlett, 1994; Kodama, 2009a).

As discussed in this book, the convergence of the ICT industry with the healthcare, welfare, insurance and pharmaceutical industries has brought about the new business models of remote treatment, remote care, remote health management and so forth, collectively called "health support innovations."

Health institutions involve themselves with other health institutions, and through collaborative innovation with medical equipment manufacturers, pharmaceutical manufacturers and ICT companies, the setting up and development of management innovation models have led to the development of better performing and new methods of healthcare and health support—better quality medical treatment, and better quality customer and patient services.

1.2 WHY IS CONVERGENCE IMPORTANT?

From the point of view of corporate growth, cleverly combining highly original and new knowledge with products, services and business models enables the creation of new markets, and raises the potential for enhanced business performance (Grant, 1996b; Kodama, 2011b; Nesta and Saviotti, 2006).

With their i-mode and iPhone ventures, NTT DOCOMO and Apple are examples of companies that have mastered the capabilities necessary to integrate the Internet, mobile communications and diverse software technologies, and have brought about new value chains and networks to bring even greater value to existing products and services (Kodama, 2002, 2011b).

Although already identified in existing research, integrating knowledge that is separated by substantive boundaries, or in other words, bringing together technical knowledge that has little or no relationship with known knowledge—combining knowledge from isolated technical areas—creates greater potential to bring about new and innovative achievements than exploiting more closely knit or path-dependent knowledge (Fleming and Sorenson, 2004; Hill, 2008; Katila and Ahuja, 2002; Kodama, 2007b, 2011a, 2014; Rodan and Galunic, 2004; Zahra, 2008). However, fusing knowledge isolated by boundaries is an extremely challenging problem and is fraught with difficulties involving personnel, capital and risks, as well as the challenge of managing the required innovation processes (Grant, 1996a; Kodama, 2011a; Kodama and Shibata, 2014).

In spite of these difficulties, recent years have seen increasing demands to merge isolated knowledge across boundaries, and in actual fact, beginning with ICT, integrating knowledge separated by boundaries (Hacklin et al., 2009; Kodama, 2011a; Zahra, 2008) has spawned new technological fields (de Boer et al., 1999; Gambardella and Torrisi, 1998), and has seen the arrival of nano-biotechnology (Roco, 2003; Shmulewitz, Langer, and Patton, 2006), mobile Internet using mobile phones (Kodama, 2002) and application and contents businesses with smartphones (Kodama, 2011b). Merging knowledge across boundaries has become indispensable to acquire competitiveness, as convergence also raises the capabilities of individuals and organizations working across boundaries between different specializations (Carlile, 2004; Kodama, 2007a, 2007b, 2007d).

However, there has not been much research in this field, despite the dramatic impacts convergence is having on the knowledge of individuals, on the organizational capabilities of companies and on entire industries. Nevertheless, in recent years, the field of innovation and technology management has arrived at the conclusion that new management innovation models to tackle these kinds of interdisciplinary challenges are required.

1.3 FORMING HEALTH SUPPORT ECOSYSTEMS THROUGH COLLABORATIVE INNOVATION

The convergence of the healthcare, nursing, insurance and pharmaceutical industries with the ICT industry[3] has brought about "health support innovation"—developments involving new business processes and business models that include remote healthcare (telemedicine), remote nursing, remote health management (telehealthcare), health data management, the dispersed development of new pharmaceuticals and information support for pharmaceutical treatment. In other words, modern corporations must quickly move away from business strategies that focus on competitiveness between companies within certain areas of business or industries, or between different business classes, and engage in collaborative innovation across a wide range of business types, business functions and industries.

Existing research (e.g., Haefliger, 2012) interprets collaborative innovation as "a development process of new and useful products [that] includes the study of user innovation, because innovations made by users can also be beneficial regardless of commercialization and market success (von Hippel, 1988). This definition focuses on activities over time rather than on states and transactions. Here, collaborative innovation refers to creation and development processes involving multiple actors and stakeholders inside and outside of companies, who collaborate for the specific purpose of generating ideas, concepts, technologies and solutions for business, or for their own use. The market for technology is moved out of focus (Arora, Fosfuri, and Gambardella, 2001), along with the similar concept of open innovation (Chesbrough, 2003), because while trading licenses and patents enable innovation inside and outside of companies, the process of generating and developing ideas is frequently excluded from, or assumed and unstated in the literature (Haefliger, 2012, p. 2)."

However, collaborative innovation as cited by Haefliger (2012, p. 2) does not only include the "collaborative innovation is defined here as a development process of new and useful products and services across and outside company boundaries" aspect, but in the broader sense, also includes collaborative innovation that transcends the boundaries across a range of organizations and areas of specialization within companies. Thus, in a wider meaning, new product and service developments carried out across different departments within a company through the acquisition of external technical licensing using open innovation are also considered to be (or are defined as) collaborative innovation in this book.

Put differently, collaborative innovation involves innovation processes through the formation of "innovation networks" (Kodama, 2009b) across a range of specialties, business classes and functions, enterprises and industrial fields of expertise within and between companies (or organizations), between industries and between companies (organizations) and their customers. Thus, from the perspective of flows sharing, exploitation and the development of diverse knowledge, including intellectual assets, collaborative innovation involves knowledge activities that have been frequently observed in corporations (organizations), not only as the conventional "closed innovation" (Pattern A), in which innovation is constrained within a company, but also as the "open innovation" (Pattern C) phenomenon that has been garnering attention in recent years, and as the ' "hybrid innovation'" (Pattern B) (Kodama, 2011b), a mixture of both the closed and open types (see Figure 1.1). These wide-ranging innovation networks (or knowledge networks) (company-internal knowledge networks or external knowledge networks) enable the convergence (integration) of diverse knowledge through collaborative innovation both inside and outside of companies, and include customers to enable the creation of new knowledge. Accordingly, from the perspective of organizations and strategy, academic research into the micro-level processes involved in the instigation, maintenance and development of collaborative innovation has become an important issue.

Collaboration is a creative activity undertaken by people to create and integrate knowledge. It has been interpreted in the existing research as described below, and has been studied in a wide variety of literature.

Gray (1989), who is often credited with formally launching the collaboration theory, defines inter-organizational collaboration as "a process through which parties who see different aspects of a problem can constructively explore their differences and search for solutions beyond their own limited visions of what is possible." Learning and innovation literature (Anand and Khanna, 2000; Kale, Singh, and Perlmutter, 2000; Larsson, Bengtsson, Henriksson, and Sparks, 1998) emphasizes that collaboration can facilitate the creation of new knowledge, not only the transfer of existing knowledge (Gulati, 1999; Powell, Koput, and Smith-Doerr, 1996). Collaboration also

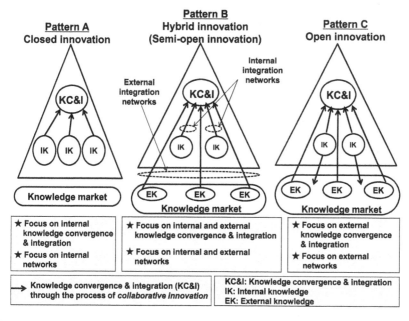

Figure 1.1   Innovation Systems

might function as a strategic tool for gaining efficiency and flexibility in rapidly changing environments (Westley and Vredenburg, 1991).

Thus, collaboration theory, which builds on empirical and theoretical perspectives from a variety of research streams, including resource dependence, learning and strategic management, etc. (Gray and Wood, 1991; Wood and Gray, 1991), is useful for the analysis of interpersonal, inter-group and inter-organizational levels within "Ba" (shared contexts in motion) (Kodama, 2005; Nonaka and Takeuchi, 1995), or of strategic communities (Kodama, 2002) such as the partnering relationships described below (Cases 1–3).

For example, collaborative innovation involving convergence with ICT in the fields of medical care, welfare and health has been accelerating rapidly— a phenomenon observed in the following cases (see Cases 1 and 2 below).

CASE 1 *COLLABORATIVE INNOVATION BETWEEN US CISCO SYSTEMS AND HOSPITALS—DEVELOPMENT OF NEW TELEMEDICINE SYSTEMS*

The US company Cisco Systems is making it possible for patients to contact doctors using methods that have never existed before, and to receive diagnoses via an advanced telemedical technology platform. Most existing telemedical approaches have focused on physical access to a medical examination, but as well as this issue, Cisco has addressed the following four important aspects of medical care: (1) Availability of diagnostic skills (insufficient specialists and productivity), (2) collaboration (between one patient and multiple doctors, or between multiple medical facilities and patients, etc.), (3) information exchange (the ability of participants to share and display important medical information), and (4) personalization (involving the patient more actively in his or her examination). Using high-quality video and audio and connections to medical equipment, Cisco has also enabled support for collaboration between doctors, and has enabled a level of patient-centered personalization that was barely possible even with face-to-face consultations.

This innovative telemedical platform has been made possible through trial-and-error experiments and prototyping at medical facilities by combining diverse knowledge, including Cisco's knowledge of ICT and medical facilities' knowledge of user interface technologies and operations. Thus, collaborative innovation through close links between Cisco and medical facilities has enabled convergence between ICT and the diagnostic skills of doctors.

As an innovation process, collaborative innovation is completely different from the ordinary outsourcing used to issue or accept systems development tasks. Essentially, it involves a unique context in a dynamic time and space— in this case, doctors take up the standpoint of the ICT developer, while the ICT developer takes up the standpoints of doctors to build mutual awareness, make judgments and implement the systems. In other words, it is important to create a "Ba" (a shared context in motion) to support collaborative innovation (Kodama, 2005; Nonaka & Takeuchi, 1995). "Ba" refers to a mutual immersion process involving the environment, organizations and individuals in time and space. Both the doctors and the ICT developer holistically accept the subjective views of others to mutually empathize, share and resonate, and the "Ba" forms through this social interaction. Transcending individuals, such inter-subjectivity in the relationships among "Ba" participants is essential to making collaborative innovation a success.

CASE 2 COLLABORATIVE INNOVATION BETWEEN JIKEI UNIVERSITY AND FUJIFILM—DEVELOPING A NEW MEDICAL CARE INFORMATION SYSTEM

Medical care support that utilizes smartphones and tablets, such as the iPhone, iPad and Android devices, has been drawing attention at medical facilities and care centers in recent years. In July 2010, the Jikei University of Japan and Fujifilm, which has been assisting with the development of ICT solutions, engaged in the joint development of a system to "save as many lives as possible," and in June 2011, made the system commercially available. The system features a new function that allows patient images or EKGs to be checked from outside the hospital, and thus enables broad support for emergency medical care. The system enables remote image diagnosis, and thus supports emergency treatment for stroke victims via a smartphone.

Transmitting a stroke patient's examination images and diagnostic information from the hospital where the patient was admitted to an external specialist also enables the specialist to efficiently communicate the information necessary for treatment to the hospital, thus enabling the hospital to diagnose and treat the patient. This system is extremely useful in emergency medical situations where the speed and appropriateness of stroke victim treatment greatly influence the chances of survival.

The system of patient admission and the speed and accuracy of diagnoses are vital to the treatment of stroke victims. Thus, in developing a new telediagnosis and treatment support system, the project built a new medical information system that enables quick access to patient information at any location, both inside and outside the hospital, to enable prompt acquisition of diagnoses and opinions from a range of specialists.

This system differs from existing remote image diagnosis systems, as it has important team treatment functions for stroke victims that enable all involved to share the information and respond quickly. In this way, smartphone and tablet-based ICT is providing efficient and broad emergency medical support at facilities around the world, is improving the quality of medical care and is contributing to general health maintenance.

While the development of this system was a pioneering effort on a worldwide scale, close mutual learning across different specialized fields and growth was needed by both doctors (the customers) and technicians on the development side. In this development process, a close community of doctors and developers that transcended the customer-led innovation processes of existing user innovation was formed. Doctors and developers became involved with each other, broke out of their shells, and through deep dialogue and discussion, mutually made great leaps forward to develop ideas and build new product concepts. As in Case 1, collaborative innovation through the formation of a dynamic "Ba" within a close community was essential for the success of this project.

As shown in the two cases, collaborative innovation aimed at the convergence of ICT with medicine, welfare and health is currently growing on a global level—the importance of health support innovation strategies to support this sort of convergence is growing each year. This convergence is not only a result of merging the ICT industry with the medical, welfare and health industries, but also springs from a whole range of high-tech industries, including pharmaceuticals, electronics, machinery, automobiles, chemicals and materials. Thus, a management innovation model based on collaborative innovation—the theme of this book—is the appropriate corporate and organizational management model for convergence.

In recent years, many countries have been promoting welfare and care information sharing networks that utilize smartphones and tablets. In countries such as the US, Canada, Sweden, Germany, Italy, France, the United Kingdom, Korea and Japan, exchanges including care advice for local residents, counseling, care consultations, information exchanges within communities (between helpers, volunteers and caregivers, etc.) and bulletin boards on the Internet have become more common—ways of using mobile information terminals have expanded across a wide range of areas. Applications have been growing rapidly in such areas as communications support, psychological and motivational support, support for social participation and support for the handicapped, as well as operational support for aged, health and medical care.

Using mobile information terminals such as smartphones and tablets starts with building networks for specific functions. These include welfare, education, industrial and administrative networks, and activity on these various networks has been growing. Conceivably then, infrastructures could be built to provide local information communication platforms based on the new cloud computing brought about by the merging and integration of these function-based networks. In advanced countries where ICT infrastructures such as broadband and wireless communications have developed, mobile information terminals and cloud computing have stimulated the creation of new and localized social communities.

These sorts of mobile information terminals, and cloud computing infrastructures in particular, are currently becoming the most important ICT platforms for smoothly driving essential health support cycles in medical care, welfare and health, which includes home medical care, care welfare, support for various types of social activities, health building and health promotion. These platforms represent one model of health support innovation, thus forming the basis for these new approaches to protecting people, which we call a "health support ecosystem" in this book (see Figure 1.2).

The building of health support ecosystems is also linked to the promotion of real telemedical care taking place around the world. The benefits anticipated from these developments include telediagnosis systems covering general hospital and home care medical services, such as telemedicine, home-visit nursing, guidance on taking medicines, medicine delivery, home monitoring equipment, guidance on operating home medical care equipment, links with medical institutions, provision of information on medical institutions and introductions to hospital admission. This is the building of overarching care and welfare systems to provide support and guidance on care and welfare services, advice, safety and security, emergency response if bodily functions falter and health insurance support, and is the building of health support systems to promote and manage health, to provide health consultancies and support preventive medicine. These systems form the core of the health support ecosystem, while the management innovation model for building these health support ecosystems is a critical issue facing stakeholders such as organizations, enterprises and local and national

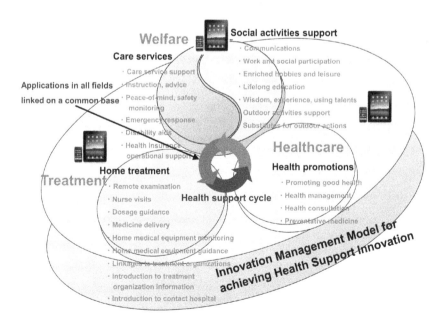

Figure 1.2 Health Support Ecosystem

governments. We believe that building this health support ecosystem will not only reduce the number of patients worldwide, but also will contribute to promoting preventive medicine and reduce the overall costs of medical care.

1.4 NEW BOUNDARY CONCEPTIONS FOR ESTABLISHING HEALTH SUPPORT ECOSYSTEMS

Health support ecosystems were established in the case studies above through collaborative innovation between a wide range of players and stakeholders. What strategic thinking and managerial elements do stakeholders need to achieve collaborative innovation and hence, health support ecosystems? In this section, as a new core concept for the achievement of collaborative innovation, we would like to describe "boundary conceptions"—strategic concepts understood by a wide range of stakeholders (people, organizations, companies, etc.). Here, boundary conceptions are based on rich data obtained through interviews with a wide range of stakeholders deeply committed to and participating in the establishment of health support ecosystems, such as the hospital organizations involved, healthcare institutions, IT businesses, government and administrative bodies, etc.

1.4.1 A New Research Agenda

From the analysis of a number of case studies, we offer the following two new insights into health support ecosystems as a knowledge convergence model (or knowledge integration model) (Kodama, 2011a, 2014). In short, we offer these insights regarding new knowledge creation (knowledge integration) to achieve value chain models that include new products, services and business models, and co-evolution models through new win-win business models, in which dynamic change in corporate (organizational) boundaries (vertical and horizontal boundaries) through collaborative innovation serves to integrate dissimilar knowledge between individuals, and dissimilar knowledge inside and outside of organizations and companies.

Specifically, these can be expressed as follows:

[Insight 1]

The value chain model arising from collaborative innovation promotes the creation of competitive new products and services, as well as innovative business models.

[Insight 2]

The co-evolution model through collaborative innovation spanning various industries promotes the creation of win-win business models.

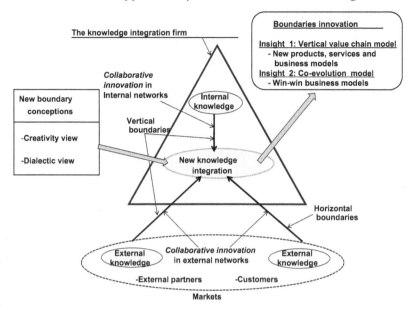

Figure 1.3 The Knowledge Integration Model (Knowledge Integration Firm)

In the knowledge integration model, the knowledge integration process occurs through networks both inside and outside of companies and organizations. Firstly, internal knowledge integration occurs through internal networks within a company, while secondly, external knowledge integration occurs through external networks that transcend vertical and horizontal boundaries outside of companies. In the knowledge integration model, knowledge is created through collaborative innovation within and between companies, enabled by the knowledge integration process and transcending corporate (organizational) boundaries through these networks. We call these activities "boundaries innovation" (Kodama, 2009a, 2014) (See Figure 1.3). As the core framework for the two new insights discussed above, we describe "new boundary conceptions" based mainly on existing research into corporate boundaries.

1.4.2 Why are "Boundary Conceptions" Important?

Much of the strategic research has been carried out from the perspective of corporate vertical boundaries, transaction costs and bargaining power (e.g., Harrigan, 1984; Porter, 1980; Williamson, 1975). This research mainly deals with the analysis of activities in the upstream of value chains (e.g., make, buy or both; Parmigiani, 2007; Rothaermel, Hitt, and Jobe, 2006) or the downstream (e.g., company-owned outlets, franchises or dual distribution; Bradach and Eccles, 1989; Dutta, Bergen, Heide, and John et al., 1995; Michael, 2000), vertical integration architecture (e.g., Kodama, 2009a) or chronological changes (e.g., Jacobides and Billinger, 2006)).

However, regarding the recent ecosystem strategies (e.g., Gawer, 2009; Iansiti and Levien, 2004) that have been gaining attention in strategic research, not much research considers and analyzes the co-evolution of corporate boundaries and capabilities (Jacobides and Winter, 2007; Mota and de Castro, 2004; Santos and Eisenhardt, 2005) with respect to the reasons why companies or organizations dynamically change their vertical and horizontal boundaries, and how they establish new ecosystems.

One of the theoretical aims of this book is to investigate the concepts of the organizational boundaries of stakeholders that enable the formation of ecosystems. Therefore, this book can offer new theoretical insights on co-evolution in regards to resources, capabilities and strategies, and address a new research agenda to develop a deeper understanding of company (organizational) boundaries and contemporary novel practices for setting company (organizational) boundaries (Santos and Eisenhardt, 2005, p. 491).

As strategic positioning, corporate boundaries (called strategy drivers in this book), which are decided by the unique conceptions of the boundaries held by individual companies, are critical factors in driving corporate strategy. One strategy driver is the industry value chain (Porter, 1980) set up to realize the objectives of the corporate-determined strategy. This strategy driver consists of business activities aimed at forming an industry value chain, and is a determining factor of a company's vertical boundaries.

A second strategy driver consists of the factors that determine a company's horizontal boundaries—factors that create new business domains by expanding and diversifying (or downsizing by selecting and concentrating) a company's existing business domains (products, services and business models), or by integrating different technologies.

Companies must always transform their own corporate governance structures and corporate boundaries to strengthen their strategic positioning in constantly changing environments (or in environments that the company itself has created). According to the research into the theory of corporate boundaries to date, corporate governance structures and decision-making on corporate boundaries involve a wide range of factors, including efficiency (the economy of transactions), power, competencies and identification (Santos and Eisenherdt, 2005) (in this book, factors that decide corporate boundaries are called management drivers). Decision-making on company activities to implement regarding innovation value chains and whether to access external resources through contractual arrangements within markets often focuses on the technology strategies of both large corporations and venture companies (Pisano, 2006).

Accordingly, dynamically changing corporate boundaries to select and decide upon appropriate corporate governance structures to suit circumstances is an important issue in executing business and innovation strategies. Companies that adopt a vertical integration strategy require the application of a closed vertical integration-type governance structure with a closed internal hierarchy to execute all business activities within the company, from R and D through manufacturing, sales and support (Pattern A in Figure 1). Moreover, like Japanese automobile manufacturers, it can also be strategically important to exert power and formulate vertical integration-type hierarchies, such as those seen in Japanese Keiretsu networks (e.g., Amasaka, 2004).

In contrast, companies that adopt a horizontal specialization strategy, typically IT and digital companies, tailor their business activities to certain areas of expertise so that they can engage in licensing to other companies or in accepting outsourcing from other companies, which means they must adopt a governance structure open to externalities and have flat relationships based on rationalized contracts with external companies in their industry structure. Even in vertical integration-type companies, some business activities constituting parts of their vertical value chains are achieved through collaborative innovation by partnering with other companies in response to changing circumstances, and there are cases in which a hybrid vertical integration/horizontal specialization governing structure is adopted to execute outsourcing (Pisano, 2006). However, the governance structure that a business adopts is heavily influenced by the circumstances at hand and the strategic aims of the company. Therefore, a company must constantly redefine the strategic objectives of its competitive products, services and business models, and optimize the design (architecture) of vertical and horizontal boundary elements of its strategy drivers to accomplish these objectives.

1.4.3 New Boundary Conceptions

Generally, one of the key deciding perspectives on corporate or organizational boundaries is the "efficiency view." This is based on the transaction cost economics view and its related exchange-efficiency perspectives. In corporate business activity, minimizing the cost of governance (Coase, 1993; Nickerson and Silverman, 2003; Williamson, 1975) is one factor that determines vertical boundaries (Harrigan, 1984; Porter, 1980; Williamson, 1975). The so-called "make or buy" decision-making problem to minimize the governance costs also involves organizational and market vertical boundaries.

Even though the efficiency view has a lot of weight in deciding corporate (organizational) boundaries, in our investigations, we have observed boundary decision factors that differ from the efficiency view in cases of convergence through collaborative innovation spanning different business classes and industries. Santos and Eisenhardt (2005, p. 503), who considered the four management drivers that decide boundaries, proposed "non-efficiency conceptions" as a new agenda for boundaries research. They described interest in the relationship between the organizational features of "flexibility," "the capacity to inspire" and "coherence" and boundary decisions while describing potentials for new research. Thus, as "non-efficiency conceptions," this book proposes the "creativity view" and "dialectic view" observed in field investigations, and describes these concepts.

(1) The Creativity View

Korean Samsung Electronics, Chinese Huawei, American Intel and Japanese Fanuc are all manufacturers who differ from the Western horizontal specialization-type model (Kodama, 2009a) and who achieve creative new products through collaborative innovation through the vertical integration of their internal networks. Moreover, in recent years, these companies have been engaging in internal and external core knowledge integration through joint developments with other companies (including competitors) through collaborative innovation on external networks.

Additionally, typified by the smartphone businesses of Apple's iPhone and so forth, currently there is explosive growth in smartphone businesses, in which unique business models featuring virtual vertical integration-type value chains have been established through collaborative innovation on external networks linking content providers, application vendors, carriers, electronics manufacturing service (EMS) vendors and components manufacturers and software developers. Regarding the "flexibility" and "the capacity to inspire" seen in the corporate cases mentioned, this book describes the "creativity view" as the concepts embraced by these companies that bring about unique, flexible and autonomous new knowledge creation in their strategic activities, and as part of their organizational capabilities.

The creativity view is a factor that drives vertical integration in a company (including the virtual type). Through the creativity view, leading global brands raise their dynamic capability by accelerating absorption of new knowledge and knowledge integration with their own knowledge through collaborative innovation by configuring external networks with external partners while raising the level of path-dependent knowledge within themselves through vertical integration (Pattern B in Figure 1.1). The out-streaming strategy, which forms a "permeable vertical architecture," a variation of vertical integration (Jacobides and Billinger, 2006), also raises corporate dynamic capability (Teece, Pisano, and Shuen, 1997), and is a driver of knowledge convergence and integration centered on one's own company.

Based on vertical integration architecture, leading manufacturers assess other companies' knowledge and business models, absorb the ideas and know-how of their external partners, and through collaborative innovation both inside and outside of themselves raise the originality of their products, services and business models (Kodama, 2009a). Moreover, the creativity view generates new products, services and business models through collaborative innovation through strategic alliances and mergers and acquisitions with businesses in other fields that have the possibilities of horizontal boundaries expansion. The cases discussed, Cisco Systems in the US, and the collaborative innovation between Cisco Systems and medical institutions in the US, and between Fujifilm and medical institutions in Japan, are cases involving boundaries conception through the creativity view. The creativity view determines the boundaries of corporations (organizations), and is a core concept that leads to [Insight 1], while the value chain model arising from collaborative innovation promotes the creation of competitive new products and services, as well as innovative business models.

(2) The Dialectic View

Santos and Eisenhardt (2005) also discuss coherence as a concept entailing the harmony or unity found in consistency between different concepts— meaning balanced, dialectic integration. Coherence enables robust and consistent business models, and drives collaborative innovation and coordination between all stakeholders to create win-win relationships. In this book, coherence, a concept that induces strategic corporate activity to create win-win co-evolution models, is referred to as "the dialectic view."

The dialectic view is based on the Hegelian approach, which is a practical method of resolving conflict within an organization. The dialectic has been applied to organization theory and has stimulated discussion on absolute truths or morality in regards to the community or the processes of corporate reform. Peng and Nisbett (1999) analyzed the psychological reactions that could easily result from two apparently contradictory propositions and, while risking crises of contradictions, proposed 'dialectic thinking in a broad sense' that judges parts of both propositions to be correct. This sort of dialectic thought has also been reported in literature on institutional theory, strategic alliances and corporate management (Benson, 1997; Das and Teng, 2000; Kodama, 2004).

The dialectic view drives the establishment of win-win, co-evolution models between stakeholders with vertical integration architecture. For example, the win-win virtual and vertical architectures structured around the Apple iPhone, which include content providers, application vendors, communications carriers, EMS vendors, components manufacturers and software developers, have brought about effective network externalities (Shapiro and Varian, 1998). In addition, the business models created with virtual vertical architecture at Sony, Microsoft or Nintendo's game businesses, which include game machine manufacturers, EMS vendors, components manufacturers and game software developers, are also examples of win-win structures (Kodama, 2007c).

The dialectic view can also expand horizontal boundaries by creating new products, services and business models through co-evolution via collaborative innovation between different industries and businesses. Examples of this are not only seen in the business alliances formed between modern-day global mobile carriers and social networking services such as Google, Facebook or LINE, or their alliances with content providers involved in video and music distribution, but are also seen in alliance strategies between mobile carriers and automotive manufacturers and broadcasters, and in business formations in which funding relationships are configured to demonstrate mutually effective business model synergies.

Moreover, global mobile carriers, which have popularized electronic money and IC cards using smartphones and mobile phones, are driving collaborative innovation along horizontal boundaries (architecture) through partnerships between different areas of specialization (finances, cards, distribution, railways and so forth) to maximize the value of the business models of individual stakeholders. As seen with the medical/welfare/IT cases (Cases 1–3) discussed earlier, and in cases of industry-government-academia collaborations, cases of collaborative innovation between different areas of expertise and industries follow co-evolution models formed from dialectic-view boundary conceptions.

A company's dialectic view acts as a springboard for strategic activities to establish new business models based on co-evolution and coexistence between stakeholders. It determines the boundaries of corporations (organizations), and thus is a core concept that leads to [Insight 2], the driver behind the creation of win-win co-evolution models across different industries through collaborative innovation.

Thus, for companies, collaborative innovation is essentially based on strategic activities that are based on the creativity and dialectic views, both of which are non-efficiency conceptions. Thus, "new boundary conceptions" is radically different from the horizontal specialization-type business structures or from sectionalism based on the standard efficiency view that puts short-term profits or the thinking of shareholders at the forefront. Therefore, as new boundary conceptions, the creativity and dialectic views are crucial to the creation of the new value chains and co-evolution models, such as those found in health support ecosystems.

However, in spite of the fact that that interdisciplinary research spanning academic areas such as economics, management, sociology, information, science and industry, medicine and pharmacology has become so important at the global level, there has been almost no theoretical or empirical research into the organizational, corporate or industrial management innovation models used to configure health support ecosystems. Thus, Chapter 2 extracts a theoretical framework for a management innovation model for success with structuring healthcare support ecosystems through collaborative innovation.

NOTES

1. According to Hacklin et al. (2013), in most cases, technical convergence is not seen as the action of social or scientific power, but is treated as power that is context-dependent (Corredoira & Rosenkopf, 2010; Lee, 2007; Srinivasan, Haunschild, & Grewal, 2007).

2. According to Hacklin et al. (2013), much of the existing research is concerned with observing and analyzing processes in which technologies are duplicated as correlating factors of corporate partnerships or mergers and acquisitions (Mowery, Oxley, & Silverman, 1996), or in which technical convergence is a variable that influences the flow of knowledge between companies (Corredoira & Rosenkopf, 2010), or in which technical convergence is a variable that influences the flow of knowledge within an organization (de Boer et al., 1999), or is concerned with the relationships between network resources and market structural elements as requisites for convergence (Lee, 2007).

3. President Satoshi Miura of NTT, a leading ICT company in Japan, states the following in Nihon Keizai Shinbun (2012), "Are you familiar with the word 'convergence?' It may not be a word you are very familiar with, but various convergences have been integrated into our society today. Convergence plays a role in the creation of new fields of study, such as financial engineering resulting from the convergence of finance and mathematics, or biogenetics and biotechnology from the convergence of biology, medicine and chemistry. However, convergence is not limited to fields such as these. The integration of one industry with another can also result in the emergence of a new industry. Because we live in an era where all kinds of things are connected to networks and information today is digitalized, the integration of advanced technology in various fields such as energy, the environment, automobiles and housing with ICT is creating various new services. In the same way, integration in personnel is also occurring, and new types of employment are emerging.

One example close to the daily lives of people is progress in the convergence of healthcare with ICT in the village of Hinoemata in the mountainous area of Fukushima Prefecture. The summer before last, the NTT group, with medical and other organizations, introduced remote health consultation in the village, where depopulation and aging are ongoing. This service networks homes, clinics and meeting places with hospitals within the prefecture via optical fiber cables to provide health consultation. ICT has enabled a system for safeguarding all residents of the village through local community cooperation with healthcare organizations. . . . We no longer live in an era where a new service or industry is launched by a single company. Open integration with external enterprises opens the door to new value creation. As the word co-creation suggests, it is more meaningful to create new synergies and innovation, rather than simply mark the time together. Japanese society needs innovation and the creation of new value, and ICT can play a role as a facilitator."

REFERENCES

Amasaka, K. (2004). Development of "Science TQM", a new principle of quality management: Effectiveness of strategic stratified task team at Toyota. *International Journal of Production Research*, 42(17), 691–706.

Anand, B. & Khanna, T. (2000). Do firms learn to create value? The case of alliances. *Strategic Management Journal*, 21(3), 295–315.

Arora, A., Fosfuri, A. & Gambardella, A. (2001). *Markets for Technology: Economics of Innovation and Corporate Strategy*. Cambridge: MIT Press.

Benson, J. (1977). Organization: A dialectical view. *Administrative Science Quarterly*, 22, 221–242.

Borés, C., Saurina, C. & Torres, R. (2003). Technological convergence: A strategic perspective. *Technovation*, 23(1), 1–13.

Bradach, J.L. & Eccles, R.G. (1989). Price, authority, and trust: From ideal types to plural forms. *Annual Review of Sociology*, 15(1), 97–118.

Carlile, P. (2004). Transferring, translating, and transforming: An integrative framework for managing knowledge across boundaries. *Organization Science*, 15(5), 555–568.

Chesbrough, H. (2003). *Open Innovation*. Boston, MA: Harvard Business School Press.

Christensen, C.M. (1997). *The Innovator's Dilemma: When New Technologies Cause Great Firms to Fail*. Boston, MA: Harvard Business School Press.

Coase, R.H. (1993). The nature of the firm: Influence. In: O. E. Williamson, S. G. Winter (eds.), *The Nature of the Firm*. New York: Oxford University Press, 61–74.

Corredoira, R.A. & Rosenkopf, L. (2010). Should auld acquaintance be forgot? The reverse transfer of knowledge through mobility ties. *Strategic Management Journal*, 31(2), 159–181.

Curran, C.S. & Leker, J. (2011). Patent indicators for monitoring convergence-examples from NFF and ICT. *Technological Forecasting and Social Change*, 78(2), 256–273.

Das, T.K. & Teng, B. (2000). Instabilities of strategic alliances: An internal tensions perspective. *Organization Science*, 11(1), 77–101.

D'Aveni, D.A., Dagnino, G.B. & Smith, K.G. (2010). The age of temporary advantage. *Strategic Management Journal*, 31(13), 1371–1385.

de Boer, M., van den Bosch, F.A.J. & Volberda, H.W. (1999). Managing organizational knowledge integration in the emerging multimedia complex. *Journal of Management Studies*, 36(3), 379–398.

Dutta, S., Bergen, M., Heide, J.B. & John, G. (1995). Understanding dual distribution: The case of reps and house accounts. *Journal of Law, Economics, & Organization*, 11(1), 189–205.

Duysters, G. & Hagedoorn, J. (1998). Technological convergence in the IT industry: The role of strategic technology alliances and technological competencies. *International Journal of the Economics of Business*, 5(3), 355–368.

Fleming, L. & Sorenson, O. (2004). Science as a map in technological search. *Strategic Management Journal*, 25(8–9), 909–928.

Gambardella, A. & Torrisi, S. (1998). Does technological convergence imply convergence in markets? Evidence from the electronics industry. *Research Policy*, 27(5), 445–463.

Gawer, A. (2009). *Platforms, Markets and Innovation*. UK: Edward Elgar Publishing.

Ghoshal, S. & Bartlett, C.A. (1994). Linking organizational context and managerial action: The dimensions of quality of management. *Strategic Management Journal*, 15(S2), 91–112.

Goktan, A.B. & Miles, G. (2011). Innovation speed and radicalness: Are they inversely related? *Management Decision*, 49(4), 533–547.

Grant, R.M. (1996a). Prospering in dynamically-competitive environments: Organizational capability as knowledge integration. *Organization Science*, 7(4), 375–387.

Grant, R.M. (1996b). Toward a knowledge-based theory of the firm. *Strategic Management Journal*, 17(Winter Special Issue), 109–122.

Gray, B. (1989). *Collaborating: Finding Common Ground for Multiparty Problems*. San Francisco, CA: Jossey-Bass Inc. Publishers.

Gray, B. & Wood, D.J. (1991). Collaborative alliances: Moving from practice to theory. *Journal of Applied Behavioral Science*, 27(1), 3–23.

Gulati, R. (1999). Network location and learning: The influence of network resources and firm capabilities on alliance formation. *Strategic Management Journal*, 20(5), 397–420.

Hacklin, F. (2008). *Management of Convergence in Innovation: Strategies and Capabilities for Value Creation beyond Blurring Industry Boundaries: Contributions to Management Science.* Berlin: Springer.

Hacklin, F., Battistini, B. & Krogh, G. (2013). Strategic choices in converging industries. *MIT Sloan Management Review,* 55(1), 65–73.

Hacklin, F., Marxt, C. & Fahrni, F. (2009). Coevolutionary cycles of convergence: An extrapolation from the ICT industry. *Technological Forecasting and Social Change,* 76(6), 723–736.

Hacklin, F., Marxt, C. & Fahrni, F. (2010). An evolutionary perspective on convergence: Inducing a stage model of inter-industry innovation. *International Journal of Technology Management,* 49(1–3), 220–249.

Haefliger, S. (2012). *Collaborative Innovation—Strategy, Technology and Social Practice* (unpublished PhD thesis). Zurich: ETH.

Harianto, F. & Pennings, J.M. (1994). Technological convergence and scope of organizational innovation. *Research Policy,* 23(3), 293–304.

Harrigan, R. (1984). Formulating vertical integration strategies. *Academy of Management Review,* 9(4) 638–652.

Hill, S. (2008). *Exploration in large, established firms: Idea generation and corporate venturing* (unpublished PhD thesis). London: Business School.

Iansiti, M. & Levien, R. (2004). *The Keystone Advantage: What the New Dynamics of Business Ecosystems Mean for Strategy, Innovation, and Sustainability.* Boston, MA: Harvard Business School Press.

Jacobides, M.G. & Billinger, S. (2006). Designing the boundaries of the firm: From "make, buy, or ally" to the dynamic benefits of vertical architecture. *Organization Science,* 17(2), 249–261.

Jacobides, M.G. & Winter, S.G. (2007). Entrepreneurship and firm boundaries: The theory of a firm. *Journal of Management Studies,* 44(4), 1213–1241.

Kale, P., Singh, H. & Perlmutter, H. (2000). Learning and protection of proprietary assets in strategic alliances: Building relational capital. *Strategic Management Journal,* 21(3), 217–237.

Katila, R. & Ahuja, G. (2002). Something old, something new: A longitudinal study of search behavior and new product introduction. *Academy of Management Journal,* 45(6), 1183–1194.

Klein, J.T. (1990). *Interdisciplinarity: History, Theory, and Practice* (1st ed.). Detroit, MI: Wayne State University Press.

Kodama, F. (1992). Technology fusion and the new R&D. *Harvard Business Review,* 70(4), 70–78.

Kodama, M. (2002). Transforming an old economy company through strategic communities. *Long Range Planning,* 35(4), 349–365.

Kodama, M. (2004). Strategic community-based theory of firms: Case study of dialectical management at NTT DoCoMo. *Systems Research and Behavioral Science,* 21(6), 603–34.

Kodama, M. (2005). Knowledge creation through networked strategic communities: Case studies in new product development. *Long Range Planning,* 38(1), 27–49.

Kodama, M. (2007a). *The Strategic Community-Based Firm.* London, UK: Palgrave Macmillan.

Kodama, M. (2007b). *Knowledge Innovation—Strategic Management as Practice.* London, UK: Edward Elgar Publishing.

Kodama, M. (2007c). *Project-Based Organization in the Knowledge-Based Society.* London, UK: Imperial College Press.

Kodama, M. (2007d). Innovation through boundary managing-case of Matsushita electric reforms. *Technovation,* 27(1–2) 15–29.

Kodama, M. (2009a). *Innovation Networks in the Knowledge-Based Firm.* Cheltenham, UK: Edward Elgar Publishing.

Kodama, M. (2009b). Boundaries innovation and knowledge integration in the Japanese firm. *Long Range Planning*, 42(4), 463–494.

Kodama, M. (2011a). *Knowledge Integration Dynamics—Developing Strategic Innovation Capability*. Singapore: World Scientific Publishing.

Kodama, M. (2011b). *Interactive Business Communities-Accelerating Corporate Innovation through Boundary Networks*. London, UK: Gower Publishing.

Kodama, M. (2014). *Winning Through Boundaries Innovation—Communities of Boundaries Generate Convergence*. Oxford: Peter Lang.

Kodama, M. & Shibata, T. (2014). Strategy transformation through strategic innovation capability—a case study of Fanuc. *R&D Management*, 44(1), 75–103.

Larsson, R., Bengtsson, L., Henriksson, K. & Sparks, J. (1998). The interorganizational learning dilemma: Collective knowledge development in strategic alliances. *Organization Science*, 9(3), 285–305.

Lee, G.K. (2007). The significance of network resources in the race to enter emerging product markets: The convergence of telephony communications and computer networking, 1989–2001. *Strategic Management Journal*, 28(1), 17–37.

Lee, S.M., Olson, D.O. & Trimi, S. (2012). Co-innovation: Convergenomics, collaboration, and cocreation for organizational values. *Management Decision*, 50(5), 817–831.

Lei, D.T. (2000). Industry evolution and competence development: the imperatives of technological convergence. *International Journal of Technology Management*, 19(7–8), 699–738.

Michael, S.C. (2000). Investments to create bargaining power: The case of franchising. *Strategic Management Journal*, 21(3), 497–514.

Mota, J. & de Castro, L.M. (2004). A capabilities perspective on the evolution of firm boundaries: A comparative case example from Portuguese moulds industry. *Journal of Management Studies*, 41(2), 295–316.

Mowery, D., Oxley, J. & Silverman, B. (1996). Strategic alliances and interfirm knowledge transfer. *Strategic Management Journal* (Special Issue: Knowledge and the Firm), 17(S2), 77–91.

Nesta, L. & Saviotti, P.P. (2006). Firm knowledge and market value in biotechnology. *Industrial and Corporate Change*, 15(4), 625–652.

Nickerson, J.A. & Silverman, B.S. (2003). Why firms want to organize efficiently and what keeps them from doing so: Inappropriate governance, performance, and adaptation in a deregulated industry. *Administrative Science Quarterly*, 48(3) 433–465.

Nihon Keizai Shinbun. (2012). Management Innovation by President Satoshi Miura of NTT, April 18.

Nonaka, I. & Takeuchi, H. (1995). *The Knowledge-Creating Company*. New York, US: Oxford University Press.

Parmigiani, A. (2007). Why do firms both make and buy? An investigation of concurrent sourcing. *Strategic Management Journal*, 28(3), 285–311.

Patel, P. & Pavitt, K. (1994). The continuing, widespread (and neglected) importance of improvements in mechanical technologies. *Research Policy*, 23(5), 533–545.

Peng, K. & Nisbett, R.E. (1999). Culture Dialectics, and Reasoning about Contradiction. *American Psychologist*, 54(3), 741–54.

Pennings, J.M. & Puranam, P. (2001). *Market Convergence and Firm Strategy: New Directions for Theory and Research*. ECIS Conference, The Future of Innovation Studies, Eindhoven, The Netherlands.

Pisano, P. (2006). *Science Business*. Boston, MA: Harvard Business School Press.

Porter, A.L., Roessner, J.D., Cohen, A.S. & Perreault, M. (2006). Interdisciplinary research: Meaning, metrics and nurture. *Research Evaluation*, 15(3), 187–195.

Porter, M. (1980). *Competitive Strategy: Techniques for Analyzing Industries and Competitors*. New York: Free Press.

Powell, W., Koput, K. & Smith-Doerr, L. (1996). Inter-organizational collaboration and the locus of innovation: Networks of learning in biotechnology. *Administrative Science Quarterly*, 41(1), 116–146.

Prahalad, C.K. & Krishnan, M.S. (2008). *The New Age of Innovation: Driving Cocreated Value Through Global Networks*. New York: McGraw-Hill.

Rafols, I. & Meyer, M. (2010). Diversity and network coherence as indicators of interdisciplinarity: Case studies in bionanoscience. *Scientometrics*, 82(2), 263–287.

Roco, M.C. (2003). Nanotechnology: Convergence with modern biology and medicine. *Current Opinion in Biotechnology*, 14(3), 337–346.

Rodan, S. & Galunic, C. (2004). More than network structure: How knowledge heterogeneity influences managerial performance and innovativeness. *Strategic Management Journal*, 25(6), 541–562.

Rosenberg, N. (1976). *Perspectives on Technology*. Cambridge: Cambridge University Press.

Rothaermel, F., Hitt, M. & Jobe, L. (2006). Balancing vertical integration and strategic outsourcing: Effects on product portfolio, product success, and firm performance. *Strategic Management Journal*, 27(11), 1033–1056.

Santos, F.M. & Eisenhardt, K.M. (2005). *Constructing Markets and Organizing Boundaries: Entrepreneurial Action in Nascent Fields*. Working paper, INSEAD

Shapiro, C. and Varian, H.R. (1998). *Information Rules*. Boston, MA: Harvard Business School Press.

Shmulewitz, A., Langer, R. & Patton, J. (2006). Convergence in biomedical technology. *Nature Biotechnology*, 24(3), 277–280.

Srinivasan, R., Haunschild, P. & Grewal, R. (2007). Vicarious learning in new product introductions in the early years of a converging market. *Management Science*, 53(1), 16–28.

Teece, D.J., Pisano, G. & Shuen, A. (1997). Dynamic capabilities and strategic management. *Strategic Management Journal*, 18(3), 509–533.

Westley, F. & Vredenburg, H. (1991). Strategic bridging: The collaboration between environmentalists and business in the marketing of green products. *Journal of Applied Behavioral Science*, 27(2), 65–90.

Williamson, O.E. (1975). *Markets and Hierarchies: Analysis and Antitrust Implications*. New York: Free Press.

Wood, D.J. & Gray, B. (1991). Toward a comprehensive theory of collaboration. *Journal of Applied Behavioral Sciences*, 27(2), 139–163.

Zahra, S.(2008). The virtuous cycle of discovery and creation of entrepreneurial opportunities. *Strategic Entrepreneurship Journal* (Special Issue: Opportunities, Organizations, and Entrepreneurship: Theory and Debate), 2(3), 243–257.

Zhang, Y. & Li, H.Y. (2010). Innovation search of new ventures in a technology cluster: The role of ties with service intermediaries. *Strategic Management Journal*, 31(1), 88–109.

von Hippel, E. (1988). *The Sources of Innovation*. New York: Oxford University Press.

von Hippel, E. (1994). Sticky information and the locus of problem-solving—Implications for innovation. *Management Science*, 40(4), 429–439.

2 Theory of Collaborative Innovation and Management Innovation

Mitsuru Kodama

As discussed in Chapter 1, with the recent digitalization and developments in ICT, there is now even greater urgency to develop products and services and create business models by converging knowledge across different industries and combining different technologies. Until now, technological innovation has been developed through the pursuit of specialized knowledge in a particular field; however, there are now a rapidly growing number of cases of new products and services developed with new and unconventional ideas that converge technologies from one area with those of another. For these reasons, dynamic business strategies for intentional positioning (new products/services/business models, etc.) in new business ecosystems to bring about new value by collaborating with a wide range of partners, including customers, have become major challenges for corporations operating in constantly changing environments.

Thus, issues such as what strategies a company (or organization) should drive and execute in these dynamically changing environments and the nature of dynamic management innovation are issues that face not only business strategy researchers, but also face many corporate leaders. Management innovation does not just simply mean creating strategies to suit the future or to respond to changing environments, but is management that also optimizes all elements of business within a company, such as its organizations, technologies, operations, leadership and human resources for the future and strategies created, and is management that achieves corporate growth and sustainability by unifying these aspects and deploying them dynamically.

Importantly, management innovation is constantly changing, and dynamically structuring and restructuring. Management innovation involves continual and ongoing activities to create new value, and is a dynamic process that brings sustainable competitiveness to a company (e.g., Montgomery, 2008). Thus, as a dynamic process, what is the management innovation model? This chapter examines the way corporate strategy should be to structure this dynamic management innovation model. In this chapter, the author would like to present a framework for the management innovation model, a dynamic model aimed at creating, growing and developing new business ecosystems in dynamic environments.

As discussed in Chapter 1, the concepts of companies (or organizations) creating new business models and ecosystems through convergence, by bringing together strategies and technological innovations using ICT, will be increasingly important future issues. Developing new ecosystems using ICT means creating new ecosystems through collaborative innovation among stakeholders. This chapter theoretically clarifies the requisites for creating diverse business ecosystems, including the health support ecosystems discussed in Chapter 1. Firstly, the author discusses the process of forming a business ecosystem. Then, the author presents possibilities for the creation, growth and development of ecosystems by driving dynamic chains of exploration and exploitation, and by forming dynamic innovation communities centered on leader corporations. From empirical data, the author extracts the concepts of the management innovation model, combining the elements of the corporate strategic activities of exploration and exploitation, which enable the creation, growth and development of sustainable ecosystems.

2.1 BUSINESS ECOSYSTEMS AS NEW MARKETS

The competitive environments accompanying the digitalization and ICT developments in recent years have brought with them new business rules. Chakravarthy (1997) identified the importance for corporations in the rapidly changing and complex ICT industries of the latter half of the 20th century to acquire a high level of competitiveness by strengthening and diversifying their core competencies. He also identified that leading innovation companies must continuously pioneer to create new value chains by managing network externality effects through positive feedback (Shapiro and Varian, 1998). However, this does not mean that it is OK for leader companies in the modern-day ICT industry to just simply act in response to environmental changes (market and technological changes) earlier than others. As discussed below, leader companies must not only engage in competition, but must also configure business ecosystems spanning entire industries by simultaneously promoting coordination among stakeholders and collaborative innovation.

A few examples of businesses accompanying the rapid advancement of ICT include the electronic money businesses, integrated circuit (IC) tag solutions businesses, businesses converging communications and broadcasting, smartphone applications and contents businesses, all of which have come about through the formation of new business networks built around the new rules of competition and business models that span different industries and fuse together different technologies through convergence. In short, this is the formation of business ecosystems. These ecosystems are formed through competition and collaboration among the stakeholders involved in a series of value chains in broadband and wireless businesses covering terminals (e.g., smartphones, tablets and PCs), communications networks, platforms (e.g., billing and payment, electronic money and all types of media distribution), applications (e.g., software, IC tags, M2M modules, etc.), through to content (e.g. broadcasting, video, music and advertising, etc.).

For example, i-mode, a pioneering Japanese information distribution business model in the ICT industry, was created through coordination, collaboration and co-evolution between content providers and the platform provider, NTT DOCOMO (Kodama, 2009b). These kinds of unique value chains have brought about new business ecosystems involving application and contents businesses with smartphones and so forth. The achievement of these new business ecosystems through convergence using ICT is the result of collaborative innovation among stakeholders, and these markets have continued to grow under the business co-evolution model with smartphones (e.g., Moore, 1993, 1996; Inanity and Levine, 2004).

Moore (1993) described business environments as ecosystems of living organisms. In this view, a company is not seen simply as a member of one industry, but as part of a business ecosystem spanning a number of diverse industries. In these business ecosystems, organizations and companies are single members of business communities—economic collectives supported by the synergies that arise between individuals and organizations. These business communities produce goods and services that are valuable to customers (these could be one's own company's vendors, partners, corporate customers or competitors); however, the customers themselves are also members of the business community. Thus, the members of these business communities (groups of companies) co-evolve their own roles and abilities, and develop their activities in directions indicated by one or many central companies. In these communities, there will be a turnover of companies demonstrating leadership with the passing of time; however, the role of the corporate leader in a business ecosystem is always going to be highly praised in the business community.

As community members of these business community-based ecosystems, all stakeholders, including the leader corporations, require the "boundaries conception" and "dialectic view" factors discussed in Chapter 1. Dialectic view thinking and action is a critical instigator of the co-evolution process involving collaborative innovation among stakeholders.

Companies such as Apple and Google that lead the way in the worldwide smartphone businesses are pursuing new business models by co-evolving through coordination and collaborative innovation among stakeholders. As a result, new dynamic business ecosystems are formed (Kodama, 2009b). Differing from older types of business structures, these new business networks simultaneously bring about both new competition and collaborative relationships. Coordination and collaborative innovation relationships in business networks is not only observed between different business classes, but also in similar business classes. A typical example of this is the digital home appliance industry, whose markets and technologies are changing rapidly. Behind the collaborative innovation between competitors in the same industry lie the strategic intentions of companies to proactively share know-how, and to reduce the risks associated with the cost of technological development in recent years.

In addition, collaborative innovation brought about through strategic partnering with external companies is also a trigger that raises the level of the "creativity view" as part of a company's boundaries conception, as discussed in Chapter 1. With open innovation (Chesbrough, 2003) and open business models (Chesbrough, 2006), companies can scrutinize both their own knowledge and capabilities as well as those of other companies, and jointly assess business models, which enables corporations to absorb the ideas and know-how of external partners, and, based on this acquired knowledge, to create new products and services through collaborative innovation both within and outside of themselves. One example of this is the US company P&G, who with their "Connect + Develop" strategy are able to raise the creativity of their own products and services (Huston and Sakkab, 2006). It's also important for the strong competitiveness of products and services to absorb customer competencies through collaborative innovation with customers (Prahalad and Ramaswamy, 2000). In this way, in industries experiencing dramatic market and technological changes, coordination and collaborative innovation between companies, including their customers, is an important factor in mutually raising the level of the creativity view, and in bringing about new business models.

2.2 CREATING BUSINESS ECOSYSTEMS THROUGH INNOVATION COMMUNITIES

First of all in this section, regarding the theoretical business ecosystem framework put forth by Moore, the author reconsiders the strategic factors necessary for a company (or organization) to configure a business ecosystem based on the existing academic knowledge. As mentioned, Moore (1993) describes business environments as ecosystems of living organisms, and also discusses the following four stages of the development of these business ecosystems: Firstly is the "birth" stage, in which a leader company explores a new ecosystem; secondly is the "expansion" stage in which a "critical mass" surrounding customers is reached; thirdly is the "leadership" stage in which the main members of the ecosystem (vendors, partners, etc.) take actions to achieve shared objectives and co-evolve through mutual coordination and collaborative innovation to reinforce their own competencies, while the fourth stage involves the "self-renewal" of existing ecosystems to achieve new objectives with even more ideas and innovation.

The spiraling execution of these four stages by leader companies and major following companies is key to the achievement of sustainable innovation (See Figure 2.1). Collaborative innovation by thinking and actions from the dialectic view among innovation community members and through coordination by leader companies are the critical factors of achieving co-evolution (See Column 2.1). Classic examples of these business ecosystems are the business models centered on leader corporations such as Apple and Google, which were mentioned earlier, or Microsoft and Sony Computer Entertainment.

However, viewed from the perspective of corporate evolutionary theory or corporate strategic theory, stakeholder corporations centered around the leader corporations acquire new knowledge and capabilities through exploration activities in the birth and self-renewal stages (March, 1991), which are also the stages in which new ecosystems (new markets) are created, and involves the processes of bringing about innovation achieved by new knowledge creation (or knowledge integration). On the other hand, the expansion and leadership stages are characterized by knowledge utilization processes that promote exploitation activities (March, 1991), in which related stakeholder companies centered around the leader companies polish existing knowledge and capabilities towards the expansion and growth of newly established ecosystems. Therefore, groups of companies (or organizations) that create ecosystems engage in the spiraling activities of exploration and exploitation through coordination and collaborative innovation in the process of creating, growing and developing ecosystems (see Figure 2.1).

The process of spirally executing exploration and exploitation centered on leader companies (or organizations) which is important in creating, developing and growing these business ecosystems, leads to the new insight below.

[Insight 3]

The process of spiraling the execution of exploration and exploitation centered on leader companies (or organizations) creates, grows and develops business ecosystems.

However, in light of Moore's theory, although the spiral execution of exploration and exploitation through the formation of the four spiral stages is necessary for the creation, growth and development of business ecosystems, these processes require collaboration (cooperation through strategic alliances, joint ventures, mergers and acquisitions (M&A), etc.) through the formation of business networks that are built around leader and major follower companies as their organizational infrastructure, which leads to the next insight.

[Insight 4]

The dynamic formation of innovation communities as business networks built around leader and major follower companies lies at the core of the formation of business ecosystems.

However, as discussed in Section 2.3, new insights can be gained from some empirical data regarding the dynamic consistency of corporate systems and the environment, including ecosystems, as well as the managerial factors of in-house systems in the execution of exploration and exploitation in this spiraling cycle. Next, the author extracts a theoretical framework derived recursively from the empirical results to date regarding the management innovation model of corporations engaging in the corporate activities of exploration and exploitation.

COLUMN 2.1 THE CO-EVOLUTION PROCESS THROUGH THE 'DIALECTIC VIEW'

The author would like to consider how and why thought and action through the dialectic view of stakeholders drive the co-evolution process through collaborative innovation. Moore's (1993) idea of a business ecosystem begins with a "social ecology." Social ecologists (e.g., Bateson, 1979; Norgaard, 1994) introduced an analogy of co-evolution into the ecological theory, perceiving co-evolution as two specific species' evolutionary patterns, and thought that the hereditary characteristics of a species mutually influence those of another (e.g., the shape of a particular insect's proboscis having evolved to fit the shape of a particular flower). These social ecologists also interpreted social systems and ecological systems both as co-evolving (e.g., insects that develop insecticide resistance, and social systems that rely on such technologies) (Norgaard, 1994). In the co-evolution approach of this social ecology, social systems are formed by ecological systems as "a 2nd nature," in which social and ecological systems are not in conflict, but rather take the position of "dialectical naturalism" that combines society and nature dialectically with a focus on natural and social perspectives (Bookchin, 1990) (See 'Social Ecology' in Figure 2.1).

Because these ecological and social systems consist of a great diversity of subsystems (elements), it is difficult to identify all of their relationships. The "Social and Ecological Theory" of recent years (e.g., Levin, 1999; Marten, 2001; Norgaard, 1994;) interprets ecological and social systems that have the characteristics of subjectivity and that are dependent on context as "complex adaptive systems" (e.g., Morel and Ramanujam, 1999; Stacey, 1996), which are described below. Thus, at the micro level, a social system is a complex adaptive system that co-evolves through the synergies that emerge as innumerable human beings interacting to adapt to the environment (e.g., Morel & Raman jam, 1999; Stacey, 1995).

Therefore, the business ecosystems involving the co-evolution processes mentioned earlier can also be interpreted as complex adaptive systems. Complex adaptive systems are self-organizing systems (various social systems, including corporations), form their own unique regions of stability and are systems that co-evolve adaptively through learning and by the interactions between the companies and organizations that make up the system with the environment. Thus, the elements of the system (people, organizations, companies, industries, etc.) engage in processes to dialectically adapt and evolve.

A complex adaptive system is not only a system that has harmonic, parallel and stable characteristics, but also has aspects of emerging nonlinear dynamics—these systems are also characterized by sudden change and novelty. These complex adaptive systems form the core concepts of the "complex theory" of recent years (see 'Complex Theories' in Figure 2.1) (e.g., Kauffman, 1993; Prigogine, 1996). Management scholars have also attempted to introduce some of these theoretical ideas into administrative science.

In business ecosystems as complex adaptive systems, a wide range of dynamically formed business networks are established through coordination and collaboration (cooperation through strategic alliances, joint ventures, M&A, etc.) between diverse partners in business communities centered around the leader corporations. Thus, diverse knowledge is integrated through the formation of inter-organizational networks. However, in this knowledge integration process (Kodama, 2011a), all kinds of abrasion, conflict and contradiction occurs between practitioners and organizations, and practitioners in innovation communities have to exercise management that can dialectically synthesize a variety of paradoxes (see 'Dialectical Management Theories' in Figure 2.1) (e.g., Benson, 1977; Das and Teng, 2000; Kodama, 2004). In this way, the dialectical thinking of practitioners drives co-evolution among partners through learning and adaptation, and is the source through which practitioners can integrate dissimilar knowledge dispersed throughout the complex adaptive system.

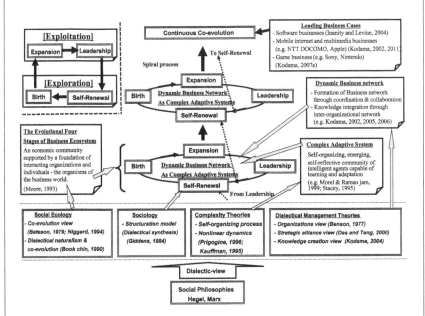

Figure 2.1 Framework of the Continuous Ecosystems Creation through the Dialectic View

Moreover, as illustrated by the leading business case in Figure 2.1 (Inanity and Levine, 2004; Kodama, 2002, 2007c, 2007d), the self-renewal step of the 4th stage mentioned above has a critical role in achieving co-evolution continuously in these kinds of business ecosystems.

For example, this is the sociological concept of the "duality of structure" that is at the heart of the continual evolution seen in software, smartphone and game businesses (see 'Sociology' in Figure 2.1). In sociology, structuration models by Giddens (1979) present organizations as continuous feedback systems in which behavior unfolds or emerges from a dialectical process. In other words, structure and actions are both involved in the process of reproducing social practice, and are interdependent. While the actions of leader corporations are dependent on existing social structures, leader corporations also introspectively transform, renew and reproduce these structures through co-evolution involving coordination and collaborative innovation with partners. The formation of business networks in business ecosystems has an intrinsic relationship with the duality of structure theory. Thus, continuous co-evolution processes in business ecosystems are rooted in the duality of corporate (or organizational) structures and the dialectic view (dialectical thinking) of practitioners—their "boundaries conceptions."

As described above, the concept of co-evolution originates from the four research streams of social psychology, sociology, complex theories and dialectical management theories. These four theories are based in the dialectic view that is proposed by the classical social philosophies of Hegel and Marx, etc. The promotion of dialectical management through the dialectical thought and actions of practitioners forms business ecosystems as complex adaptive systems that introduce an analogy of co-evolution within a "social ecology."

2.3 CREATING A MANAGEMENT INNOVATION MODEL WITH COLLABORATIVE INNOVATION

In this section, the author would like to present our empirical evidence for the conditions for business ecosystems to be formed through collaborative innovation, and the concept of the management innovation model. From field research, it became clear that the theoretical concepts cited below are critical for leader and follower corporations in the performance of their central roles in creating, growing and developing business ecosystems. Specifically, as illustrated in Figure 2.2, business ecosystems founded on collaboration among stakeholders require dynamic consistency between environmental (ecosystem) and corporate systems, and require dynamic internal consistency within corporate systems.

In this research, we derived first-order concepts as empirical observations from extensive interviews with a wide range of stakeholders such as companies, healthcare institutions, administrative bodies and local governments and customers—stakeholders who make up business ecosystems through

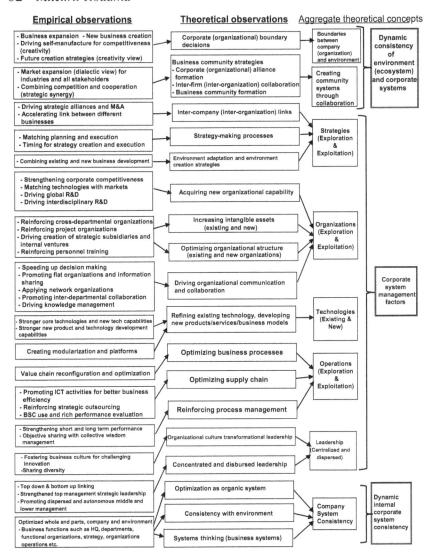

Figure 2.2   Management Innovation Model Data Structures

collaborative innovation. From these first-order concepts, we extracted second-order themes as theoretical observations, themes necessary for establishing business ecosystems through collaborative innovation, finally leading to the main aggregate theoretical concepts ((1) boundaries between companies and environments, (2) establishing community systems, (3) strategy, (4) organizations, (5) technologies, (6) operations, (7) leadership as a factor of management of corporate systems, and (8) corporate system consistency) as the eight core frames derived from these second-order themes.

The following can be stated regarding (1) boundaries between companies and environments and (2) establishing community systems through collaboration. It is crucial that community systems are established as innovation communities for the creation, growth and development of the ecosystem, as a driving factor for establishing a business ecosystem. It is also important that as stakeholders in establishing community systems, companies (organizations) aim for dynamic and appropriate consistency through their interactions with the environment (the structure) as the ecosystem. Furthermore, it is necessary to execute dynamic and appropriate consistency ((8) corporate system consistency) between the internal corporate managerial elements of (3) strategy, (4) organization, (5) technology, (6) operations and (7) leadership. Next, the author presents the framework for a new management innovation model from these aggregate theoretical categories.

2.3.1 Dynamic Strategic Management through the Management Innovation Model

In constantly changing environments (or in the new environments that they create), companies must reinforce their strategic position by actively changing corporate boundaries and their own governance structures (Kodama, 2009b). According to existing research into corporate boundaries, decision-making about corporate governance structures and corporate boundaries relies on a variety of factors, such as transaction costs, capabilities and competencies and identity[1]. Thus, decision-making about the types of business activities executed in companies, or how external resources are accessed through contracts in the marketplace to configure value chains as strategic objectives, is an important factor of corporate strategy not only for large corporations, but also for venture companies (e.g., Kodama, 2009a; Pisano, 1991).

Santos and Eisenhardt (2005) presented four characteristic factors that determine corporate boundaries: Efficiency, power, competencies and identity. Thus, because these four factors are critical issues that determine the boundaries of the company, they are also fundamental managerial issues that confront business leaders in corporate activities—i.e., costs (efficiency), autonomy (power), growth (competence) and uniformity (identity). Notably, with the strategic outsourcing of recent times, decisions about corporate boundaries to reduce costs have taken the efficiency of corporate activity to a higher level, while the Keiretsu networks, which are rooted in relationships of trust built up over a long period, typical of subcontracting in the automotive industry, both drive autonomy in subcontracting companies and wield influence through power in corporate activities.

On the other hand, the following can be said about the research implications regarding competence as identified by Santos and Eisenhardt (2005). As the new creativity view boundaries conception centered on leader corporations, the decisions about corporate boundaries drive self-manufacture for competitiveness (creativity) or the expansion of business territory, and are linked to the achievement of strategies for corporate long-term future creation. Thus, decisions about corporate (or organizational) boundaries are important managerial factors for defining boundaries between companies (organizations) and environments, creating environments as new business ecosystems, and growing and developing these ecosystems (see Figure 2.2).

For example, the mobile and smartphone application and contents businesses, the game industry and the foundry businesses involved in semiconductor manufacture all have created new environments as business ecosystems through the co-evolution process among stakeholders, and that dramatically influence the boundaries between companies and industries (e.g., Kodama, 2011b). As discussed in Chapter 1, market expansion for entire businesses and stakeholders depends on bringing about collaborative innovation by building business communities (community systems) by combining both competition and cooperation (strategic synergies) through the dialectic view centered on the leader companies and major follower companies, as new boundaries conceptions (see Figure 2.2).

Thus, considering the integrity that corporations have with environments, the way corporate boundaries are dynamically changed and applied to environments as existing ecosystems (expansion and leadership in Figure 2.1, or self-renewal and birth in the creation of new ecosystems as environments in Figure 2.1) is a major issue in executing corporate strategy. In short, dynamic consistency between environments (ecosystems) and corporate systems is critical [Insert Figure 2.2]. Thus, companies have to establish strategic objectives for sustainably competitive products, services and business models, and have to optimize the design of their vertical (value chains required to achieve the strategic objectives set down by a company) and horizontal (diversification and expansion of business domains) boundaries to achieve these aims. The design of corporate boundaries adapted for ecosystems as environments must be a design to optimize corporate systems consisting of the business elements of strategy, organization, technologies, operations and leadership, as discussed below (see Figure 2.2).

To optimize corporate systems consistent with ecosystem environments, individual business elements (strategy, organizations, technologies, operations, leadership) must be optimized both partially and entirely (headquarters and each business division, each organizational job function, strategy, organizations, operations and so on—optimization of all business functions). Therefore, systems that think about optimization as organic systems and are consistent with ecosystem environments require consistency in corporate systems. In other words, there needs to be dynamic consistency in the internal parts of a corporate system, because these parts are the individual business elements that make up the corporate system (see Figure 2.2).

Achieving business models as new objective ecosystems with architecture thinking (management architecture) about corporate systems made up of individual business elements lies in the achievement of an optimized management innovation model that includes all stakeholders. Thus, the idea of "business architecture" is a similar concept to the management innovation model. For example, in the information system (IS) research and systems research view, the concept of business architecture is the integrated design thinking of optimized ICT and organizations and business processes in order to achieve the intended corporate strategy[2].

According to the leading researchers, business architecture refers to the uniform structures between concepts in business, and to the composite structures relating to the relationships with stakeholders targeted for strategic corporate activity, and a range of business activities involving such things as products, services, organizations, business processes and ICT, etc. (the way that interdependencies and relationships are formed between elements of business activities). However, there have been conflicting ideas among researchers about business architecture, and there have not been any comprehensive concepts relating to the general contexts of management. In contrast, the concept of the management innovation model described in this book includes IS design and product and service architecture, and is a comprehensive concept that considers consistency with environmental changes, consistency between business elements in corporate systems, and considers dynamic consistency over time.

Therefore, corporations must aim for consistency in their corporate systems (in-house managerial elements of strategies, organizations, technologies, operations, leadership, etc.), i.e., for the management innovation model, so that they can adapt to dynamically changing environments, including ecosystems, such as leader corporations (for example, markets, technologies, competition and cooperation, structures). It is the boundaries between corporate systems and environments—corporate boundaries—that define ecosystems, relationships with entire environments and a company's business models.

In turn, changes across entire environments (or ecosystems) bring about changes in corporate boundaries, and thus simultaneously influence the individual business elements in corporate systems. Similarly, actively changing business elements in corporate systems brings about changes in corporate boundaries, and thus simultaneously influences entire environments (or ecosystems). Dynamic strategic management is then both adaptation to changing environments (or ecosystems), or creating new environments (or ecosystems) by applying appropriate strategies for the future, while tailoring all business factors of the management innovation model and optimizing the whole as a corporate system.

As shown in Figure 2.3, the management innovation model consists of the business elements of strategy, organizations, technologies, operations and leadership, and thus requires consistency between these elements, elements that are matched to their environments, including ecosystems. Therefore, in perceiving the dynamic processes of the management innovation model, both academics and practitioners must pay attention to the dynamic

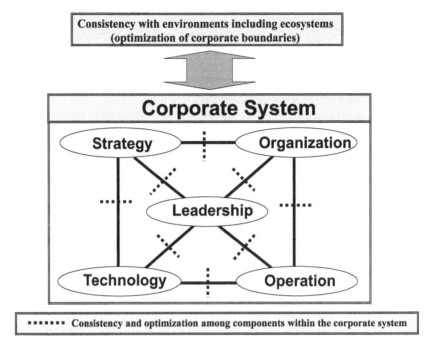

Figure 2.3   Management Innovation Model

changes in corporate systems (strategies, organizations, technologies, operations, leadership, etc.) that are adapting to the dynamically changing environments (markets, technologies, competition and cooperation, structures)
surrounding corporations.

It is the boundaries between environments and corporate systems—
corporate boundaries—that define the relationship between corporations
and environments and the forms of corporation business models and ecosystems. Changes in environments (or ecosystems) bring about changes in
corporate boundaries, and thus simultaneously influence the individual
business elements in corporate systems. Similarly, actively (or passively)
changing business elements in corporate systems brings about changes in
corporate boundaries, and thus simultaneously influences environments (or
ecosystems).

Thus, for a company to adapt to changes in environments that include
ecosystems (setting down and executing an environment adaptive strategy),
or to actively work on environments that include ecosystems to create a new
environment (setting down and executing an environment creation strategy),
companies must intentionally change their internal business elements, such as
strategy, organizations, technologies, operations and leadership, and must aim
for consistency in the boundaries between these business elements. Due to the
similarities with existing research (Dixon, Meyer, and Day, 2014) (described

later), the author calls the capabilities of companies (or organizations) that set down and execute these environmental adaptive and creation strategies "dynamic adaptation" and "dynamic innovation" capabilities, respectively.

Regarding short- and long-term corporate strategy and organizational makeovers, Dixon et al. (2014) presented a theoretical framework for a dynamic capability cycle from the in-depth longitudinal case studies of a Russian oil company. In this concept, they discuss the two capabilities that a company must demonstrate in the process of developing over the short and long term. The first of these capabilities is a "dynamic adaptation capability," involving exploitation activities to acquire short-term and temporary competitiveness by the regular polishing of extant knowledge (the operational capabilities, etc., in a company to respond to environmental changes). The second capability is a "dynamic innovation capability" that involves exploration activities to acquire sustainable competitiveness over the long term with new and unique creative thinking and action that is not reliant on other companies.

Dixon et al. call this pattern of executing strategy, in which these two mutually dissimilar capabilities are demonstrated cyclically over time by leader companies (both asynchronously and synchronously), the "dynamic capability cycle." Thus, in contrast to the dynamic capabilities (Teece, Pisano, and Shuen, 1997) series of dynamic resources reconfiguration, divestment and integration in response to environmental changes, this theory is also a framework that considers the capability factors necessary for achieving new innovations through the process of new knowledge creation (Nonaka and Takeuchi, 1995) as even further exploration (March, 1991) and path creation (Graud & Karne, 2001). As discussed in Moore's (1993) theoretical framework earlier, this means that dynamic capability cycle factors that operate through this dynamic adaptation capability (exploitation) and dynamic innovation capabilities (exploration), are required as corporate organizational capabilities to achieve the creation, growth and development of ecosystems (see Figure 2.5).

The capabilities of companies that set down and execute the environment adaptive and environment creation strategies mentioned earlier can be interpreted as "dynamic adaptation" and "dynamic innovation" capabilities, respectively. However, Dixon et al. (2014) do not go into any detail about how companies demonstrate dynamic adaptation and dynamic innovation capabilities, and whether these happen asynchronously or synchronously. As the subject of field investigations for this book, it has been observed and reported that companies and organizations that have achieved convergence across different industries successfully and sustainably innovate through the creation, growth and development of ecosystems by simultaneously managing distinct and dissimilar contexts in the five managerial elements of their corporate systems (strategy, organizations, technologies, operations and leadership) through ambidextrous business activities (e.g., Gibson and Birkinshaw, 2004; Kodama, 2003; He and Wong, 2004) (see Figure 2.2).

The importance of the dynamic strategic management mentioned earlier is how practitioners see and recognize boundaries between environments and corporate systems, boundaries between various business elements within corporate systems, and the changes within those boundaries, in relation to the processes of change in corporate systems in these environments and corporate systems, and how practitioners bring consistency to these boundaries. In rapidly changing circumstances, of particular importance are the factors of boundary consistency between corporate systems and environments, and internal corporate system boundary consistency in business management, which are required for practitioners to execute the processes of changing strategy management to achieve the environment adaptive and environment creative strategies mentioned earlier (see Figure 2.4).

The theoretical framework of the management innovation model presented in this book aims to embrace the theories brought forth from existing research—the positioning-based view (e.g., Porter, 1980, 1985), the resource-based view (e.g., Barney, 1991; Wernerfelt, 1984) and the dynamic capabilities cycle (Dixon et al., 2014). This is because the internal and external viewpoints on corporate boundaries must be dynamically integrated in a strategic theory of business ecosystems that includes a wide range of stakeholders (see Column 2.2).

Thus, for a company to sustainably develop and grow, it is essential that practitioners bring about processes to change business strategy (incremental

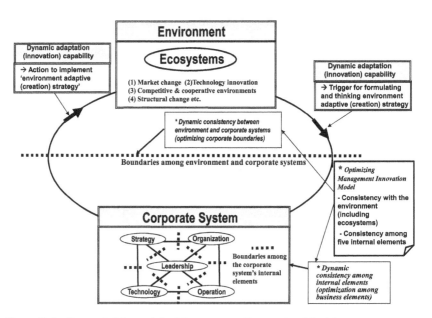

Figure 2.4　Dynamic View of the Management Innovation Model

and radical processes) over time to create new business models. Therefore, as mentioned, the concept of boundaries consistency and its execution are of importance, and lead to the following new insight (see Figure 2.4):

[Insight 5]

Dynamic consistency in the boundaries between environments and corporate systems and the boundaries between the individual business elements within corporate systems builds ecosystems and achieves sustainable corporate development and growth.

To understand the mechanism of boundaries consistency, analysis and considerations must focus on the practical processes of practitioners. Not only does "practical process" refer to specific activities in the public organizations of practitioners, both within and outside of organizations, but it also refers to the bridging processes of knowledge boundaries that form through business networks and transcend organizational and corporate boundaries (both in real space and in virtual space, using ICT). As will be discussed later, the formation of business networks also means the formation of organizations from the perspective of organizational theory: For example, communities of practice (Wenger, 1998), strategic communities (Kodama, 2002, 2007a, 2007b, 2009a) and the "small-world networks" (Watts, 2003) from the viewpoint of social network theory. Through practical processes,

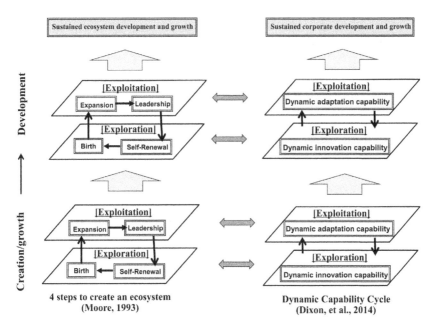

Figure 2.5 Continuous Ecosystems Creation, Growth and Development

practitioners set down and execute strategy by forming business networks, which brings about "boundaries consistency." Business networks formed in this way are examples of the innovation communities (community systems) discussed earlier. The way that practitioners achieve consistency in business activities and environments to set down and execute strategies in dynamically changing environments and on a variety of knowledge boundaries within and outside of a corporation is the essence of dynamic strategic management with the management innovation model.

COLUMN 2.2 STRATEGIC MANAGEMENT IN DYNAMICALLY CHANGING ENVIRONMENTS

Companies do not only have to compete within the same industry in the conventional theories of competitive strategy, but they also face the major challenge of creating new business models through collaborative innovation between different industries, known as convergence. Thus, the way these major shifts in environments are sensed and how new strategies are executed are critical matters for companies, because such collaborative innovation is accelerating in a wide range of industries.

These new business models are leading to major shifts in external environments, bringing about market changes, technology innovations, competitive and cooperative environments and structural changes, and are redefining new corporate boundaries, and thus require new management models. This means redefining corporate systems in relation to internal elements such as strategy, organization, technology, operation and leadership to achieve consistency with the corporate boundaries and systems as environments change. In addition, corporate systems need to be consistent with their internal elements (see Figure 2.3) while achieving and maintaining consistency with environmental changes.

A practical theoretical model to describe dynamic environmental changes and corporate systems is a topic that greatly concerns both researchers and practitioners. Among past models of consistency between companies and the environment, one area of interest is the positioning theory, or Porter theory (Porter, 1980, 1985), which describes a company's ideal strategic position from a static analysis of the external environment. This leading strategy theory provides a framework for a company to discover an advantageous position through a structural analysis of the market (including an analysis of competitive and transactional structures among companies). The positioning theory is an excellent competitive tool for judging a company's superiority (or deficiencies) through the past, present and future (predictive) analysis of an industry and the competition within it. However, for the businesses described above, which are operating across different industries in dramatically changing environments, the Porter theory has the disadvantage of being static, and neglects to analyze a company's internal resources.

A second area of interest is the resource-based view (e.g., Barney, 1991; Wernerfelt, 1984). This theory also describes differences in competitiveness and profitability among companies, as well as the importance of a company's innovation processes and the efficiency of its operations from intrinsic competences, resources and capabilities. The resource-based theory is based on the idea that a company's internal resources should determine competitive capabilities that are difficult to copy, and takes the position that a company should enter markets that exploit its unique business resources. Thus, the resource-based view has the great advantage of describing a company's strategic position from an analysis of its internal resources. The major disadvantage remains, however; it is a static theory (like Porter's), and it lacks a detailed analysis of external environments.

Nevertheless, these two theories provide frameworks that can be adequately applied in situations where grasping market structures or making projections for relatively stable environments is possible (Chakravarthy, 1997; D'Aveni, 1995; Eisenhardt, 2002). In contrast, dynamic capability theories that take a dynamic view of strategy conceptualize change in a company's core capabilities in line with environmental change (Teece, 2007; Teece et al., 1997). The dynamic capability approach is a path-dependent, market positioning approach in which practitioners' thoughts and actions redefine their company's capabilities, and thus strengthen its market position. It is also a theory that extends from the internal (organizational view) to the external (market view), and is thus a development of the resource-based theory.

Therefore, in the existing research, the positioning theory with its focus on the external environment and the resource-based theory with its focus on internal resources show two sides of the same coin (Wernerfelt, 1984). As mentioned, in rapidly and dynamically changing cross-industry competitive environments where change cannot be easily predicted, it is essential to organically link both the external environment and internal resource concepts to create a new dynamic strategic management theory. Consistency between a corporate system and a changing environment, and between the internal corporate system's elements, are indicative of a framework for a dynamic strategic management theory that organically links the external environment with internal resources, as suggested in this book.

2.3.2 Adaptation Dynamic Capability for Environment Adaptive Strategies

The dynamic innovation management framework is suggested in this book as an approach to "change process management." Changes happen in external environments and internal corporate systems, thus, creating and maintaining dynamic consistency in corporate boundaries is the first stage of processing change. How do companies (practitioners) recognize changes in the external environment, how far and in what way should a company's corporate system be changed with regard to this, and how should dynamic consistency be formed between the external environment and the corporate system? To answer these questions, practitioners must interpret the degree of change in a company's external environment over time, asking themselves how markets, technology, competition and cooperation, and structure are changing now and into the future, and then modify their corporate systems accordingly to suit those changes. This means consistency between external environmental change and internal elemental changes in the company—consistency with external, environmental changes such as market changes, technological innovations, competitive and cooperative environments, and structural changes, as well as changes within the corporate system including strategies, organizations, technologies, operations and leadership (see Figure 2.4).

Second is the dynamic consistency between the individual internal elements of the corporate system, such as strategy, organization, technology, operations and leadership. Such consistency between the degrees of change in the individual elements is important. Building and maintaining consistency also involves questions such as how far and in what way should existing strategies be changed, how should existing organizations be reformed, how far should existing technologies be improved or radically restructured, how should existing business flows be reformed, what kind of personnel are required, how and whether to cultivate or acquire staff or technologies, and how to acquire consistency to resolve these issues. Despite the existence of research discussing corporate strategies for adapting strengths and weaknesses to environmental changes (e.g., Chakravarthy, 1997; D'Aveni, 1995; Eisenhardt, 2002), not much of it deals with the elements of strategy-supported organizations, operations, technology and leadership.

Tushman and O'Reilly (1997) and Nadler and Tushman (1989) demonstrate the importance of a "consistent model of organizations" for innovation and organizational change. They posit that the basic structure of organizations consists of the four elements of critical tasks, culture, formal organizations and people. The consistency among these blocks has to be aligned with the pace of innovation (the periods of incremental change), and also achieved as the four elements change. They also indicate that the management of these periods of change with this kind of organizational consistency is a source of sustainable competitiveness.

According to Tushman and others, the organizational consistency model is important in practical terms, and with regard to sudden, pan-industry environmental changes, "business architectures that" achieve consistency among the options and elements of strategy, technology, operations and leadership must also be considered in addition to the "organizational consistency model." Furthermore, the changes in the internal elements of these corporate systems must dynamically link to, and be consistent with, the changes in the external environments. The ability to enhance an organization's adaptability is also required to deal with the strategic uncertainty surrounding changing patterns in the external environment. Organizational adaptability is also the ability of a corporation's strategy, organizations, technologies, operations and leadership to keep up with changes in the external environment.

Raynor (2007) suggests that sudden and gradual environmental changes occur simultaneously, and that it is impossible to deal with the demands of an unpredictable environment, no matter how adaptable the organization may be, without some other entirely new element. Many companies find it difficult to accurately predict change from the complex factors influencing external environmentals, such as markets, technological innovation, competitive and cooperative environments, and structural change over time. As a corporate strategy for environmental adaptation in such situations, Raynor suggests the need to synthesize core strategies with no risk (defined as risk of failure occurring when making strategic commitments) common to multiple outstanding strategies (these can also be described as strategies whose success can be adequately projected in the planning stage) with contingency strategies contributing to a small number of specific outstanding strategies (alternative strategies with uncertain elements, yet having the potential to help future business). These approaches enable companies to adapt to strategic uncertainty and enhance their organizational adaptability to environmental change.

Here, core strategy is planned (deliberate) strategy (Mintzberg, 1978), which establishes a reliable competitive edge as existing business enhances core competences or related business exploits core competences. With core strategy, it is important to drive business through improvements and best practices resulting from continuous organizational learning.

Core strategy should also be implemented when environmental change is slow or moderate. However, in business domains with high-paced environmental change, "strategic learning" through multiple strategy scenarios and trial and error with 'intentional emergent strategies' (see Figure 2.6) become important. To implement robust adaptive strategies to deal with the unpredictable, a company must enhance its 'dynamic adapation capability' (Dixon et al., 2014) by implementing a range of business investments, incubations and real-option strategies (Beinhocker 1999). Thus, the synthesis of deliberate and intentional emergent strategies enhances a company's 'dynamic adaptation capability'. In this book, the author calls this paradoxical strategy-making and implementation an "environment adaptive strategy" (see Figure 2.6).

"Intentional emergent strategies" differ from deliberate strategies that are executed through decision-making at the top level of companies, in that these proposals originate from the frontline or often from middle management. With intentional emergent strategies, originators intentionally anticipate, foresee and predict new meaning from the relationships between dissimilar and existing knowledge (or empirical knowledge), and repeatedly verify hypotheses by taking advantage of flashes of inspiration and their imagination to create new strategies. Thus, intentional emergent strategies

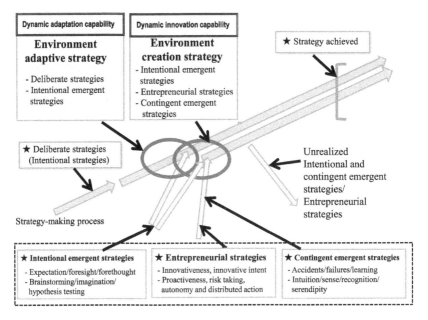

Figure 2.6   Environment Adaptive and Environment Creation Strategies

are bottom-up strategic proposals that are for the most part in step with a company's missions and directions, and are not often just purely emergent.

On the other hand, the environment adaptive strategy is an objective "passive strategy behavior" for adapting to environmental change, and redefines a company's strategic positioning from the positioning-based view while renewing core competences (core knowledge) in response to environmental change from the resource-based view. Adaptation with these approaches is important in facing environmental change and improving core knowledge.

Apple and Samsung are examples of leading smartphone and digital product companies that create business ecosystems. As shown in Figure 2.1, these companies improve their knowledge and expand their product lineup while introducing new versions one after the other, and are maintaining their positions and shares as global leaders as they work to expand and establish their leadership in the ecosystem. As customer demands for these new digital goods (product aspects such as quality, price and functionality) diversify around the world, and as technologies develop (in particular device miniaturization, high functionality and low power consumption, etc. through software development and components), and against the backdrop of environments of competition and cooperation, these companies simultaneously improve their core knowledge, i.e., their technological capabilities (by improving hardware and software development capabilities and introducing manufacturing systems for cost reductions and quality improvements) and their operating capabilities (configuring supply chains for efficient sales, production and support on a global scale) to maintain competitiveness in their digital product markets in the ecosystem. These high-tech companies execute environment adaptive strategies by dynamically and sustainably changing their knowledge to adapt to environmental change. Their approach is an example of the dynamic adaptation capability discussed earlier.

In spite of that, countless past examples of failed environment adaptive strategies exist, including the cases of failure to adapt to technological changes described below. Any company hoping to grow continuously must be able to successfully manage the transfer from current to new technology. A large body of research carried out in the US and Europe has highlighted cases of established, outstanding companies that succeeded with existing technologies, but failed to overcome the challenges of new technologies. Thus, the bringers of new technologies were not the established major corporations, but the new start-ups. For example, when technology transferred from vacuum tubes to semiconductors, which emerged in 1955 and dominated for a quarter-century, the only two companies to survive the transition were RCA and Philips (Foster, 1986).

Research into this technology transfer undertaken in the US and Europe has offered various explanations (e.g., Henderson and Clark, 1990). Among these, Foster suggested the S-curve technology theory and emphasized the dilemma of technological transfer that arises from it. Christensen (1997) undertook a historical analysis of the hard-disk industry and asserted that the outstanding companies failed due to the missing requisite of truly outstanding management—that of listening to the demands of their customers. Nevertheless, leader companies able to ride the wave of new technologies certainly exist, and many Japanese companies especially have successfully handled the technology transfer. Examples of these companies that survived the switch from vacuum to semiconductor technologies mentioned above include Japanese majors such as Toshiba, Matsushita (Panasonic) and Hitachi, companies that continue to play a leading role in the technology transfer.

The recent example of the technology transfer from analog silver halide cameras to digital cameras highlights a difference between US and European companies on the one hand, and Japanese companies on the other. The US camera manufacturers Polaroid and Kodak have already withdrawn from the digital camera market, whereas Japanese film and camera manufacturers such as Canon, Fujifilm, Olympus and Nikon continue to dominate with both digital and conventional cameras. There is little clarification at the management level as to how this difference arose or why some companies achieve so many successful strategy and technology transfers. One explanation (asserted in this book) is that of the optimal "change process management" with boundaries consistency using the management innovation model to adapt to environmental change.

2.3.3 Innovation Dynamic Capability for Environment Creation Strategies

In reality, while "environment adaptive strategy" forms the greater part of corporate strategy behavior, the academic research on the subjective aspects of "active strategy behavior" has been much debated. Hamel (1998, 1996) cited strategic innovation as the key to successful value creation. With the strategic intent of corporate leaders playing a crucial role (Hamel and Prahalad, 1989), strategic innovation emphasizes the kind of business change that radically reforms (or restructures) existing business models, provides new value to the customer, anticipates competition and creates value for all stakeholders.

When thinking about corporate strategy in the light of his business experience, the author considers that the essence of corporate strategy is a company's ability to dynamically and mutually complement and reinforce its core knowledge, and to constantly change its market positions to suit its targets while sustainably formulating and implementing strategy. Markets (the external environment of positioning theory) and organizations (the internal resources of resource-based theory) are not diametrically opposed; rather, companies (practitioners) must dynamically synthesize these elements from a strategic perspective. How should practitioners think and act when opening up new markets? How should companies dynamically build and implement strategy? These questions also tie in with the issues discussed in this chapter.

Strategy-making in companies that transcends their own core knowledge and spontaneously and deliberately formulates new positions (products, services and business models) is an essential part of practitioners' day-to-day business, especially in uncertain environments characterized by dramatic change. Thus, companies must continuously work to create the new knowledge needed to establish new market positions and deliberately create new environments while simultaneously establishing new competitive positions through trial and error. Therefore, in practice, this dynamic thinking and action is an approach that simultaneously shifts from the external to the internal (in the corporate system perspective) and from the internal to the external (Kodama, 2007a).

The author would like to emphasize an aspect that has rarely been the subject of academic research—that of companies (practitioners) that spontaneously create environments for new markets and technologies. Here, in questioning how to create innovative strategies through drastic means, Hamel (1998) developed his strategy, the "S-curve."

For example, the achievement of the Apple iPhone and NTT DOCOMO i-mode business ecosystems did not just come about due to environmental changes such as customer demands or technological advances, but were born through these companies' intentions to create new markets and technologies. By transforming existing mobile telephones and creating new markets, Apple and NTT DOCOMO built new ecosystems (the examples of self-renewal and birth in Figure 2.1). Also, recent years have seen typical examples of ecosystems such as those fusing the home appliance, broadband and multimedia to create ubiquitous communications markets (M2M—machine to machine, IoT—Internet of things), and the telematics market, which brings together electronics, IT and automotive technologies. These cases can also be represented by a new strategic S-curve.

Accordingly, to achieve future innovation, the most important issues facing companies are both adapting to environmental change and adopting processes for creating environments by deliberately forming new market positions with the intention of innovation through new emergence. In the high-tech industry, where environmental change is especially dramatic and investment in new products and services is essential, companies must have a dynamic view of strategy (e.g., Markides, 1999) to adapt to environmental change while creating their own environments to acquire competitive dominance. Thus, the dynamic view of strategy must go beyond the continuous creation of new products and services to sustainably construct major business concepts or models.

Therefore, this strategy-making process does not just include the intentional emergent strategies mentioned earlier, but also requires the execution of entrepreneurial strategies through the entrepreneurial spirit within companies (see Figure 2.6). Entrepreneurship involves businesspeople seeking out opportunity in uncertainty, and achieving innovation while shouldering the burden of risk, which can be viewed as actions and processes in pursuit of entrepreneur rent (Collis and Montogomery, 2005) obtained. Entrepreneurship is not only found in the actions of start-ups, but is also a critical element of existing companies, including the majors (e.g., Low and Mac-Millan, 1988; Stevenson, Roberts, and Grousbeck, 1989; Wortman, 1987). Therefore, as well as meaning activities to get a company off the ground and bring about an organization from zero, as seen in venture companies, it also means corporate entrepreneurship seen in new products and services developments or new corporate venture activities in existing companies (e.g., Shane and Venkatraman, 2000; Sharma and Chrisma, 1999).

Thus, entrepreneurial strategies have a lot of weight in configuring new and previously unseen business models, such as ecosystems. For these reasons, practitioners need to engage in innovativeness (Lumpkin and Dess, 1996) to establish innovative intent, proactivity (Lumpkin and Dess, 1996) combining thought and actions with risk taking (Miller and Friesen, 1978), and autonomy and distributed actions through strategic learning (Kodama, 2003).

In addition to these strategy-making processes, contingent emergent strategies (see Figure 2.6) are also required. Contingent emergent strategies enable strategy creation in the sense of the purely emergent, in other words, strategies from ideas that bubble up suddenly from the thoughts of proposers, and are strategies often observed in discovery and invention processes such as science or new product developments. Called "contingent emergent strategies," they are often the birthplace of new inventions and products created from the intuition, sense, recognition or serendipity, etc. of scientists and researchers in the process of sustained learning through coincidence and failure. Some of these include new product developments such as 3M's Post-It product, P&G's Ivory Soap and Pfizer's Viagra, and new scientific discoveries and inventions such as Fleming's penicillin, Pasteur's vaccines and Leo Esaki's tunnel diode.

Integrating these intentional emergent strategies, entrepreneurial strategies and contingent emergent strategies raises the level of a company's dynamic innovation capability (Dixon et al., 2014). In this book, the author calls integrating and implementing these strategy-making processes "environment creation strategies" (see Figure 2.6).

2.3.4 The Framework of the Management Innovation Model—Strategic Innovation Capability

Companies actualize these environment adaptive and creation strategies within their corporate systems to grow existing business in a way that is adapted to environmental change and to realize new business to create environments, and in so doing, to establish a sustainable competitive edge. Figure 2.7 shows a strategy framework for a company to continuously

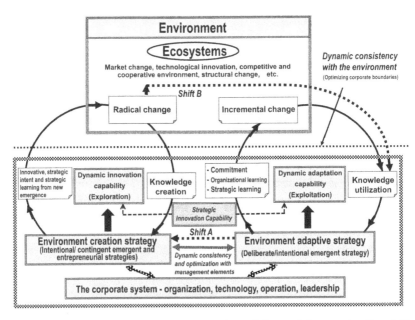

Figure 2.7 Dynamic Strategic Management through Strategic Innovation Capability

implement both environment adaptive strategies to grow existing business through knowledge utilization, and environment creation strategies to build new market positions through knowledge creation to achieve future innovations and acquire new knowledge.

The implementation cycle of the environment adaptive strategy enables a company to adapt to environmental change (through gradual or sudden progress, or a mixture of the two), and spontaneously synthesizes or separates deliberate strategies through daily commitment and organizational learning (improving daily activities), from or with intentional emergent strategies that come about through learning arising from trial and error in situations characterized by uncertainty and high hurdles. Nevertheless, in implementing cycles of environment creation strategies, it is important for a company to implement intentional, contingent emergent and entrepreneurial strategies (Mintzberg, 1978) through strategic learning through trial and incubation, and thus create sudden environmental change through the innovative and strategic intent resulting from new emergence. As described below, these two cycles are not independent, but interdependent.

The implementational shift from environment adaptive strategies to new environment creation strategies (Shift A in Figure 2.7) consists of actions to enter completely new fields (and sometimes industries) and create new business domains through new technologies emerging in the growth processes of existing businesses.

NTT DOCOMO's i-mode service (Kodama, 2002) and the IC card businesses of telecommunications carriers and transport/distribution companies are examples of this strategy- making process. Another example of this can be seen in the case of Fanuc (Kodama and Shibata, 2014), a global leader in the machine tool field, which engaged in the strategy-making process by undertaking technological and organizational transformations to raise quality and cut costs, while newly expanding the machine tool market. As well as those, the strategy transformation of Apple in its shift from computer business to music distribution and smartphone businesses (Kodama, 2011a) are examples of creating new ecosystems through the self-renewal and birth illustrated in Figure 2.1.

Another example of the strategy-making process can be seen in an environment creation strategy that redefines newly emerging business domains as a company's core business, and a company that achieves a sustainable environment adaptive strategy by committing to and investing in new resources in this core business (Shift B in Figure 2.7). For example, this is seen when a venture company with a special technology starts out with an environment creation strategy, but then rivals enter the newly emerged markets, and these competitive new markets steadily change as they grow while the venture company (already grown to a medium-sized enterprise) gears itself toward environment adaptive strategies.

Cases of this include the Sony game business corporate venture "Sony Computer Entertainment (SCE)" (a subsidiary) (Kodama, 2007c), or the split off from Fujitsu in Japan of Fanuc as an internal venture (Kodama and Shibata, 2014), which are examples of the Shift B strategy-making process. Through these corporate ventures, the start-ups created ecosystems as new markets (described as self-renewal and birth in Figure 2.1), after which competitors moved in to reconfigure the ecosystem. Thus, to adapt to the shift to a competitive environment, the start-up companies had to reinforce their environmental adaptation strategies in the ecosystem to maintain their lead, which is described by Shift B (as the establishment of expansion and leadership in the ecosystem—see Figure 2.1).

Moreover, in the sustainable growth of a business ecosystem, as shown in Figure 2.1, the renewal stage in which new businesses are created becomes a key condition for sustainable co-evolution between stakeholders. Here, leader companies within the business ecosystem set down timely environment creation strategies while driving the shift from environment creation to environment adaptive strategies with the stakeholders. Then, cycling from environment creation to environment adaptive strategies and back again becomes the motive force behind the growth of sustainable business ecosystems. As shown in Figure 2.5, this is an example of a sustainable corporate growth process brought about through the "dynamic capabilities cycle" (Dixon et al., 2014).

In the corporate activities of recent years, the time for a strategy to take effect has shortened, while the focus-expand-redefine cycle of strategic activity has accelerated (Zook, 2007). Accordingly, companies must pioneer new business domains and promote existing business growth while implementing this spiral of sustainable strategy practice by achieving dynamic consistency in environmental change with their corporate systems, and while skillfully managing environment adaptive and creation strategies.

Consistency both within and outside of corporate systems ((1) strategy, (2) organizations, (3) technologies, (4) operations and (5) leadership) is a factor that brings about the dynamic adaption capability needed to execute environmental adaptive strategies, and the dynamic innovation capability needed to execute environment creation strategies. In this book, as a framework supplemental to the dynamic capabilities cycle (Dixon et al., 2014) [Insert Figure 2.5], the author calls the integration of dynamic adaption capability and dynamic innovation capability (asynchronously and synchronously) in the dynamic capabilities cycle in strategic corporate activity "strategic innovation capability" (Kodama and Shibata, 2014) (see Figure 2.6).

[Insight 6]

Consistency both within and outside of corporate systems ((1) strategy, (2) organizations, (3) technologies, (4) operations and (5) leadership) brings about the dynamic adaptation and dynamic innovation capabilities.

[Insight 7]

The integration (asynchronous and synchronous) of dynamic adaptation and dynamic innovation capabilities brings about the strategic innovation capabilities of companies that execute both environmental adaptation and environmental creation strategies.

Hamel mentions that 21st century management innovation has to enhance both operational efficiency and the strategic aspects of adaptability (Hamel, 1998). This means that companies should continuously implement environment adaptive strategies for innovation. Hamel also talks about the importance of successively creating daring, rule-breaking innovations, saying, "first picture the future, then create that future." Thus, companies should also always implement environment creation strategies. In this way, strategic innovation capability also includes and conceptualizes Hamel's two assertions. Leading cases of strategic innovation capability can be seen in the Japanese automakers Toyota Motors and Honda, machine tool manufacturer Fanuc, digital equipment manufacturers Apple, Samsung and Canon, and communications carriers NTT DOCOMO and SoftBank. These companies deliberately and simultaneously implement incremental innovation through sustainable improvement as their environment adaptive strategies, and radical innovation through innovative behavior as their environment creation strategies (see Figure 2.7).

Modern-day business activities are complex, and the implementation of "strategic innovation capability" poses problems and challenges. As Raynor (2007) points out, the future is uncertain, and it is unclear what strategies will succeed (cases abound where commitment to specific strategies that seemed sure to succeed resulted in very little gain). This is truly a strategic paradox—however outstanding a technology appears, its value from the customer's point of view might be quite different.

As discussed, the following insight can be derived from the discussion about environmental adaptation and environmental creation strategies.

[Insight 8]

Dynamic strategic management involving the strategic innovation capability embedded in a corporate management innovation model achieves the creation, growth and development of ecosystems.

However, to achieve the strategic innovation capability to create, grow and develop an ecosystem, as mentioned, dynamic boundaries consistency is required both inside and outside of corporate systems, and for this, an optimized organizational model must be configured through collaborative innovation among stakeholders such as leader corporations and follower corporations. As already stated in [Insight 4], the key is to establish innovation communities as business networks that make up the ecosystem. In other words, there need to be dynamic community systems built through collaboration between stakeholders (see Figure 2.2). Chapter 9 in Part 3 analyzes and considers the framework for dynamic community systems to achieve management innovation models as optimized corporate systems, and to sustainably execute strategic innovation capability, through the case studies discussed in Part 2.

NOTES

1. Refer to Klein (1988), Williamson (1975) for the transaction cost economics view. Refer to Penrose (1959), Nelson and Winter (1982) for the capabilities and competencies view. Refer to Kogut and Zander (1992) for the identification view.
2. For example, see Versteeg and Bouwman (2006) and Hasselbring (2000). Refer to Gharajedaghi (2005) for business architecture concepts in the systems theory view.

REFERENCES

Barney, J. (1991). Firm resources and sustained competitive advantage. *Journal of Management*, 17(3), 99–120.
Bateson, G. (1979). *Mind and Nature*. New York: Brockman, Inc.
Beinhocker, E. (1999). Robust adaptive strategies. *Sloan Management Review*, 40(3), 95–106.
Benson, J. (1977). Organization: A dialectical view. *Administrative Science Quarterly*, 22, 221–242.
Bookchin, M (1990). *The Philosophy of Social Ecology: Essays on Dialectical Naturalism*. Black Rose Books Ltd US.
Chakravarthy, B. (1997). A new strategy framework for coping with turbulence. *Sloan Management Review*, 38(2), 69–82.
Chesbrough, H. (2003). *Open Innovation*. Boston, MA: Harvard Business School Press.
Chesbrough, H. (2006). *Open Business Models: How to Thrive in the New Innovation Landscape*. Boston, MA: Harvard Business School Press.
Christensen, C.M. (1997). *The Innovator's Dilemma: When New Technologies Cause Great Firms to Fail*. Boston, MA: Harvard Business School Press.
Collis, D.J. & Montgomery, C.A. (2005). *Corporate Strategy: A Resource-Based Approach* (2nd ed.). New York: Irwin-McGraw-Hill.
Das, T.K. & Teng, B. (2000). Instabilities of strategic alliances: An internal tensions perspective. *Organization Science*, 11(1), 77–101.
D'Aveni, R. (1995). Coping with hypercompetition: Utilizing the new 7S's framework. *Academy of Management Executive*, 9(3), 45–60.
Dixon, S., Meyer, K. & Day, M. (2014). Building dynamic capabilities of adaptation and innovation: A study of micro-foundations in a transition economy. *Long Range Planning*, 47(4), 186–205.
Eisenhardt, K.M. (2002). Has strategy changed? *MIT Sloan Management Review*, 4(2), 88–91.
Foster, R. (1986). *Innovation: The Attacker's Advantage*. New York:Summit Books.

Garud, R. & Karnoe, P. (2001). Path creation as a process of mindful deviation. In: R. Garud, P. Karnoe (eds.), *Path Dependence and Creation*. London: Lawrence Erlbaum, 1–38.

Gharajedaghi, J. (2005). *Systems Thinking: Managing Chaos and Complexity: A Platform for Designing Business Architecture* (2nd ed.). Oxford: Butterworth-Heinemann.

Gibson, C. & Birkinshaw, J. (2004). The antecedents, consequences, and mediating role of organizational ambidexterity. *Academy of Management Journal*, 47(2), 209–226.

Giddens, A. (1979). *Central Problems in Social Theory: Action, Structure, and Contradiction in Social Analysis*. London: University of California Press.

Hamel, G. (1996). Strategy as revolution. *Harvard Business Review*, 74(6), 69–82.

Hamel, G. (1998). Strategy innovation and the quest for value. *MIT Sloan Management Review*, 39(2), 7–14.

Hamel, G. & Prahalad, C.K. (1989). Strategic intent. *Harvard Business Review*, 67(3), 63–76.

Hasselbring, W. (2000). Information system integration. Communications of the ACM, 43(6), 32–38.

He, Z. & Wong, P. (2004). Exploration vs. exploitation: An Empirical test of the ambidexterity hypothesis. *Organization Science*, 15(4), 481–494.

Henderson, R. & Clark, K. (1990). Architectural innovation: The reconfiguration of existing product technologies and the failure of established firms. *Administrative Science Quarterly*, 35(1), 9–30.

Huston, L. & Sakkab, N. (2006). Connect and develop inside Procter & Gamble's new model for innovation. *Harvard Business Review*, 84(3), 58–66.

Iansiti, M. & Levien, R. (2004). *The Keystone Advantage: What the New Dynamics of Business Ecosystems Mean for Strategy, Innovation, and Sustainability*. Boston, MA: Harvard Business School Press.

Kauffman, S. (1993). *The Origins of Order: Self-Organization and Selection in Evolution*. Oxford: Oxford University Press.

Klein, B. (1988). Vertical integration as organizational ownership: The Fisher-Body-General Motors relationship revisited. *Journal of Law and Economic Organization*, 4(2), 199–213.

Kodama, M. & Shibata, T. (2014). Strategy transformation through strategic innovation capability—a case study of Fanuc. *R&D Management*, 44(1), 75–103.

Kodama, M. (2002). Transforming an Old Economy Company through strategic communities. *Long Range Planning*, 35(4), 349–365.

Kodama, M. (2003). Strategic innovation in traditional big business. *Organization Studies*, 24(2), 235–268.

Kodama, M. (2004). Strategic community-based theory of firms: Case study of dialectical management at NTT DoCoMo. *Systems Research and Behavioral Science*, 21(6), 603–634.

Kodama, M. (2007a). *The Strategic Community-Based Firm*. London, UK: Palgrave Macmillan.

Kodama, M. (2007b). *Knowledge Innovation—Strategic Management as Practice*. London, UK: Edward Elgar Publishing.

Kodama, M. (2007c). *Project-Based Organization in the Knowledge-Based Society*. London, UK: Imperial College Press.

Kodama, M. (2007d). Innovation and knowledge creation through leadership-based strategic community: Case study on high-tech company in Japan. *Technovation*, 27(3), 115–132.

Kodama, M. (2009a). *Innovation Networks in Knowledge-Based Firm—Developing ICT-Based Integrative Competences*. UK: Edward Elgar Publishing.

Kodama, M. (2009b). Boundaries innovation and knowledge integration in the Japanese firm. *Long Range Planning*, 42(4), 463–494.

Kodama, M. (2011a). *Knowledge Integration Dynamics—Developing Strategic Innovation Capability*. Singapore: World Scientific Publishing.

Kodama, M. (2011b). *Interactive Business Communities-Accelerating Corporate Innovation through Boundary Networks*. London, UK: Gower Publishing.

Kogut, B. and Zander, U (1992). Knowledge of the Firm, Combinative Capabilities and the Replication of Technology. *Organization Science*, 5(2), 383–397.

Levin, S. (1999). *Fragile Dominion*. New York: Perseus Publishing.

Low, M.B. & MacMillan, I.C. (1988). Entrepreneurship: Past Research and Future Challenges. *Journal of Management*, 14(2), 139–161.

Lumpkin, G.T. & Dess, G.G. (1996). Clarifying the entrepreneurial orientation construct and linking it to performance. *Academy of Management Journal*, 21(1), 135–172.

March, J. (1991). Exploration and exploitation in organizational learning. *Organization Science*, 2(1), 71–87.

Markides, C. (1999). *All the Right Moves: A Guide to Crafting Breakthrough Strategy*. Boston, MA: Harvard Business School Publishing.

Marten, G. (2001). *Human Ecology*. New York: Earthscan Publication Ltd.

Miller, D. & Friesen, P.H. (1978). Archetypes of strategy formulation. *Management Science*, 24(9), 921–933.

Mintzberg, H. (1978). Patterns in strategy formation. *Management Science*, 24(4), 934–948.

Montgomery, C. (2008). Putting leadership back into strategy. *Harvard Business Review*, 86(1), 54–60.

Moore, J. (1993). Predators and prey: A new ecology of competition. *Harvard Business Review*, 71(3),75–86.

Moore, J. (1996). *The Death of Competition: Leadership and Strategy in the Age of Business Ecosystems*. New York: Harper Business.

Morel, B. & Ramanujam, R. (1999). Through the looking glass of complexity: The dynamics of organizations as adaptive and evolving systems. *Organization Science*, 10(3), 278–293.

Nadler, D. & Tushman, M. (1989). Organizational frame bending: Principles for managing reorientation. *Academy of Management Executive*, III(3), 194–204.

Nelson, R. & Winter, S. (1982). *An Evolutionary Theory of Economic Change*. Cambridge, MA: Belknap Press.

Nonaka, I. & Takeuchi, H. (1995). *The Knowledge-Creating Company*. New York: Oxford University Press.

Norgaard, R. (1994). *Development Betrayed*. London, UK: Routledge.

Penrose, E.T. (1959). *The Theory of the Growth of the Firm*. New York: Wiley.

Pisano, G. (1991). The governance of innovation: Vertical integration and collaborative arrangements in the biotechnology industry. *Research Policy*, 20(3), 237–249.

Porter, M. (1980). *Competitive Strategy: Techniques for Analyzing Industries and Competitors*. New York: Free Press.

Porter, M. (1985). *Competitive Advantage*. New York: Free Press.

Prahalad, C.K. & Ramaswamy, V. (2000). Co-opting customer competence. *Harvard Business Review*, 78(1), 79–88.

Prigogine, I. (1996). *The end of certainty*. New York: The Free Press.

Raynor, M. (2007). *The Strategy Paradox: Why Committing to Success Leads to Failure*. US: Broadway Business.

Santos, F.M. & Eisenhardt, K.M. (2005). *Constructing Markets and Organizing Boundaries: Entrepreneurial Action in Nascent Fields*. Working paper, INSEAD

Shane, S. & Venkataraman, S. (2000). The promise of entrepreneurship as a field of research. *Academy of Management Review*, 25(2), 217–226.

Shapiro, C. & Varian, H.R. (1998). *Information Rules*. Boston, MA: Harvard Business School Press.

Sharma, P. & Chrisman, J. (1999). Toward a reconciliation of the definitional issues in the field of corporate entrepreneurship. *Entrepreneurship Theory and Practice*, 23(3), 11–27.

Stacey, R. (1995). The science of complexity: An alternative perspective for strategic change process. *Strategic Management Journal*, 16(6), 477–495.

Stacey, R. (1996). *Complexity and Creativity in Organizations*. San Francisco: Berett-Koehler Publishers.

Stevenson, H.H., Roberts, M.J. & Grousbeck, H.I. (1989). *New Business Ventures and the Entrepreneur*. Homewood, IL: Irwin.

Teece, D. (2007). Explicating dynamic capabilities: The nature and microfoundations of (sustainable) enterprise performance. *Strategic Management Journal*, 28(12), 1319–1350.

Teece, D., Pisano, G. & Shuen, A. (1997). Dynamic capabilities and strategic management. *Strategic Management Journal*, 18(3), 509–533.

Tushman, M.L. & O'Reilly, C.A. (1997). *Winning Through Innovation*. Cambridge, MA: Harvard Business School Press.

Versteeg, G. & Bouwman, H. (2006). Business architecture: A new paradigm to relate business strategy to ICT. *Information Systems Frontiers*, 8(2), 91–102.

Watts, J. (2003). *Six Degrees: The Science of a Connected Age*. New York: W.W. Norton and Company.

Wenger, E.C. (1998). *Community of Practice: Learning, Meaning and Identity*. Cambridge: Cambridge University Press.

Wernerfelt, B. (1984). A resource-based view of the firm. *Strategic Management Journal*, 5(1), 171–180.

Williamson, O.E. (1975). *Markets and Hierarchies: Analysis and Antitrust Implications*. New York: Free Press.

Wortman, M.S., Jr. (1987). Entrepreneurship: An integrating typology and evaluation of the empirical research in the Field. *Journal of Management*, 13(2), 259–279.

Zook, C. (2007). Finding your next core business. *Harvard Business Review*, 85(4), 66–75.

Part II
In-Depth Case Studies

3 Building a Health Support Ecosystem Between Hospitals

Toshiro Takahashi, Daisuke Koide,
Mu-Ho Liu and Takenori Aoki

So far, this book has presented the proposition of [Insight 2] in Chapter 1, that "[t]he co-evolution model through collaborative innovation spanning various industries promotes the creation of win-win business models," and the proposition of [Insight 3] in Chapter 2, that "[t]he process of [the] spiraling execution of exploration and exploitation centered on leader companies (or organizations) creates, grows and develops business ecosystems." This chapter looks at cases of medical institutions in Canada that execute environment adaptation strategies as exploitations to adapt to changing environments, and that execute environment creation strategies as explorations to create new environments. This chapter also analyzes and considers the propositions of [Insight 5] in Chapter 2, that the "[d]ynamic consistency of boundaries between environments and corporate systems, and boundaries between the individual business elements within corporate systems builds ecosystems and achieves sustainable corporate development and growth."

3.1 THE HEALTH SUPPORT ECOSYSTEM OF CANADIAN BLOOD SERVICES (CBS)

3.1.1 Canadian Blood Services (CBS) Overview

Excluding Quebec, CBS is an organization headquartered in Ottawa in Ontario Province that provides blood services across Canada, and that was established by the Canadian federal government. Having around 5,000 staff, this organization has annual revenues in excess of $1 billion. With blood collection facilities widely deployed in 42 locations throughout Canada, the organization collects about 1 million units of blood every year from Canadian citizens, which it distributes along with blood products and stem cells to the more than 700 hospitals around the country.

There are four main areas of business covered by the CBS health support ecosystem. The first of these is the business involved in anything to do with blood. This entails recruiting donors, collecting and independently testing blood constituents and manufacturing blood products, and providing these to Canadian hospitals.

The second of these businesses is involved in operating stem cell planning across Canada. CBS operates a national registry for patients who require or are waiting for stem cell or bone marrow transplants. The organization links its registry globally to form an international registry of patients requiring transplants and suitable donors.

The third area of business is the organization's blood plasma operations. This entails collecting plasma from donors and using it to make particular medicines. CBS does not only provide therapeutic agents for hemophiliacs and sufferers of immune disorders, but also functions as an importer of human biological products, using a unified import system. The organization imports and distributes some 35 types of medicine required by hospitals.

The fourth area of business is carried out in CBS's diagnostic laboratories across Canada, in which clinical trials are performed on behalf of a wide range of hospitals and healthcare institutions. In addition, CBS is also active as the central body in Canada coordinating organ donation (liver, heart, lungs and kidneys) and contributing to organ provision and transplant. The organization also operates a tissue bank and collects mainly skin, eye and bone tissue from patients for processing. Thus, in spite of what the name suggests, Canadian Blood Services is not just involved in the area of blood, but is actually active across a range of different specializations. CBS is an organization that operates its businesses across Canada and stands at the center of a health support ecosystem.

3.1.2 Adapting to Environments, Consistency of Business Systems with Environments—Implementing the BSC Tool

Splitting from the Canadian Red Cross, CBS was established in 1998 to take over its blood services in Canada, a country that experienced serious problems with HIV infection in the 1980s and 1990s. The Canadian government decided to establish CBS in 1997. Graham Sher, a contributor to this chapter, started his career at CBS in 1998, became vice president of its medical department, and then became its CEO in 2001.

At the time, CBS was facing problems with strategic planning and execution. There was a range of measures in place within its organizations that were in competition with each other, while its management was diffuse and unable to clarify objectives. Furthermore, in 1998, when CBS began operations, the organization was in a constant state of crisis management for the first few years, which became the most significant impetus for the implementation of the balanced scorecard BSC.

In these first years, as soon as one crisis was alleviated, another one appeared. There were problems everywhere. It began everything with crisis management, and finished everything with crisis management.

At the time, Sher felt unable to implement any reforms while his focus was entirely on crisis management, and he was thus strongly aware of the need for scientifically persuasive management to replace the unsatisfactory conditions of crisis management. Thus, CBS needed to unhinge itself from crisis management and shift to strategic management—Sher needed to find an enabler to break free from the constant crisis management mode. It was here that BSC came into play.[1]

Sher described how the company was excellent at crisis management, but needed to move forward with more strategic management. It was problematic to remain solely focused on crisis management. This was the beginning of a new movement, and was the main impetus for the implementation of BSC.

CBS took this action because deploying BSC techniques in a company or organizational system in this way enables the company to transform its entire systems by setting down and executing environmental adaptation strategies to adapt to changes in its environments, while at the same time providing dynamic consistency between environments and company (organizational) systems.

3.1.3 Internal Consistency in Company (Organizational) Systems

Kaplan and Norton (2008) assert that strategic and operational breakdowns are the cause of stagnant corporate results. While a management system can reinforce workplace activities and forge strong links between specific strategic aims using strategic tools such as a strategy manual (explicit knowledge) to support practical corporate activities, it is not the essence of strategy. The key is not only to engage in strategic planning, but also to have a comprehensive view that takes in the "human system" aspect of operations, technologies and the actions and leadership of the practitioners (including customers who are closely connected with the organization) working both inside and outside of the corporation. If the "human system" is ignored, it will be impossible to achieve an outstanding management system. Strategy is thus an organic thing, and really looks much more like a "human process."

Therefore, to successfully implement and use BSC, it is of particular importance to have internal and external cohesion between the aspects of the corporate systems discussed in Chapter 2 ((1) strategies, (2) organizations, (3) technologies, (4) operations and (5) leadership). The following discusses the individual internal managerial factors of a company (organization) system:

(1) Implementing the BSC Technique—Initial Staff Training
CBS cooperated with Kaplan and Norton over two years and sent many of its executives to their research society. As well as that, CBS has engaged in BSC deployment and staff training while partnering with three or four other Canadian companies that already have experience in implementing BSC.[2]

Sher has also attended a number of research meetings held by Kaplan and Norton. He also brings people from the research society into CBS, and has CBS staff participate in meetings and external organizations. In all these cases, Sher has made efforts to enable his executives to have contact with authentic BSC and become accustomed to it.[3] The authors believe the most significant aspect of CBS's execution of BSC is the joint efforts it has made with the guidance it has received from Kaplan and Norton and the experience of authentic BSC. Over a two-year period, Kaplan and Norton and the CBS staff were engaged in this endeavor, during which there was always someone from Kaplan's instructional group stationed at CBS. This can be seen as one of the important factors of success.

At the time, Sher concluded that although BSC was a costly investment, CBS needed to get training in it and learn it, and to absorb it into its culture. On reflection, Sher spoke of how BSC was crucial to success. Even though the investment cost well over $1 million, the results proved that it was worth it. After using BSC for almost eight years, business at CBS has been dramatically transformed. By thinking about priorities, the staff can concentrate on business, and have also been able to sufficiently accumulate the organizational capability needed to achieve reforms. The personal and organizational capabilities (knowledge) that enable the reformation of an organizational culture in this way are examples of valuable intangible assets.

(2) *Setting Down and Executing Strategy—From Preparing a Strategy Map to Actual Operations*

CBS completed its first strategy map in 2003, but it took at least a year for it to become widely used. Tables 3.1 and 3.2 describe part of the CBS strategy map and scorecard. This was created in 2009—the company rethinks the strategy map and scorecard every year, when CBS thoroughly checks all of the criteria it uses to measure performance, and reconsiders their validity in relation to the targets. It is of the utmost importance that consistency is brought about between strategy making and BSC as a tool in these operations.

(3) *Operations—Consistency with BSC*

There are many operational mechanisms of BSC. Because BSC is used in conjunction with business cycles, a strategy is set down at the beginning of each fiscal year using BSC. Every month, all departments assess their business performance using a scorecard. In addition, all departments meet each quarter term to assess their performance for that quarter. Sher himself also presents a performance report on the whole of CBS to the Board of Directors each quarter. Thus, this is one type of management cycle operating at CBS. BSC is used for strategic planning and for monthly and quarterly performance reporting, and is used to thoroughly convey intentions. Therefore, there are a number of tools used. Performance reports are created and

Table 3.1   CBS Strategy Map (Partial)

Items	Contents
Mission	Commitment to safety and security of CBS high-quality blood and blood products, supplied at an affordable price, to gain the trust of the Canadian people and to supply blood in Canada
Excellence in customer service	Operating systems to provide blood services effectively, efficiently and reliably to Canadians
Strategic actions	-The right products in the right placeat the right time - Better efficiency and productivity - Efficient recruiting and maintenance of blood donation - Promoting optimized product use
Resource usage	- Improve staff techniques, talent and knowledge - Business support with IT - Quality systems and organizational cultural development

Table 3.2   Scorecard for Efficient Blood Donor Recruiting and Maintenance

Strategic objectives	Scale	Target values	Action plans
Efficiently recruiting and maintaining blood donation	Frequency of blood donation	Leukocytes: 2.2 Plasma: 10 Platelets: 5.4	E.g. Training in customer service

Source: Compiled from interviews.

distributed regularly to organizations using the company intranet. BSC at CBS is used for reporting, monitoring and measuring performance. CBS meets once a year to rethink its approach to its strategy map, performance measurement, criteria and numerical targets.

(4) Organizational Forms that Drive Transformation—Consistency with BSC

While it was implementing BSC, CBS was facing a number of organizational issues (see Column 3.1). In 2005, the company set up and began operating its Office of Strategy Management (OSM). Under Sher, a vice president was assigned the job of director of strategy management to lead a team managing strategic processes on behalf of top management. Thus, the OSM was responsible for maintaining consistency between BSC, strategy and operations. While the vice presidents in charge of the actual business operations are also responsible for executing strategy, it is the OSM that manages the overall processes centered on BSC.

The OSM gathers a variety of data, engages in reporting and checks that all reports are properly made available. Next, the OSM consults with Sher, and Sher consults with the management team. The management team engages in strategy creation and operational management, but also takes charge of a wide variety of reporting and analysis tasks.

The vice president in charge of managing strategy in the OSM works directly under CEO Sher, but must also require information from other vice presidents. Although Sher has authority, coordination tasks become difficult when there are discrepancies between the opinions of the vice presidents in charge of operations and the vice president in charge of strategy, because authority and accountability are not always perfectly clear. Therefore, sometimes there is friction between the OSM and the vice presidents in charge of operations, but it is up to the top management team, including Sher, to make efforts to transform such friction or discord into "creative abrasion" and "productive friction."

(5) Leadership Driving BSC

There are four factors of business that are linked within corporate (organizational) systems as organizational forms to create strategies and execute operations on the axis of the BSC as a tool, and it is leadership that drives consistency among these. At CBS, this leadership comes from Sher[4], the OSM and the vice presidents who are actually in charge of business operations

The organization has seven vice presidents, three of whom were not initially in favor of BSC. These three were critical of BSC and resisted it, but Sher made efforts over a long period to educate them and get them on board. Sher felt that the CBS top management needed to have a unified viewpoint on the kind of strategies to set down and what should be prioritized. Thus, this meant people combining efforts and aligning vectors to move forward in the same direction, rather than individuals moving in different directions. Speaking of this in terms of shared language, how an organization preserves its common language among individuals with different backgrounds is critical. Here, CBS certainly uses BSC as a unified communications tool to enable the sharing of a common language.

However, it took considerable time and effort to get middle management's understanding and willingness regarding BSC. It is essential that the staff is thoroughly supportive and accepting of BSC. The staff had to be trained, which took a long time. With the middle management, this required much more patience than it did with the top management.

Middle management training was performed both within and outside of the company's organizations. Externally, this meant dispatching staff to meetings, other companies, institutions and seminars—some staff in middle management even attended business school to acquire an MBA or similar qualifications from other educational institutions. The company provided wide-ranging training opportunities, such as managerial training, leadership development and coaching, etc. Observational visits were made to public and private sector organizations that had already deployed BSC. One of the public institutions visited was the Royal Canadian Mounted Police (RCMP), because that organization had deployed BSC before CBS. CBS staff made many visits to the RCMP. CBS staff also made field trips to observe private companies, financial institutions and insurance companies using BSC both inside and outside of Canada. These visits also covered the Hospital for Sick Children in Ontario Province, and the University Health Network (UHN) discussed in the case described below.

As described above, the most important aspects of the continued use of BSC are the contribution of top management and the leadership of top and middle management to integrate strategic, organizational, technological and operational factors to maintain consistency within corporate (organizational) systems and bring about consistency with changing environments (see Figure 3.1). It is also important to produce better business results—failure to do so will obviously defeat the purpose of the exercise.

In the end, the strategy map and scorecard play major roles in driving the attainment of results, and therefore, outcomes that have actually been

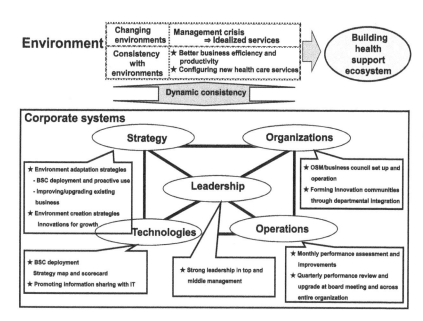

Figure 3.1   Consistency of CBS Organizational Systems

achieved must be presented to all staff. This is another crucial aspect of the leadership of top management.

3.1.4 Shifting Between and Combining Environmental Adaptive Strategies and Environment Creation Strategies

The most remarkable and significant change that happened in CBS with the deployment of BSC was that related staff became aware of setting business priorities. Before BSC was deployed, actions in the company were taken without direction or a strategic objective. The actual business efforts and projects underway were dispersed and lacked sufficient regulation. Sher and the top management are convinced that while BSC is effective on a number of fronts, the most noticeable change was the setting of priorities for strategic objectives, thus enabling the focus to be narrowed onto core business actions.

It is noteworthy that CBS engaged in environment adaptive strategies as exploitations based on BSC to respond to the environmental changes involving business crises, and then engaged in environment creation strategies as explorations to forge ahead with new business when organizational performance improved—new businesses such as the company's organ provision and tissue bank.

The CBS strategies are simple. To date, they have been based on three themes: (1) By making full use of CBS's organizational capability, (2) the company aims to save lives and improve the quality of life, while (3) improving the productivity and efficiency of these actions. CBS sets down three or four strategic objectives for each of these three themes. These involve proactive cost management, improving the quality of processes and sustainably improving and upgrading business models to drive business transformation and raise the levels of productivity and business efficiency through the deployment of high technology. Furthermore, to achieve its objective of saving lives and improving the quality of life, CBS also engages in measures to produce its own innovations, and thus grow sustainably into the future.

As described in Column 3.1, CBS promotes collaborative innovation by forming innovation communities that span the different departments within its own organizations. As a result, the process of spiraling the execution of exploration and exploitation centered on the CBS leader organizations creates, grows and develops health support ecosystems [Insight 3]. Thus, the dynamic consistency of the boundaries between corporate systems and environments, and of the boundaries between the individual business elements within corporate systems is of critical importance. CBS therefore dynamically reconfigures its corporate and organizational systems using the BSC technique to build its health support ecosystems and to achieve sustainable corporate development and growth [Insight 5].

The most important thing for Sher and the top management is creating a strategy map, and while, reading information in from the bottom-up, bringing about the sustainable reform and innovation of the top management leadership, corporate culture and organizational resources (strategy, technologies, operations). By investing in the individual elements of its corporate (organizational) systems, and by focusing efforts on the three central themes mentioned above, the CBS top management confidently achieves sustainable growth and business performance.

COLUMN 3.1 ORGANIZATIONAL REFORM TOWARDS BSC DEPLOYMENT

CBS CEO Sher recalls that some on the board were skeptical of BSC—a number of vice presidents looked on BSC with serious reservations. In addition to their distrust and dislike of BSC, some had interest in other managerial frameworks that were available. Thus, Sher had to make some changes. There were three vice presidents who had no affinity with BSC and were relieved of their posts. This meant that there had to also be some changes made to the management team, which was a serious hurdle to overcome. Looking at this from a different perspective, there was a clash between the optimistic and skeptical attitudes towards BSC.

CBS does not employ many physicians. Of its 5,000 staff, only 25 are doctors, who were not in favor of BSC, although CEO Sher is a doctor who trusts it. As opposed to a hospital, BSC deployment was easier at CBS because of the limited number of doctors involved.

BSC completely changed the CBS organizational structure—transforming the very fabric of the organization itself. BSC involves integrating organizational structures split into departments and divisions to form working groups. These groups are referred to as "business councils," and are formed for each area of business. For this reason, the membership of each business council consists of staff working in those respective areas and those supporting that business. Departments such as human resources, finances and IT are integrated into the business councils, which are responsible for managing each area of business as an integrated organization. Thus, with the introduction of the scorecard, CBS dramatically changed its organizational structures. CBS achieved organizational reform through collaborative innovation by forming the innovation communities discussed in Chapter 2 across its various departments.

CBS lists improved decision making as one of its important strategies. Before BSC was introduced, decision making took time and was extremely difficult to handle. The company focused on improving decision making by driving collaborative innovation through the formation of these innovation communities.

3.2 THE HEALTH SUPPORT ECOSYSTEM OF UNIVERSITY HEALTH NETWORK (UHN)

3.2.1 Overview of UHN

In the beginning of the 1990s, there was a major shakeup of the hospitals in Toronto, Ontario Province. As part of Ontario's reforms to its medical system, UHN was established by integrating the management of the university schools of medicine at three of Toronto's teaching hospitals—Toronto General Hospital, Toronto Western Hospital and Princess Margaret Hospital (and Toronto Rehabilitation Institute, currently). UHN covers some of the largest teaching and research hospitals in Canada providing tertiary and quaternary care. UHN objectives include patient health care, research and education, which are clarified as the UHN mission.

The organization's main areas of activity are in the seven fields of organ transplants, cardiovascular treatment, oncology, the sensory neuroscience involved with musculoskeletal and arthritis treatment, localized healthcare, including emergency treatment, general medicine and mental healthcare. The organization is also active in the fields of advanced medicines and surgery provided to dialysis, digestive system and benign lung disease patients. The organization covers the wide catchment area of Ontario Province, and accepts patients from all over Canada. With its large research headquarters, called the Mars Building, UHN has configured a health support ecosystem in the areas of healthcare and education with itself at the center.

3.2.2 Creating New Environments and Consistency between Environments and Corporate Systems—Implementing BSC as a Tool and Creating New Organizational Cultures

UHN implemented BSC as one method of effecting organizational reform as a structural form necessary to execute strategic management. Unlike the CBS case described above, UHN was not facing a crisis, nor did it face an unfavorable business condition that required it to change the culture of its hospital organizations. Instead, UHN introduced BSC as a proactive strategic action to create a new culture with everybody involved. In other words, introducing and using BSC enables the organizations to set down and work towards its visions, and enables strategies to be presented to the UHN Board of Directors and clinicians working on the healthcare frontline and other stakeholders—BSC is an active approach taken by the organization.

The former CEO, Robert Bell, who took up the post in 2005, made prior active efforts to hold meetings with researchers, educators and staff in all three hospitals. On these occasions, Bell presented strategic targets to achieve a "global impact" (discussed later) as a vision for UHN hospitals, and thoroughly exchanged opinions with all involved.

This entailed discussing the strategic vision of achieving a global impact with the emergency departments, and clarifying which parts of that vision were not properly understood. Put simply, emergency wards were aware of nothing other than the fact that they were working hard for their local society.

Bell, the new CEO, engaged in discussions with the Board of Directors, and began to think deeply about how to enable staff to participate in working towards the grander target of achieving a global impact. As a result, Bell created a statement of purpose that enabled the strategic objectives and the shared values of working with the utmost effort for patients and the global community from the perspectives of caring, creativity and academia.

3.2.3 Internal Consistency in Company (Organizational) Systems

(1) Implementing BSC as a Technique

UHN started out by reading literature of Kaplan and his cohorts, and finally ended by getting the support of Kaplan and his cohorts to implement BSC. This specifically involved sending executives to America to learn at the BSC Collaborative[5]. In this way, it can be said that UHN and CBS traveled the same route, although there were fundamental differences between them in terms of their stance towards BSC.

UHN recognized BSC as a management tool, and used it in a manner that faithfully encapsulated the ideas of Kaplan and his cohorts. On the other hand, although CBS also recognized BSC as a management tool, the organization studied BSC in detail and executed it while aligning with Kaplan and his cohorts, and became infatuated with BSC, supporting it enthusiastically. In other words, CBS CEO Sher felt there was something more to BSC than just a simple management tool—there are about five or six people who work in CBS's Office of Strategic Management (OSM), and CBS staff has also been invited to lecture at seminars held by Kaplan and others. The Sunnybrook Health Sciences Center, the Hospital for Sick Children and Toronto East General Hospital in Toronto also are proactively using BSC, although without the fervor of CBS.

In addition, there are also hospitals in Toronto, such as the Mount Sinai Hospital and the St. John's Rehab Hospital, that use BSC in their own way, using only the basic ideas of Kaplan et al., because BSC is a management tool that confers autonomy. Upon interviewing the CEOs of these hospitals, the authors were able to make the following classifications (see Table 3.3).

Table 3.3 Hospital Stance on Deploying and Developing BSC

BSC deployment	Contents
Orthodox BSC in line with the thinking of Kaplan and his cohorts	- Organizational capability and leadership that embraces BSC passionately and produces results - Organizational capability and leadership that uses BSC dispassionately and produces results - Lack of organizational capability and leadership, which does not produce results
BSC modified by individual interpretation	- Only properly understanding BSC and organizational capability and leadership produce results - Improperly understanding BSC does not produce results

Source: Compiled from interviews.

(2) Setting Down and Executing Strategy

The strategy map of UHN was created based on the objectives of UHN. The UHN vision entails the achievement of a global impact. UHN top management instructs staff working for UHN to find their own individual purpose. The strategic objectives of UHN are caring (in other words, enthusiastically considering people), being active, accountability and also engaging academically. UHN's aim is to pour all of its efforts into its patients, as well as global health in general.

UHN has a statement of purpose, which also describes the attention the organization gives to accountability. UHN pursues consideration of people, creativity and academia in its pursuit of its global impact mission. UHN's strategy map has been created by drawing relationships between these aspects (we, caring, creativity, accountability and academia).

Domains for each of these aspects are set down in the purpose statement. These are the domains in which the hospitals face challenges. The purpose statement contains goals for each of these challenges—attracting the best people, making budgetary savings, and measuring resources, impacts and targets, just as in the strategy map. UHN then produces monthly and quarterly reports, using these targets. These reports are submitted to the UHN Board of Directors, who then makes the information available to all staff online.

(3) Operations—Consistency with BSC

As a characteristic of BSC at UHN, strategy maps are not limited to the management level or Board of Directors, but are created with participation from middle management upwards. This is rare for such large hospitals. Moreover, although those on the frontline do not participate in the creation of BSC, the fact that BSC cascades down to the frontline is also rare for such large hospitals.

The second characteristic of BSC at UHN is the changes that were brought about through the recent implementation of the business intelligence school "Cognos" computer tool. Cognos is a Canadian software company. To cascade its strategy maps, UHN uses this software, as it makes it easy to stretch the cascades to the departmental ends, thus enabling the assessment of results and performance for each department. The tool enables staff to check performance aspects from their own offices, such as how much overtime is being done or how much of the budget has been used, etc.

Whether the UHN hospitals implement this system and use it is up to the individual hospitals. UHN does not only use this software for BSC purposes, but also uses it for financial reporting and enterprise data housing purposes, etc. However, creating reports on various results at the unit level has not been satisfactory.

Various business programs also have individual BSCs. These individual program BSCs are reported to the Board of Directors. In addition to that, BSC for entire hospitals are reported to the Board of Directors.

UHN believes in a holistic strategy. In other words, the overall strategy of UHN is designed to cover everyone, including those working on the frontline, and enable them to make a sincere effort.

(4) Organizational Forms that Drive Transformation—Consistency with BSC

At the time of performing the survey, there were some 14,000 people working in the UHN organization—it was an organization in which communication strategies were particularly difficult. Moreover, it is difficult to thoroughly execute strategies that change with time. The organization found that it was critical that it formulate four action plans, improve communications and make action plans that were linked to its purpose statement in order for it to succeed.

It is UHN's corporate planning team that drives BSC usage. This team is also in charge of disseminating the results of BSC throughout the entire organization. Thus, based on these results, actions are cascaded downwards. For example, if there is excessive overtime, it is reported to the managers. Then, the CEO talks with the executive and management teams about the problem and how to eliminate it, and cascades down the problem by conveying it to the various departments and departmental managers. Then it becomes a ground level, i.e., frontline departmental manager-centered question of thinking about how to reduce overtime. Then, the results of those actions are conveyed back up to the top. As a best practice, this mechanism is structured so that it can be implemented with the other departments across the entire organization and throughout all hospitals.

When UHN engaged with Kaplan and his cohorts' Collaborative to introduce BSC, the CEOs of some hospitals which did not participate in UHN had absolutely no interest in BSC, and some senior leaders did not seem to be making a contribution. However, the response from UHN hospitals was completely different—the CEOs themselves had great interest in BSC and voluntarily participated. Of course, the UHN CEO says that it is advantageous to have separate teams to achieve targets, and it is also good to have those teams monitoring and paying attention to units that are not performing very well. Despite that, UHN did not move in that direction.

The organization has no plans to have individual teams. Instead, the UHN executive believes it is better to more thoroughly review strategy, and more thoroughly reinforce reporting functions. Therefore, currently, BSC is managed in each department informally. UHN suggests that this will bring about the potential to create bodies like management committees within organizations. In other words, innovation communities can flexibly take on both informal and formal forms to suit changing situations.

(5) Leadership Driving BSC

UHN's executive team contributes greatly to BSC by demonstrating the strong leadership needed to drive BSC in individual people. Thus, at UHN, they believe it is not necessary to have individual organizational forms or teams set up to achieve results. Instead, UHN has a range of target business domains, and pours efforts into achieving its objectives of accountability, caring and academia in each of these domains. Here, the organization has supervisors in senior management for each of these domains who are charged with reporting directly to the CEO. This means UHN's top management is extremely strict about reviewing results, while there is also a shift in the organization towards strong leadership that drives BSC in middle management on the frontline.

As described above, and as described by the CBS case, the most important aspects of the continued use of BSC is the contribution of top management and the leadership of top and middle management that integrates strategic, organizational, technological and operational factors to drive consistency within corporate (organizational) systems and maintain consistency with changing environments.

3.2.4 Combining Environment Creation and Environment Adaptation Strategies

As described above, UHN implemented BSC as one method of affecting the organizational and structural reforms needed to execute its strategic management. UHN was not facing a crisis, nor did it face an unfavorable business condition that required it to change the culture of its hospital organizations. In other words, the UHN case differed from the CBS case mentioned above, in that the implementation of BSC was not a response to setting down and executing an environmental adaptation strategy.

In contrast, UHN implemented BSC as part of setting down and executing environment creation strategies, as a dynamic strategic activity to create a new organizational culture for all staff. Thus, by implementing BSC, UHN was able to set down targets and find strategic directions to create new environments.

For UHN staff to achieve a global impact, staff had to ask themselves how they could participate to achieve even bigger objectives, such as the achievement of a global impact, which began with them thinking deeply about how to pursue absolute value as idealized hospital management. As a result, the organization created a statement of purpose that enabled all staff to understand the strategic objectives and the shared values of commitment to patients and the global community from the perspectives of caring, creativity and academia—the prominent characteristics of the organization's achievements.

What is noteworthy about this case is the fact that only the four perspectives of the Kaplan and Norton strategy map were first used as tools at UHN. However, UHN eventually introduced five perspectives (we, caring, creativity, accountability and academia) into its strategy map with its statement of purpose[6]. Therefore, the actual framework of BSC was modified to suit the hospitals involved, which meant that the UHN case was characterized by the setting down of an environmental creation strategy by implementing BSC with the purpose statement containing these five perspectives.

However, these perspectives are aligned (integrated) with Kaplan and Norton's framework. The five perspectives contained in the purpose statement include caring, which is patient-related, creativity, which concerns itself with research, academia, which is concerned with education, and accountability, which is concerned with finance. UHN also has an organizational characteristic of "we" (meaning all staff and doctors, etc.)[7].

Centered on BSC, UHN engages in the execution of its environment creation strategies as explorations. It also is noteworthy in its simultaneous setting down and execution of environment adaptation strategies as exploitations to improve and upgrade its business. UHN has engaged in upgrading and improvement measures for some years, and has employed a range of tools to these ends. For example, the organization has adopted Six Sigma, green initiatives and 5S to improve its business efficiency and productivity. In one case, the organization envisioned reducing the long waiting times in the emergency ward, which entailed rethinking the entire processes therein. In addition to the emergency ward, the organization was able to rethink its overall processes, from transferring and releasing patients to a range of hospital wards, while eliminating waste and inefficiency. To achieve these aims, UHN has been making efforts by investing in new technologies and introducing new processes. In this way, the organization was able to adapt a range of business issues to its hospital management environments.

Similar to the CBS case above, the process of spiraling the execution of exploration and exploitation through collaborative innovation through the formation of innovation communities formed across different organizations and departments centered on UHN leader organizations creates, grows and develops the organization's health support ecosystems [Insight 3]. Thus, the dynamic consistency of the boundaries between corporate systems and environments, and the boundaries between the individual business elements within corporate systems is of critical importance. UHN therefore dynamically reconfigures its corporate and organizational systems using the BSC technique to build its health support ecosystems and achieve sustainable corporate development and growth [Insight 5].

3.3 SUMMARY OF THIS CHAPTER

The corporate activities of the CBS and UHN cases described above specifically realize the notions of Insights 3 and 5 described above, and simultaneously lead to the specific practice of the three propositions below, which are described in Chapter 2.

[Insight 6]

Consistency both within and outside of corporate systems ((1) strategy, (2) organizations, (3) technologies, (4) operations and (5) leadership) brings about dynamic adaptation and dynamic innovation capabilities.

[Insight 7]

The integration (asynchronous and synchronous) of the dynamic adaptation and dynamic innovation capabilities brings about the strategic innovation capabilities of companies that execute both environmental adaptation and environmental creation strategies.

[Insight 8]

Dynamic strategic management involving the strategic innovation capability embedded in a corporate management innovation model achieves the creation, growth and development of ecosystems.

In the above two cases, the efforts made to maintain dynamic consistency between environments and business (organizational) systems and within the business systems entail a combination of setting down and executing both environmental adaptation and environment creation strategies. In this way, the strategic innovation capability described by [Insight 7] comes about by integrating the adaptation dynamic capability and innovation dynamic capability through organizational activity as medical institutions. The strategic innovation capability embedded in a corporate management innovation model achieves the creation, growth and development of health support ecosystems.

NOTES

1. The main aim of using the BSC was to achieve CBS's mission. This was an extremely complicated strategy to execute. Similarly, in 1998, when the Canadian Red Cross was providing blood services, there were 14 centers across Canada that engaged in activities independently. Because there was no coordination among these 14 centers from everything from blood collection through to testing, constituent manufacture, delivery and finances, CBS aimed to integrate business strategies that entailed massive reforms because blood collection was one area of business, while testing was another and so forth.

   For Sher, the BSC clarified CBS strategy, and became a tool that enables the organization to execute, measure and convey its strategies. Sher became even more confident that BSC was a tool that would enable response to all of these issues. Furthermore, for CBS, BSC is also a comprehensive management framework.
2. There were also corporations who had already enshrined BSC. Encounters with these companies were also useful for implementation. In other words,

many organizations, whether they are for-profit or non-profit, face the same basic obstacles to the implementation and operation of BSC. Thus, there is significance in the fact that CBS, a nationally operated non-profit organization, sought out existing case studies of for-profit organizations within Canada.

3. Sher certainly feels that these actions are extremely helpful.
4. Sher's leadership is characterized by patience. If Sher had not been at the helm, CBS's organizational reforms may not have succeeded. It is well known that the direct commitment of the CEO is a crucial factor.
5. Strictly speaking, as the investment in BSC, about $100,000 was paid to the BSC Collaborative for personnel training, BSC understanding and training for leaders. This included workshops held on eight occasions, and is an investment for the continued future growth of the organization.
6. American hospitals that have deployed BSC can and do increase or decrease the four basic perspectives instructed by Kaplan and his cohorts. The literature on the subject describes between three and seven perspectives in use. However, if too many perspectives are used, the basic BSC characteristics of being able to talk about strategy creatively but simply and to increase communication with staff through the strategy map will be lost.
7. Before introducing BSC, UHN reported publicly on the performance of its organizations. For example, the organization announced various results to the community, such as hospital infections and death rates. This information is available to anyone on the organization's website. Such public disclosure is also part of the UHN's organizational culture.

REFERENCE

Kaplan, R. & Norton, D. (2008). Mastering the management system. *Harvard Business Review*, 86(1), 62–77.

4 A Product Innovation of a Timeline System as a Health Support Ecosystem

Yoshiaki Kondo

4.1 BACKGROUND AND RESEARCH OBJECTIVES

With the continued falling birth rates and aging of society, the medical and healthcare fields are facing issues such as increases in lifestyle-related diseases and the uneven distribution of medical resources. To solve these problems, it is important that the roles that are assigned to various healthcare institutions be based on their individual capabilities, rather than one institution trying to provide all forms of healthcare, so that patient illness can be detected and treated as quickly as possible. Thus, there is great promise for ICT to bring about partnerships between local healthcare providers, that, as one approach, entails the linking of healthcare information between these institutions using ICT (e.g., Cruz-Correia et al., 2007; Kilic, Dogac, and Eichelberg, 2010; Serbanati, Ricci, and Mercurio, 2011; Wozak, Ammenweth, Hörbst, Sögner, and Mair, 2008).

In this chapter, the authors discuss management processes for forming innovation communities through strategic partnering between corporations and university hospitals as their customers, the way corporations include the knowledge of customers with high-level experiential learning (called innovative customers in this chapter) in innovation communities, and how the achievements of innovation communities are spread to many other related customers as the communities produce new products.

The authors also present a case study of product innovation using ICT in healthcare in Japan. The Tohoku University School of Medicine Hospital in Japan (Tohoku University Hospital hereinafter) has engaged in close-knit collaborative innovation with Nippon Telegraph and Telephone East Corporation (NTT East hereinafter) to develop a system to display the medical information stored in electronic records with different specifications for different medical institutions on a single screen using a timeline. This joint venture began to trial the timeline system, a system that enables the partnered medical institutions, with the consent of the patients, to access medical information such as a patient's history of illness as well as his or her prescriptions and examinations at a glance.

Here, the corporation, NTT East, and the medical staff involved with its innovative customer, Tohoku University Hospital, have formed an innovation community to bring about new products and set up new business models in the healthcare field using ICT. The achievements of this innovation community have spread new products throughout Japan through the formation of chains of communities of large numbers of related customers.

Nevertheless, collaboration through the formation of business networks centered on leader corporations and major follower corporations as the organizational infrastructure to build, grow and develop these kinds of business ecosystems is required, and leads to the following insight, as presented in Chapter 2.

[Insight 4]

The dynamic formation of innovation communities as business networks built around leader and major follower companies lies at the core of the formation of business ecosystems.

As these new ICT healthcare systems are expanding to medical institutions around Japan, this chapter identifies the dynamic formation of innovation communities involving innovative customers and corporations as a factor contributing to the formation of business ecosystems, even though these developments are only small when viewed at the market level.

4.2 THE IMPORTANCE OF CUSTOMER COMPETENCE AND USER INNOVATION

The typical corporate strategy of the latter half of the 20th century focused on strategies to proactively take in knowledge and core competences from outside companies by strategic partnering between companies such as main business partners, suppliers and distributors. For example, classic automotive businesses such as GM, Ford and Toyota have long established partnerships with their component suppliers, while in the ICT field involved in smartphones, tablets and computers, business styles characterized by strategic alliances between the commercial appliance industries, telecommunications industries, PC, software and entertainment industries are commonplace.

The strategies enacted through these kinds of business styles have been understood and accepted by many corporations as a requisite for expanding existing markets or pioneering new ones. However, even though the right to make a decision about purchasing products and services offered by corporations is ultimately up to the customer, it has been widely thought that there is a natural tendency for customers to passively accept products and services.

However, the rapid expansion of the Internet and ICT in recent years has enabled the gathering of information and the acquisition of high-quality data about products and services, while raising customer interest in diverse applications, content and social networking services (SNS) using PCs and smartphones has spawned in-depth learning and familiarity on the customer side with the products and services provided by these companies and with the business models through which they are provided. Thus, high-level learning experiences and the rigorous evaluation of products and services and their associated business models on the customer side can dramatically affect the popularization of the products and services provided by companies.

Looking out to the 21st century, Prahalad et al. (2000) emphasize the increasing importance of corporate product and service marketing and developing issues involving co-opting customer knowledge and competence as the core elements of business strategy.

Therefore, due to these external challenges, which necessitate high degrees of innovation to satisfy customer needs, many businesses need to transform their entire approach to product and service development through continuous innovation and learning processes (Kodama, 2007b). The learning and knowledge creation process (Kodama, 2007b; Nonaka and Takeuchi, 1995), which integrates different knowledge in companies and involves customers, and which reduces product development cycle time, has come to be characterized by collaborative innovation between companies and customers.

Who then, as core to corporate strategy, is responsible for innovation (new products, services and business models)? It is a widely held belief that companies, as the developers and vendors of products, are responsible for their innovations. Nevertheless, an important emerging aspect of innovation is user innovation, in which the user, in other words, the consumer of innovation, also becomes the producer of it. Users are also thus becoming innovators. It was von Hippel of MIT who first clarified the concept of user innovation. According to von Hippel's research in 1994, users had innovated some 67% of production assets, such as equipment to assemble printed circuit boards.

As described below, user innovation changes the roles of the user and the vendor in the innovation process. Conventionally, the innovation process is a sequence that starts out with searching out user needs, designing products that will fulfill those needs, developing prototypes, and then moving on to mass production once a prototype is designed that works well. In the past, all of these steps were carried out by companies, as the vendors of the development. However, with user innovation, the vendor is only involved in mass production—users are involved all the way through to the development of prototypes. Users do not just stop at conveying information about needs—they also contribute to the development itself.

Why are users becoming innovators?

One of the reasons is the learning process called "learning by using." When a user actually uses a product or service, they deepen their understanding of the characteristics or methods of use of the product or service, and in so doing clarify related knowledge and needs (Rosenberg, 1982). Rosenberg (1982) conceptualized this learning process as "learning by using." Learning by using entails acquiring knowledge that is clarified through the actual experience of using something, which is knowledge that can be measured as such things as maintenance costs indices, and observed as maintenance cost reductions—obviously, users with rich usage experiences will have valuable opinions regarding product defects or how products can be improved.

For example, in software development, rapid prototyping is one of the ways that learning by using is included in product development. In this production technique, prototype software products are shipped as early as possible, so that users can start using them in the early stages of development, which means that the users' desires can be reflected in the final product quickly. Knowledge that cannot be properly understood in the product design stage can be acquired through the user experience and then included in the product design.

In other words, "using" is not just a matter of consuming some product or service, but also has a concomitant aspect as a learning activity. Thus, in some cases, the user will have richer knowledge and experience than the vendor, and so has potential as an innovator.

Therefore, the authors would like to define the "innovative customer" mentioned earlier as follows: Customers that have the high-level knowledge and competence needed to achieve user innovation through rich learning experiences in particular fields of specialization can be called "innovative customers."

4.3 COLLABORATIVE INNOVATION USING ICT IN THE HEALTH-CARE AND WELFARE FIELDS—A CASE STUDY

Japan is currently experiencing the most serious decline in birth rate and increase in societal aging in the developed world. For this reason, a range of chronic afflictions such as cancer, stroke and diabetes are on the rise, which is making it increasingly difficult for the healthcare and nursing industries to secure resources. Therefore, to use the limited healthcare resources available more effectively, our modern societies urgently need to drastically revise the healthcare and healthcare supply systems, and clarify the most rational picture for the future of these systems.

Kondo had the opportunity in the 1990s to play a central role in the operation of the medical information system at Tohoku University Hospital, and encountered a range of contradictions surrounding the hospital's information management, and became aware that the critical issue facing the medical workplace was implementing systems that would enable all involved with healthcare institutions to be able to share information and organically link business so that business and linked information could transcend the borders of single medical institutions, thus improving the quality and efficiency of healthcare, nursing and welfare services.

4.3.1 Joint R and D to Develop Electronic Medical Records to Assist Physicians and Contribute to Treatment in the Workplace

Upon recognizing the need to develop and operate such a medical information system, Kondo and the contributors to this book began researching a rational electronic medical record interface at Tohoku University Hospital. In 2002, NTT East expressed its desire to jointly research medical information systems with the University Hospital, and made a research proposal to the hospital healthcare information department associated with Tohoku University Hospital (the healthcare information department hereinafter). At the time, NTT East proposed a joint research theme of communications tools such as TV phone systems using ICT, but with Kondo supervising the medical information department, it became clear that research into a new electronic medical record interface would be the most useful solution to the social problem of medical information systems rather than researching TV conferencing or security database systems, etc.

Based on this conclusion, Tohoku University Hospital and NTT East closed a joint research contract and embarked on research into an electronic medical record interface chiefly to aid doctors in the delivery of care. Research funds were originally to be made available from both NTT East and the Japanese government, but because the government funding was canceled, the bulk of R and D funding was made available by NTT East, with some coming from Tohoku University Hospital itself.

Firstly, the research project involved itself with visualizing idealized forms of an interface for electronic medical records. To achieve this, the researchers established a system for creating model software, and extracted the basic elements of the interface under the leadership of Kondo and the contributors to this book. Having taken the lead, Kondo had served as a doctor expert on a wide range of pediatrics cases from primary to tertiary treatments prior to specializing in medical informatics. When bringing his know-how to the fore, the researchers clarified the necessary elements of the electronic medical records interface by investigating the form that the records should take when a pediatrician actually makes a diagnosis. They did this by asking a neighboring after-hours emergency center to participate in the research after getting ethical approval relating to personal information, so they could clarify the requirements for the interface in pediatric emergency care, a fundamental area of pediatrics.

These requirements included the following (for more details refer to Column 4.1):

(1) Medical records must be able to be handwritten by doctors, in the same manner as the older, non-electronic records.

(2) The records must enable quick and easy input by button pushing, etc., for medical actions such as prescriptions and tests.

(3) The medical records must be able to be opened and closed instantly so that valuable treatment time is not wasted.

(4) Recording images with treatment must also be quick and easy.

(5) Information such as external test results must be reflected in the medical records semi-automatically.

COLUMN 4.1 REQUIREMENTS FOR THE ELECTRONIC MEDICAL RECORD INTERFACE

(1) *Medical records must be able to be handwritten by doctors, in the same manner as the older, non-electronic records.*

Because doctors from all age groups work in shifts in the medical center dealing with patients, the researchers concluded that the interface must be easy to use regardless of age, and that handwritten input with a pen must be included in addition to typing to circumvent the limitations of typed input, and because the medical records that reused information as text and codes had not been very convenient. Thus, the researchers presented a visionary interface model of an electronic medical records system equipped with handwriting capabilities with the potential for future implementation in a large number of healthcare facilities.

(2) *The records must enable quick and easy input by button pushing, etc., for medical actions such as prescriptions and tests.*

Because standardized medical actions such as prescribing medicines and medical tests are systemized with unique codes, the researchers concluded that the inclusion of buttons and other easy, formulated input methods rather than a handwritten-only records system was the correct approach to take. In other words, it became clear that the medical information system must combine both the recommendations of (1) above for an interface that enabled handwriting with contrasting input methods. Due to its clear advantage, there was also a proposal for an efficient information selection screen on the interface that would enable doctors to select medical information from a personalized list rather than having to search for medical information that they often used—an aspect of the interface called a "user pallet."

(3) *The medical records must be able to be opened and closed instantly so that valuable treatment time is not wasted.*

The number of patients treated in clinics such as the pediatrics facilities in Japan is far more than in Western countries. Also, in many cases, treatment does not involve a clerk system, and therefore an electronic medical record interface that would lengthen treatment time would not be feasible. Thus, in this modeling research, it became clear that the best option was to develop Java-based software that would run on web-based applications. For this reason, the processes of developing the integrated Java application with Java-Script were also a significant aspect of NTT East's commercialization of the product. The high-speed electronic medical records interface that this research achieved enables doctors to deal with one patient every minute.

(4) *Recording images with treatment must also be quick and easy.*

Many doctors also expressed a wish for the quick and easy recording of digital camera images, etc., with the interface in their treatment rooms. Being a technically simple thing to handle, this aspect was also included in the model.

(5) *Information such as external test results must be reflected in the medical records semi-automatically.*

For information from external sources to be reflected in records, it must be standardized. Here, as well as configuring the interface model, standardized codes such as YJ codes and JLAC 10 are used for pharmaceuticals and clinical tests respectively in databases.

After that, the joint research finished in a year, and the achievement belonged to both Tohoku University Hospital and NTT East. NTT East continued for the following two years to develop its own product, and commercialized a fully-fledged electronic medical record system with database and user administration structures and so on for use in healthcare centers (see Figure 4.1). Called "FutureClinic21," these electronic medical record systems were released throughout Japan, and are currently used in more than 300 locations around the country, including in specialist institutions dealing with internal medicine, surgery, pediatrics, gynecology and maternity, otolaryngology, dermatology and so forth, as well as general healthcare providers. Notably, in pediatrics, the specialist area of Kondo, the system has been favorably evaluated for its ease of use, and has developed a fan base among its users.

Later, FutureClinic21, a Tohoku University venture, engaged in the research and development of the new FutureClinic21 warp, which NTT East bought as successor software and which the company continues to sell. Currently, the medical institutions using this product are gradually on the rise.

This joint research was carried out to enable the use of an electronic medical records system in the healthcare workplace, which could be easily used by doctors of all ages and thus overcome the digital divide.

Researched as a model system for emergency pediatrics, the easy-to-use system was developed to enable (1) handwriting in the familiar way with a pen, (2) buttons for input for prescription and tests etc, (3) high speed software, (4) image data referencing, and (5) test result info linking.Photography is actually used in pediatrics, and is useful in raising the quality of healthcare with electronic records

Healthcare in Metoki Children's Clinic

Photo.: Courtesy of Dr. Hisaya Metoki

Figure 4.1   NTT East/Tohoku University Hospital Joint Development of a Pen-Input-Capable Electronic Medical Record System

4.3.2 Timeline Medical Information Systems R and D by a University Venture Company

In 2003, there were incentives to plan or establish university-originated venture companies as part of the movement in Japan for universities to incorporate. Wise Solutions (WS hereinafter), a Tohoku University venture company, which started with three non-executive directors from the teaching staff at the Tohoku University School of Medicine and Akita University Faculty of Medicine, thus set out on new R and D into electronic medical records.

Six months after WS was established in 2003, Kondo became a non-executive director of the company to research and develop new software, and suggested that the company patent the research results to protect them from the competition. Thus, regarding the theoretical research on the structure of the software, the development of patented technologies on which prototypes were based was greatly expanded by Kondo. In its second year, the company applied for patents for the Core of Act (CoA) concept as units for distributing healthcare information and the basic configurations of the timeline view tools, which entailed particular applications for eight patents related to timeline view editing, and was thus a full-scale deployment of the information theory research. These patents were jointly applied for by Kondo and WS, but later on, the software developed by WS and the patents held by WS were sold to NTT East, after which WS only continue to involve itself in international patent applications. In the end, there were 11 related patents in Japan that were assessed.

Then, it was decided that NTT-ME would actually provide the product, although NTT East had been advised on the research and development of the electronic medical records, including FutureClinic21, by Kondo, and it was decided that the WiseScope, with its timeline function researched and developed by WS (refer to Column 4.2 for details), would be adopted as the software to succeed FutureClinic21.

Meanwhile, even before its acquisition of the timeline software, NTT East had aimed for the commercialization of local networks linking healthcare, and had engaged in a wide-ranging exchange of information with Aizawa Hospital in Matsumoto City, Nagano Prefecture. With this background, it was proposed that WS deploy the timeline interface software as a tool to link local healthcare providers on a trial basis. Thus, the WS timeline software was introduced to Aizawa Hospital through NTT East. Aizawa Hospital itself had been extremely interested in the problems surrounding medical information systems at the time, and, as part of its efforts to link local healthcare, was aware of the favorable assessment of the timeline software as a hospital medical information system. Thus, the timeline software was implemented to begin testing as an initiative taken by the hospital director.

Under the superior, rationally progressive top-down bottom-up healthcare management system of Aizawa Hospital, the testing and verification of the software began in earnest in June of 2011. After NTT East was granted patent rights in March of 2012, the company accelerated the commercialization of the product, and has been selling it as the "Hikari Timeline" since the summer of 2012.

Moreover, the product has been adopted as a healthcare info network platform in the Tohoku area, the area affected by the Great East Japan Earthquake, and the timeline system is expected to become a popular method of linking local healthcare providers, especially around the Miyagi Prefecture.

COLUMN 4.2 WISESCOPE WITH TIMELINE FUNCTION

WiseScope put efforts into developing an electronic medical record system for clinics. This standalone, PC-based timeline software enables the drawing and editing of clinical timelines. It is software that is specialized for university medical training staff and clinical trainees, and contains descriptions of Internet-based software sales sites. It is also described in catalogues, etc., as an official product by University Co-ops. As a result, in spite of the initial sales price of several tens of thousands of yen, there were a number of enquiries and sales, while promotional sales promotion measures such as setting campaign prices were also carried out.

However, the attempts that were made to develop this standalone software had great impacts on later timeline software licensing for systems linking local healthcare providers. This was because the systems linking local healthcare providers did not need a general interface for entering medical treatment actions into the electronic medical records used in clinics, but required tools that would enable on-screen timeline editing, and thus, because of this stand-alone software development, and because the on-screen timeline editing tools had been already developed to some degree, NTT East was able to run its local healthcare provider timeline linking business on a trial basis in Matsu-moto City in Nagano Prefecture.

NTT Medical Center Tokyo also adopted the timeline interface into hospi-tal electronic medical records on one screen. This case was also based on the standalone software development as the platform. In this way, the achieve-ments of the R and D that split from the clinical software R and D provided a foothold into the in-hospital timeline interface trial deployment.

4.4 PROMOTING CREATIVE DIALOGUES AND COLLABORATIVE INNOVATION WITH INNOVATIVE CUSTOMERS

As is typified by ICT, providing products and services to customers essen-tially entails companies both marketing and developing products, services and business models from the perspective of the customer, as well as absorb-ing a wide range of opinions, hopes and criticisms from customers familiar with the related products and services.

In particular, as the most important piece of this case study, the formation of innovation communities from innovative customers and companies to bring about new products and business models through proactive dialogue and collaboration within these communities, and horizontal expansion to other related customers as a result of these community activities has become a business process of previously unseen importance.

The first issue is the promotion of close dialogue with innovative custom-ers through proactive contact with them. Unlike in the past, when com-panies one-sidedly established products and business models and provided products to customers, modern companies must work to conceptualize new business models and products by engaging in dialogue with innovative cus-tomers. In other words, innovative customers are just like company staff, and do nothing other than jointly develop business models and product concepts. The important point is for development project leaders in compa-nies (called community leaders in this chapter) and innovative customers to share and resonate their ideas and visions with each other towards bringing about new product concepts and new business models.

Innovative customers have ideas and visions about many customers, including themselves, being able to enjoy high-quality, low-cost products and services brought about through new products and business models. Thus, it is the mission of the company, as the community leader, to provide competitive products and services to as many customers as possible, and to achieve high levels of customer satisfaction through such products and business models. Here, community leaders and innovative customers must repeatedly engage in dialogue to share and resonate their values with each other so that they can establish new concepts. It is also important to form innovation communities that include innovative customers and company project teams. Members of these innovation communities must resonate their values with each other, and the innovative customers must be treated as members of the project team, while business processes must be driven so that innovative customers are regarded as community members, and take action together.

In this case, the joint R and D project that finally motivated NTT East was positioned as part of the ICT business of the large company, because the innovative customer had the ideas and strong opinions required to inform the healthcare practices. Collaborative innovation for the creation of a future image of medical services using ICT that not only the end users (customers and patients) but also the company itself could understand through the persuasiveness of innovative customers and mutual creative dialogue was of great importance for this development. In this way, through working to share and resonate values among all community members, the contributions of the innovative customer and the University research staff to this business venture were significant.

Moreover, the authors analyzed in detail this case, and extracted the following perspectives as important aspects of this determined innovation community structure.

The first of these is the element of "high involvement" (Kodama, 2005). High involvement maximizes the commitment of companies and customers in joint projects. Innovation communities built around "Ba" (Kodama, 2005) entail the sharing of contexts through mutual interaction with others, and are places in time and space where new knowledge is inspired based on the new meanings and actions that come about through these dynamically changing contexts. As well as that, innovation communities create time and space where tacit knowledge can be shared, which is the source of commitment.

Innovation communities are fundamentally different from the "communities of practice" (e.g., Wenger, 2000). This is because, as seen in this case, communities that are motivated by issues in business or social activities are also groups that instigate action on pressing issues and problems. Pressing problems are problems that immediately generate interest, and are also business opportunities that will disappear if not grasped quickly. Therefore, these communities are required to move in an instant. Communities that are motivated by business issues in this way are qualitatively completely different from "communities of practice," in that there are big differences in the sense of urgency and diversification between these two types of communities. In general, a community of practice has few members, and is not a community that is motivated by issues, and thus does not have the same sense of urgency.

The second point is the element of "high embeddedness" (e.g., Granovetter, 1985). High embeddedness deepens the level of sharing of knowledge and information within the innovation community. In other words, it illustrates the qualities of deeply connected human networks.

The third point is the element of "resonance of values" (Kodama, 2001). Resonance of value brings about shared values related to the project objectives between innovative customers and project members, and promotes the sharing and resonating of these within innovation communities. Through the process of resonating values, community members build trust with each other.

From the perspective of innovative customers, such as those involved with university hospitals, there are currently serious deficiencies in hospital information systems that must be overcome, and there are interests at play—healthcare workers, rather than administrators, want to research and develop highly effective software, and raise research performance so that patents can be acquired as intellectual property. Thus, the imperatives brought about by this social contribution gave rise to a sense of values through which the University would want to raise its social contribution through the products.

Conversely, the value for NTT East stemmed from how the company was able to invigorate its ICT-related business. For this reason, the company researched and developed software that would contribute as its sense of value accelerated the spread of the new products through release for sale, ultimately contributing to the success of its ICT business. Thus, these shared values between the University and the company about the project objectives were intrinsically linked to the formation of a determined innovation community.

Nevertheless, it is necessary for project members and innovative customers to have common interests (Kodama, 2007c) to bring about high involvement and high embeddedness. Here, repeated and mutual dialectical and creative dialogue (Kodama, 2007a) is important. High-quality, productive dialogue is a medium that leads to the discovery of shared solutions and ties together shared objectives. Thus, these processes result in the discovery and sharing of common interests. Conversely, common interests can act as a trigger for the processes of resonating values.

Moreover, resonating values promotes learning within innovation communities. Organizational learning brings about new knowledge, and is an important process that drives best practices within organizations (e.g., Huber, 1991; Walsh and Ungson, 1991). "Awareness gained from improvised learning" is inspired by these ad-lib knowledge creation processes. The process of handling the knowledge embedded among the individual members of communities is an important perspective from which to create new knowledge among members from awareness gained through improvised learning.

Originally, in this case, NTT East proposed testing real-time communications tools, such as TV phones in healthcare workplaces, to its innovative customer. However, from the perspective of the innovative customer, communications tools such as TV phones were already commercialized technologies. Thus, rather than test the practicality of these in the medical area, NTT East gained awareness of the significance of the innovative customer perspective, even as it proceeded with its own sales through its normal sales planning and existing channels. Thus, the innovative customer gained "awareness" through strong opinions that there was no software that could be used, what kind of basic structure the electronic medical records should take, and under what sort of mechanisms they should operate, especially considering the workers and doctors who had to use them—the research continued and accumulated in parallel into a business linking electronic medical records with local healthcare providers that was centered on innovative customers.

Knowledge-handling processes entail knowledge transfer (e.g., Argote, 1999; Szulanski, 2000), knowledge access (Grant and Barden-Fuller, 2004), knowledge acquisitions, knowledge storage, knowledge retrieval (Hargadon and Sutton, 1997), knowledge transformation (Carlile and Rebentisch, 2003) and processes for handling the knowledge embedded in actors and organizations (e.g., Carlile and Rebentisch, 2003; Hargadon and Sutton, 1997; Kodama, 2001). From the perspective of this case, it became clear that "knowledge accumulation," "knowledge sharing," "knowledge inspiration" and "knowledge creation (including knowledge integration and knowledge transformation)" lie on the critical handling process axis as important knowledge-handling processes and as knowledge-creation processes (e.g., Kodama, 2006a, 2006b).

Through the formation of innovation communities with innovative customers, new knowledge is created among community members (specifically, this is described as community knowledge here, and includes examples of new products, services or business models) and then put into practice on worksites and in organizations. Thus, knowledge such as competencies, skills and know-how (tacit knowledge and explicit knowledge) becomes embedded and accumulates in the community members themselves and between members. In this chapter, the authors call this chain of knowledge-handling processes the "community knowledge-creating cycle."

The authors would like to describe the community knowledge-creating cycle as an important core concept of the six factors in the next section.

4.5 PROMOTING INCUBATION WITH INNOVATIVE CUSTOMERS

The issue facing the innovation community is producing specific incubation through the trial and error of the business models configured and the products developed. In promoting this incubation, innovative customers are positioned as central characters driving projects, and are also positioned as partners in executing such things as incubation planning and scheduling. This enables the extraction of the issues required for incubation through the valuable knowledge and core competencies possessed by innovative customers.

For example, this entails including specifics about the actual field monitoring of customers and the methods of execution, etc., in strategy and tactics. Thus, through collaborative innovation in innovation communities with innovative customers, project teams can perform experiments in the actual field, and then, through surveys and interviews with many customers, the appropriateness of a new product or business model can be confirmed while raising the level of the product and service quality.

4.5.1 Community Knowledge-Creating Cycle

Community knowledge innovation is an important process in incubation as part of both the community learning and creative processes. This entails the important series of processes of the sharing of the existing knowledge held by members in the community, including innovative customers, and then creating new community knowledge through mutual inspiration and propagation, which is then accumulated organizationally.

As an example, these processes can be described as follows regarding this case study. Firstly, the sharing of community knowledge step is the stage in which project teams and innovative customers thoroughly discuss mutual objectives in the community, and share and understand each other's knowledge. Initially, in this case, NTT East proposed joint research into communications tools such as TV phones and so forth using ICT as the research theme; however, Kondo (the innovative customer), who was at the time supervising the medical information department of Tohoku University Hospital, was considering the research issues with the company, and explained thoroughly that rather than R and D of TV conferencing systems or security database systems, the electronic medical record interface, which was a social problem to be solved for information systems related to healthcare, should be researched. NTT East then indicated its understanding of the importance of the need to solve the problem.

Thus, as the innovative customer, Kondo, who was a doctor working in pediatrics before specializing in medical informatics, and was an expert on a wide range of pediatric treatments from primary through to tertiary treatments, brought the full weight of his know-how to clarify the requirements for an electronic medical record interface in emergency pediatric treatment, a major area of the profession, and his knowledge and information was shared with NTT East.

In this way, the knowledge that NTT East had about ICT, and the knowledge that the innovative customer had about clinical treatments and information was thoroughly shared and understood within the community. The innovative customer understood the technology that NTT East had, and wondered what could be achieved with it. In contrast, NTT East thoroughly understood the opinions and demands of the innovative customer, considered what kind of products and services could be brought about with the technologies the company had, and engaged in planning for the incubation of a healthcare and welfare service.

The second step, the inspiration step, was the stage in which a wide range of community knowledge was mutually inspired and propagated to uncover problems and issues and their solutions to establish new product and business models for a healthcare and welfare service based on this shared community knowledge. Specifically, through the trial of incubation, many issues and demands were extracted by the healthcare workers and institutions involved, which acted as feedback for improving services. However, in this case study, the community members directly faced a wide range of realistic problems and issues in executing the development project. These included commodity measures, area measures, customer layer measures, sales measures, customer measures, organizational measures, capital measures, time measures and so forth—there were various serious issues, and the community members had to deal with all of these problems rationally.

In contrast, "awareness" came about through improvised learning among the community members through the process of trial and error in this inspiration step. In the sharing and inspiration steps, community members had to have the capabilities of dialectical and creative dialogue (Kodama, 2007a), creative confrontations or abrasion (Leonard-Barton, 1995), productive friction (Hagel III and Brown, 2005) and political negotiating practice (Brown and Duguid, 2001), because high-quality dialogue and practice is crucial for the subsequent process, which is knowledge creation.

The third step, the creation step, is the stage in which new community knowledge is created based on the community knowledge inspired and propagated within the community. Specifically, this means services being improved and upgraded through incubation, new services and products being created to provide customers with sufficient satisfaction, and new business models being established.

The fourth step, the accumulation step, is the stage in which the community knowledge acquired through the process of sharing, inspiring and creating accumulates in organizations as valuable know-how. Specifically, this is a range of accumulated developmental processes and operational skills related to the healthcare and welfare services, as well as technical know-how obtained through incubation. Through these community knowledge innovation processes, the quality of incubation is raised, and the creation of new products and services that can provide many customers with satisfaction is enabled.

4.5.2 Forming Linked Innovation Communities with Many Customers

The next issues facing the community were that of establishing, expanding and popularizing the products and business models created through incubation. In this case study, the achievements of community knowledge, such as the wide-ranging developmental processes, operating skills, technical know-how and so forth related to the health and welfare services that were accumulated through the activities of the innovation community, including the innovative customer, were utilized through the formation of other communities of related customers. As a result, new value could be offered to many customers through the product, which in turn enabled the smooth popularization and deployment of the business models through the continuous formation of linked innovation communities with customers. By expanding these external innovation networks between customers and corporations (including universities), and by expanding the absorption of customer competencies, the project team was able to create new community knowledge, and accumulate new know-how and skills.

The mechanism through which success in the innovation community with innovative customers forms another new innovation community to achieve a business is an important process for achieving continued innovations in corporate activities. For example, this is like a spiraling management system, in which the success of a large project with a corporate customer wanting to develop strategic products or services leads to similar expansion with other customers.

In the case study, the point was to propagate and extend the achievements of the innovation community consisting of a project team and innovative customers in the fields of medicine and welfare to many other customers throughout Japan. By taking maximum advantage of ICT, the core competencies of the project team, the project team's own company and forming linked innovation communities with customers in several hospitals, it was possible to establish effective new business models utilizing ICT in the fields of medicine and welfare while also providing new value to even more customers though competitive new services.

Thus, through repeated improvised learning with innovative customers, the project team absorbed customer competencies and was able to acquire the ICT-based integrative capability to bring together the knowledge and competencies of the customers and the project team.

4.6 INNOVATION THROUGH EXTERNAL INNOVATION NETWORKS WITH CUSTOMERS

As is typified by ICT, there are substantial corporate risks involved with new product and service developments. Great new products and services with competitive functionality and price may not be accepted by large numbers of customers. Certainly, in the past, companies have traditionally reflected the results of market surveys done on large numbers of customers in their new product developments and sales, many of which were the marketing and business strategies based on the business models as the seeds of the companies.

However, the new perspectives gained through the case study described in this chapter entail innovative customers being taken up as corporate partners, innovation communities being formed with innovative customers, and the formation of new business processes conceptualized and enacted alongside those innovative customers. The following five points are critical for these business processes.

4.6.1 Forming External Innovation Networks with Customers

To bring about never-before-seen product concepts or new business models using the products or services of a company, face-to-face dialogue with customers is indispensable. The opinions of the customers must be heard to absorb novel ideas to improve and upgrade products and services or to create new product concepts or business models. Therefore, it is wise to hold periodical customer forums, forums to promote product or service usage and forums for showing gratitude to customers.

Also, virtual forums using SMS can be set up on the Internet, which is a tactic that is useful for gathering ideas for new products and business models. It is important that a company position itself so that it can proactively collect constructive criticisms, opinions and desires by making contact with many customers to expand its human networks. Put differently, this is like the first steps towards discovering new and valuable veins of gold in a giant mine.

4.6.2 Resonating Values with Innovative Customers

Innovative customers can be discovered and uncovered in the human networks created by many customers, which subsequently leads to the issue of proactively creating connections with those innovative customers. Innovative customers have their own unique visions and views, and voice their constructive opinions regarding the products and services offered by companies, although these are often criticisms, and may include excessive expectations or demands.

However, the new and novel ideas born of the knowledge they gained through high-level learning and their competencies are of value, and so it is important for the community leaders to understand their ideas by engaging thoroughly in dialogue. Sometimes, it takes patience just to accept excessively critical opinions graciously, but it is this patience that enables understanding and empathy with the thoughts and visions of innovative customers.

Taking such a patient approach enables company members to uncover their common interests with innovative customers and to mutually resonate and share these values with innovative customers, and thus create new product concepts and business models based on new ideas.

4.6.3 Creating Innovation Communities with Innovative Customers—Resonating Values and Building Trust

Community leaders perceive innovative customers as members of their companies, and build innovation communities with them based on mutual trust and resonance of values. All company team members (community members) share the same values in the community, and work to build mutual trust with innovative customers in the community. It is important that community leaders demonstrate the organizational leadership needed to resonate values among all community members, including innovative customers, and to build mutual trust.

4.6.4 Innovating Community Knowledge—Promoting Incubation through Improvised Learning

It is important that innovation communities built on mutual trust among all community members, including innovative customers, who resonate and share the values proactively, drive the "organizational learning and creation process" as community knowledge innovation (see Figure 4.4). Thus, the "awareness" of new ideas and concepts will be born in the innovation community. With incubation through proactive and mutual dialogue and collaboration among community members, including the innovative customers, the knowledge of individual members can be shared, inspired and propagated to create new community knowledge and accumulate know-how and skills, etc., organizationally through that process.

4.6.5 Promoting Innovation Communities through Community Management

Successful innovation communities with innovative customers lead to the formation of subsequent innovation communities to achieve business. This mechanism is an important process to achieve continuous innovation in corporate activity. In this case, this can be seen as the spiral management system that enabled a successful large-scale project with customers, and as a corporate objective to develop strategic products and services and then in the same way extend these to even more customers.

The point of this case study is to demonstrate how the achievements of this innovation community, as a project team formed of NTT East and the innovative customers in the healthcare and welfare fields, were disseminated and expanded to many the customers involved in healthcare and welfare throughout Japan. The NTT East project team made the maximum use of its competence in ICT, while establishing effective new products and business models using ICT in the healthcare and welfare areas by creating and linking together innovation communities consisting of customers in other medical institutions and at the same time, offering new value to even more customers in new service areas, thereby enabling the company to gain a competitive edge.

4.7 CONCLUSION

This chapter described the importance of a company consciously and strategically incorporating the knowledge and core competencies of customers into its product and service developments, engaging in strategic partnerships with core innovative customers that have high-quality learning experiences, and creating innovation communities to generate new products and business models through these communities. The chapter also discusses the corporate management processes to disseminate and expand new business models and products by strategically creating communities with other related customers, linking them together, and extending the achievements of the innovation communities to these new communities. This is the community management framework with customers.

Being charged with managing communities with customers, community leaders will have to emulate the persona of a new and never-before-seen breed of leader both inside and outside of their corporate organizations, while corporate organizations must strategically spawn and nurture good community leaders to take charge of corporate innovation in the 21st century in the future ICT-based society. Increased benefit will come about by paying continued attention to the business innovation enabled by forming innovation communities.

REFERENCES

Argote, L. (1999). *Organizational Learning: Creating, Retaining and Transferring Knowledge*. Norwell, MA: Kluwer.

Brown, J.S. & Duguid, P. (2001). Knowledge and organization: A social–practice perspective. *Organization Science*, 12(6), 198–213.

Carlile, P.R. & Rebentisch, E.S. (2003). Into the black box: The knowledge transformation cycle. *Management Science*, 49(9), 1180–1195.

Cruz-Correia, R.J., Vieira-Marques, M.P., Ferreira, M.A., Ferreira, C.F., Wyatt, C.J. & Costa-Pereira, A.M. (2007). Reviewing the integration of patient data: How systems are evolving in practice to meet patient needs. *BMC Medical Informatics and Decision Making*, 7, 14.

Granovetter, M. (1985). Economic action and social structure: The problem of embeddedness. *American Journal of Sociology*, 91(3), 481–510.

Grant, R. & Baden-Fuller, C. (2004). A knowledge accessing theory of strategic alliance. *Journal of Management Studies*, 41(1), 61–84.

Hagel, J., III & Brown, J.S. (2005). Productive Friction. *Harvard Business Review*, 83(2), 139–145.

Hargadon, A. & Sutton, R. (1997). Technology brokering and innovation in a product development firm. *Administrative Science Quarterly*, 42(3), 716–714.

Huber, G. (1991). Organizational learning: The contributing processes and the literature. *Organization Science*, 2(1), 88–115.

Kilic, O., Dogac, A. & Eichelberg, M. (2010). Providing interoperability of eHealth communities through peer-to-peer networks. *IEEE Transactions on Information Technology in Biomedicine*, 14(3), 846–853.

Kodama, M. (2001). Creating new business through strategic community management. *International Journal of Human Resource Management*, 11(6), 1062–84.

Kodama, M. (2005). Knowledge creation through networked strategic communities: Case studies in new product development. *Long Range Planning*, 38(1), 27–49.

Kodama, M. (2006a). Strategic community: Foundation of knowledge creation. *Research-Technology Management*, 49(5), 49–58.

Kodama, M. (2006b). Knowledge-based view of corporate strategy. *Technovation*, 26(8), 1390–1406.

Kodama, M. (2007a). *The Strategic Community-Based Firm*. UK: Palgrave Macmillan.

Kodama, M. (2007b). *Knowledge Innovation—Strategic Management As Practice*. UK: Edward Elgar Publishing.

Kodama, M. (2007c). *Project-Based Organization in the Knowledge-Based Society*. UK: Imperial College Press.

Leonard-Barton, D. (1995). *Wellsprings of Knowledge: Building and Sustaining the Sources of Innovation*. Boston, MA: Harvard Business School Press.

Nonaka, I. & Takeuchi, H. (1995). *The Knowledge Creating Company*. Oxford: Oxford University Press.

Prahalad, C.K. & Ramaswamy, V. (2000). Co-opting customer competence. *Harvard Business Review*, 78(1), 79–88.

Rosenberg, N. (1982). *Inside the Black Box: Technology and Economics*. Cambridge: Cambridge University Press.

Serbanati, L.D., Ricci, L.F. & Mercurio, G. (2011). Steps towards a digital health ecosystem. *Journal of Biomedical Informatics*, 44(4), 621–636.

Szulanski, G. (2000). The process of knowledge transfer: A diachronic analysis of stickiness. *Organization Behavior Human Decision Processes*, 82(1), 9–27.

Walsh, J. & Urgson, G. (1991). Organizational memory. *Academy of Management Review*, 16(1), 57–91.

Wenger, E.C. (2000). Communities of practice: The organizational frontier. *Harvard Business Review*, 78(1), 139–145.

Wozak, F., Ammenweth, E., Hörbst, A., Sögner, P. & Mair, R. (2008). IHE based interoperability—benefits and challenges. *Studies in Health Technology and Informatics*, 136, 771–776.

5 Building a Health Support Ecosystem through Links Across Industry, Academia and Government

Mitsuru Kodama

In local societies in the 21st century, the effective use of ICT in achieving local revitalization, especially in the creation of virtual communities in the fields of medical care, welfare and health, has been an important issue in the creation of new value within and between communities. Remote-area medical and home care support utilizing ICT have the potential to build new health support ecosystems.

This chapter presents a strategic framework for configuring health support ecosystems through corporate strategies for collaborative innovation across different industries in Asia and the West. It also discusses how collaborative innovation in medical practice centered on telecommunications carriers as ICT businesses and carried out between stakeholders, including healthcare institutions, medical equipment manufacturers and communications equipment manufacturers, drives the configuration of health support ecosystems.

As well as the congruence between the five managerial elements of corporate systems presented in Chapter 2 (strategy, organizations, technologies, operations and leadership), this chapter presents a management innovation model to drive consistency between environments and corporate systems, a requirement for telecommunications carriers to succeed with collaborative innovation across different industries. In particular, the chapter describes the importance of "triad network" structures that span the internal and external aspects of corporations as elements of telecommunications carrier corporate strategies.

5.1 COLLABORATIVE INNOVATION CENTERED ON TELECOMMUNICATIONS CARRIERS

In recent years, business systems have changed rapidly with changing industrial structures and business environments and the development of ICT. Many businesses face the challenge of developing a strategic business that takes into account resources such as knowledge and personnel that exist across diverse industries, both those of the company and those outside—not only resources limited to existing business units, but resources that are accessible through strategic alliances, M&A, corporate ventures and strategic outsourcing.

Particularly in leading businesses fields, such as IT, e-business, contents, electronics and biotech, the leading core technologies and diverse business models are becoming more and more innovated and dispersed throughout the world. It is becoming more and more difficult for the old-style hierarchical organizations of the mass production era or companies with closed and autonomous systems to retain their independence and full control over their innovations. The theoretical frameworks of open innovation (Chesbrough, 2003), distributed innovation (Haour, 2004) and hybrid innovation (Kodama, 2011) point to the importance of managing knowledge both inside and outside of a company (core competencies or core capabilities) and generating new collaborative innovation across businesses and industries.

Despite playing the central role in configuring health support systems, before the emergence of the Internet, telecommunications carriers worked with business models centered on providing telephone services. In this old era of telephone services, the business models of telecommunications carriers were technologically well defined, and core technologies and know-how was developed in closed systems within the company, or in 'Keiretsu'-type alliances that included communications equipment manufacturers, and the development results were possessed by the telecommunications companies and Keiretsu networks. Furthermore, product and service development cycles were comparatively longer than they are today. This was an era in which companies were able to provide vertically integrated telephone services independently.

However, with the rapid technological revolution in the 1990s involving the development of digital technologies, the Internet, broadband and mobile Internet, etc., conventional business models changed dramatically. Figure 5.1 illustrates how the vertically integrated, telephone service-centered business models were destroyed in the Internet protocol era, to be replaced by new opportunities to expand and pioneer markets, with entry by a wide range of players in individual layers. These layers include the terminal layer with its PC, mobile music players, mobile telephones, smartphones, tablets, mobile information devices and so forth, the network layer, which offers optical fiber communications and high-speed mobile communications through Long-Term Evolution (LTE), the platform layers that provide functions for contents authentication (music, video, games software, e-commerce and so forth), billing, content delivery and functions for copyright management, as well as the contents and application layers that provide wide-ranging application and contents services to end users (including medical, welfare, health and educational services).

In short, the advent of the Internet has caused a massive shift from vertically integrated business models to horizontally integrated ones. While competing on layers, players on the individual layers also engage in strategic

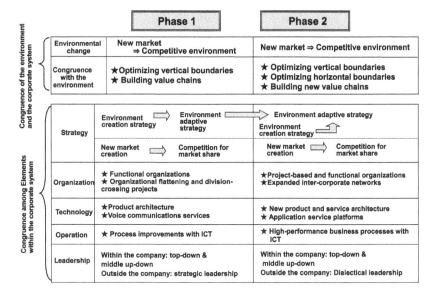

Figure 5.1   Congruence with Environments and between Corporate System Elements

alliances and mergers and acquisitions with players on adjacent layers to mutually expand business opportunities.

These changing business models have enabled telecommunications carriers to converge and integrate not only their own core R and D competencies in telecommunication technology that were accumulated over time, but also to create new knowledge through the convergence of these competencies with core competencies outside of the company across a range of different industries (diversified information terminals, software, contents, applications, etc.). In turn, this has enabled the configurations of co-evolution models through positive feedback across different industries and of vertical value chain business models—two insights discussed in Chapter 1.

[Insight 1]

The value chain model arising from collaborative innovation promotes the creation of competitive new products and services as well as innovative business models.

[Insight 2]

The co-evolution model through collaborative innovation spanning various industries promotes the creation of win-win business models.

The massive changes to business models like those above are a common business model framework found in telecommunications carriers (both fixed line and mobile) all over the world. In particular, collaborative innovation between telecommunications carriers and related businesses and industries to develop diverse social services by combining ICT with medical, welfare and health is creating new markets in Westernized, developed countries, including Japan.

For example, in present-day Japan, the primary business strategies of carriers NTT DOCOMO, KDDI, and SoftBank are to propagate and expand 3.9G. Up to now, to develop technical platforms for hardware and software to realize new services, these carriers have pursued strategic alliances with leading communications device manufacturers, computer manufacturers and software vendors. To realize electronic settlement services, for example, NTT DOCOMO also actively pursued collaborative innovation with various industries and organizations in different businesses. NTT DOCOMO engaged in the joint development of its mobile e-cash and mobile e-credit services through strategic alliances with companies such as Sony, which has electronic money card technology, Japan Railway, Japan's largest railway company, which has prepaid card service know-how, and the Mitsui Sumitomo VISA card, which is a member company of a major finance group in Japan. Through these partnerships, NTT DOCOMO launched its mobile e-cash and mobile e-credit services.

With developments like these, the need to search out these new business models puts pressure on players in all layers to acquire dissimilar knowledge across the boundaries of their own companies. Westernized, advanced communications carriers such as NTT DOCOMO in Japan are also pouring their efforts into creating personalized "behavioral support" services that are tailored to the needs of individuals. Thus, while working towards sustainable growth in society, many new social support businesses in a number of fields, such as environment and ecology, safety and security, medical, welfare and health management are being rolled out to create value in new areas.

One of these services, called "docomo Healthcare," is a service that has been providing health management and illness prevention support to DOCOMO customers since December 2011. Collaborative innovation with medical equipment manufacturer Omron Healthcare to utilize the business resources of both companies in planning, developing and providing health support services led to the establishment and operation of the company docomo Healthcare, Inc. As well as that, DOCOMO began providing cloud services in August of 2014 starting with 15 hospitals to enable the sharing of patient images and diagnostic results data, etc.

Furthermore, in advanced countries in Europe and Asia, the deployment of optical fiber to the home (FTTH) is accelerating, and home care and remote healthcare services available with tablet PCs and smartphones are spreading in countries such as Germany, France, Italy, Sweden, Finland, Japan, Korea and Singapore (See Column 5.2). These services have been achieved by telecommunications carrier-centered collaboration between stakeholders involved in medical institutions and care facilities, and with national and local government financial support and cooperation between industries, governments and universities to drive remote and home health-care development. These localized health support ecosystems are more and more often seen in developed countries (See Column 5.3), and are offering some of the solutions to the problems involved in achieving sustainable social growth (environmental, medical, welfare and healthcare issues).

Advanced telecommunications carriers around the world are continuing to work on solutions to such social problems with their mobile phone and smartphone customer base. Mobile communications carriers can expand the scope of mobile and smartphone use with mobility, real-time perfor mance and personalization by advancing their strengths in networks, mobile terminals and services. These companies set down and execute strategies to improve the efficiency of individual behaviors and consumption and pro-ductivity in society as a whole.

In addition to the huge contribution that mobile phones and smartphones enable through telecommunications providers using their social infrastruc-ture building capabilities and the driving capabilities of their alliances, the social support platforms configured by telecommunications carriers for the efficient exchange of information and promotion of collaborative innova-tion across a variety of industries and other businesses, etc., has become of major social significance.

The health support ecosystems discussed in this book are a part of those social support platforms. The development of these social support services ties in with the approaches by individuals, companies and associations to solving social problems with mobile and smartphones. While these develop-ments lead to the formation of new markets, they also contribute to sus-tainable social growth, as they promote the invigoration and efficiency of the actions of individuals and companies, etc. In the case of a mobile com-munications carrier, one of the major challenges is how to ignite collabora-tive innovation through the convergence of diverse industries and services through cooperation with partner companies in business areas where there are high synergistic effects with mobiles for creating new markets.

5.2 TRANSFORMATION IN TELECOMMUNICATIONS CARRIER R AND D PROCESSES—THE SHIFT TO COLLABORATIVE INNOVATION

The changing R and D processes in telecommunications carriers lie behind the achievement of the new and diverse Internet businesses and healthcare, welfare and health services, as described above. The array of communi-cations devices and services developed by telecommunications carriers to date has come about through collaboration with external communications device manufacturers and so forth.

This is because although most of the world's telecommunications carriers have R and D functions, they do not have the manufacturing functions required to achieve the specific hardware and software to further their technical achievements in R and D (their knowledge assets, such as patents and know-how). Therefore, out of necessity, telecommunications carriers must engage in collaboration as joint developers with external manufacturing partners and outsourced manufacturers.

In the current Internet era of optical fiber and high-speed mobile communications, modern telecommunications carriers have to provide diverse services with software technologies in network environments using cloud technologies. To adapt to these technical and market environments, telecommunications carriers have been shifting their R and D processes from "hardware types" to "software types."

This "software-type R and D" does not simply mean focusing on the idea of developing software, but involves shifting from circuit design and implementing processes for architecture and protocol investigation, and achieving specific new services by developing software, which, in a broader sense, means shifting resources over to software development.

Not only are modern telecommunications carriers shifting the focus of their developments from hardware to software, but they also have to change their R and D methodologies due to these trends. In the old telephone service era, these companies created technical specifications to develop hardware that were passed on to business divisions within the company. In this case, these business and R and D divisions were connected to manufacturers who would produce the hardware (commercial equipment) based on the technical specifications and then deliver it. The R and D and business divisions would share the technical specifications as explicit knowledge, but were only connected via the channel of the manufacturer. Thus, knowledge sharing and utilizing were restricted to the telecommunications carrier and the manufacturer.

However, as development processes to achieve services become more software-oriented, it has become necessary to unify R and D and business divisions and to absorb customer demands and workplace feedback to develop new services. Therefore, using the core software developed by the R and D division to achieve services, the business division engaged in system engineering (SC) for the entire new service under development, and flexibly customized software to meet user needs. In this way, carriers have had to promote the sharing of necessary knowledge through collaborative innovation across different organizations within the company, and have had to reinforce their software-type R and D processes so that this knowledge can be developed and put to further use.

Moreover, the explosion of diversified Internet businesses of recent years has seen an extremely large number of examples of joint software development come about through partnerships and strategic alliances with external companies at the R and D stage. This dynamic collaborative innovation instigated by telecommunications carriers across different industries has brought about a range of new services based on software architecture.

In this way, the shift to software-type R and D has triggered the promotion of the knowledge integration process through collaborative innovation across different organizations and businesses (Kodama, 2009)[1]. These changing R and D processes are common frameworks seen in the value networks (value chains) of telecommunications carriers around the world, and are increasingly driving the collaborative innovation spanning dissimilar businesses and industries.

5.3 THE MANAGEMENT INNOVATION MODEL OF TELECOMMUNICATIONS CARRIERS

In this section, the author discusses a corporate management innovation model to promote collaborative innovation among stakeholders across different industries to configure health support ecosystems. This requires the analysis of the congruence between corporate systems and environments, and of the congruence between individual business elements within the corporate systems of telecommunications carriers, because it is they that play the central role in health support ecosystems.

The author has engaged in ongoing research into the strategies and organizations of the major global telecommunications carriers in the 11 years from 2003 to 2013. From the analysis of the business strategies of telecommunications carriers, including those in Japan (NTT group, KDDI, SoftBank), Germany (Deutsche Telekom), France (France Telecom), Italy (Telecom Italia), Britain (British Telecom), America (AT&T group), Taiwan (Chunghwa Telecom) and Korea (SK Telecom), the author has derived the following common framework for these business strategies, as discussed below.

As well as expanding services using existing infrastructure businesses, telecommunications carriers are also driving new business developments through convergence with other industries, enabled by the explosive spread of the Internet in recent years. In other words, these companies have to create "hybrid networks" of "exploitative networks" to drive existing infrastructure business, and "exploratory networks" to develop new business both inside and outside of the company, and must combine "environment creation strategies" and "environment adaptive strategies" on the networks that span different organizations and businesses. Below, the author revisits the insights discussed in Chapter 2.

[Insight 3]

The process of spiraling the execution of exploration and exploitation centered on leader companies (or organizations) creates, grows and develops business ecosystems.

[Insight 5]

The dynamic consistency of boundaries between corporate systems and environments and boundaries between the individual business elements within corporate systems builds ecosystems and achieves sustainable corporate development and growth.

Thus, in executing these corporate strategies, the networks within companies, between companies and across organizations become deeply embedded as the nexus of the socio-economic relationships of related organizations. These network ties mutually influence organizations and their network contacts in terms of information, power, resources and trust. Such ties provide benefits such as trustworthy relationships, detailed information sharing, knowledge transfer and sharing, and joint problem-solving arrangements (Burt, 1992; Granovetter, 1985; Gulati, 1998; Powell, Koput, and Smith-Doerr, 1996).

Here, we focus on a new perspective of organizational networks—the hybrid networks that span companies internally and externally, and which are formed from exploitative networks and exploratory networks. This section describes the concept of hybrid networks, which entails the exploitative and exploratory networks required to execute environment creation strategies and environment adaptive strategies.

Next, this section describes the processes of dynamically advancing strategy management in telecommunications carriers. As mentioned earlier, in each phase of shifting business models away from telephone services to new services that involve different businesses and diverse Internet services, telecommunications carriers have demonstrated dynamism in their efforts to establish congruence between their environments and their corporate systems, and congruence between the individual business elements within their corporate systems.

5.3.1 Integrating Exploitative and Exploratory Networks

As discussed in Chapter 2, businesses have to both grow their existing businesses and establish new strategic positions to remain competitive in the market. To grow existing business (e.g., upgrading existing products and services to expand profits, etc.), companies must adapt to environmental changes and set down and execute business plans for the short term. Except in cases of massive structural environmental change, business practitioners are able, to some extent, to predict business changes and respond with their existing business activities. Practitioners regularly engage in activities to improve and upgrade routine business by making use of know-how such as path-dependent technologies, corporate customs and so forth accumulated over time. Thus, in these activities, practitioners are required to engage in regular organizational learning for incremental innovation (e.g., Nelson and

Winter, 1982; Tushman and Anderson, 1986). These types of business strategies are also the environment adaptive strategies discussed in Chapter 2.

In contrast, when a company engages in activities to search out a future, not only must it become involved in new scientific research or technical development, but it must also configure new business models to pioneer markets. Practitioners must brave the challenges of market uncertainty and risk, and seek out new business through experiments, incubation and trial and error (March, 1991). Architectural innovation through the integration of existing technology based on technical knowledge (Henderson and Clark, 1990) and radical innovation with scientific knowledge as new technical developments based on new theories and principles (e.g., Fleming and Sorenson, 2004) are critical goals for the researchers and engineers who drive exploration.

Realistically, not only are technical and scientific knowledge important, but marketing perspectives that radically transform existing business systems are also important to practitioners in their business activities. In short, to radically change existing value chains and construct new business models, new marketing knowledge is required. Customer value-creating marketing knowledge is an important factor in bringing about radical innovation to generate new business and transform lifestyles. Business strategies like these are equivalent to the environment creation strategies used to create new environments discussed in Chapter 2.

To acquire customer value-creating marketing knowledge, organizational leaders need ways of thinking that break free from the existing mental models and enable them to experience space and time in which diverse and dissimilar knowledge intersect (e.g., Kodama, 2014). They also need to leverage and stretch existing resources and capabilities by strategic intent (Hamel and Prahalad, 1989) to come up with new ideas, avoid competency traps (Levitt and March, 1988; Martines and Kambil, 1999) and core rigidities (Leonard-Barton, 1995), destroy information filters in organizations, break down organizational power structures and creatively dismantle resources, and abolish organizational inertia (Hanna and Freeman, 1989), and must be able to let go of experiences of success while continually setting down forward-looking strategies (Ackoff, 1981). It is also necessary for practitioners to be put off balance from their "thought world" of their individual backgrounds and specialties (Dougherty, 1992) consciously by the customer perspective.

Exploratory activities do not only entail acquiring knowledge through regular organizational learning through exploitative activities, but also require that practitioners engage in challenging and transformative activities for radical innovation (Nelson and Winter, 1982). Moreover, leaders in organizations who are making precise decisions about carefully selecting a number of exploratory strategies must also have a "disciplined imagination" (Weick, 1989). As described above, corporations need to combine the two factors of exploration through exploratory networks, and exploitation through exploitative networks to acquire and maintain a sustainable competitive edge through innovation.

Practical processes through exploration are of particular importance in executing the environment creation strategies discussed in Chapter 2. The practice of exploration is the engine that brings about the radical innovation to create new markets. Exploration is also required to execute environment adaptive strategies to adapt to new environmental change while engaging in practical processes based on existing capabilities. The practice of combined exploration and exploitation brings about incremental and radical innovation to adapt to environmental change.

The following two items of knowledge were derived from an analysis of the business strategies of telecommunications carriers in developed countries. Firstly, telecommunications carriers deploy specialist project-based organizations that are separate from their existing bureaucratic organizations, form exploratory networks across different industries, and engage in dynamic processes to achieve radical innovation with environment creation strategies to form new business for the future, and engage in environment adaptive strategies to respond to large changes in their environments. Nevertheless, functional organizations are required to spread, upgrade and improve and embed the new businesses formed through these exploratory networks. These functional organizations also form exploitation networks for routine activities for incremental innovation with environment adaptive strategies. These exploitative networks play a major role in expanding and growing existing business.

These two types of networks (exploratory and exploitative) are seamlessly linked, and have not only dramatically expanded the market for telecommunications, but have also created and expanded new markets using ICT, through the execution of these environment creation and environment adaptive strategies enabled by dialectic and recursive processes (Barley, 1986; Barley and Tolbert, 1997; Giddens, 1984) with environments/markets (structure) and organizations/individuals (practice), through the practical processes of practitioners and the formation of these hybrid networks. Leading telecommunications carriers simultaneously pursue the dissemination and embedding of existing business and the creation of new markets through activities in hybrid networks consisting of exploratory networks and the functional organization exploitative networks.

The nodes of these hybrid networks are the "small-world networks" (SWNs)—tertiary network formations created by project-based organizations spanning organizational boundaries and the leaders and managers of the function-based organizations in telecommunications carriers. Small-world networks, the networks that play the role of clustering together hybrid networks, are characterized by tertiary network formations of "leader teams" consisting of the managers in organizations. The network integration capabilities of these leader teams play a central role in the dialectic execution of environment creation and environment adaptive strategies.

From my analysis, it became clear that the existence of "triad networks" consisting of these leader team tertiary networks and the exploratory and exploitative networks mentioned above are common features of a number of telecommunications carriers. This is discussed in more detail in section 5.4.

5.3.2 Dynamic Strategic Management of Telecommunications Carriers

In this section, the author discusses the evolution of dynamic strategic management in telecommunications carriers. Labeling the era of telephone-only services "Phase 1," the shift to business models involving diversified Internet services and new services across different industries can be called "Phase 2," ideas which the author uses to develop the discussion below.

This depends on how telecommunications carriers bring about congruence between the corporate system and the environment, and between the various business elements within the corporate system (See Figure 5.1). In each phase of deploying services, telecommunications carriers have always executed environment adaptive strategies in response to environmental changes in the existing service markets. Nevertheless, these companies also bring forth environment creation strategies by planning and executing business models to bring about new markets in each of these phases.

(1) Telephone Service Establishment and Expansion (Phase 1)

In Phase 1, after Alexander Graham Bell's invention of the telephone, telecommunications carriers had to engage in environment creation strategies, both in terms of marketing and technology, to create a telephone service market to commercialize the service in developed countries, where there was almost no penetration. Telecommunications carriers also created new markets and value chains for telephone services markets. These were vertically integrated value chains that included users, the telecommunications carrier, communications equipment manufacturers, facility construction and maintenance through to sales agencies. As corporate systems, telecommunications carriers optimized their vertical boundaries, and dynamically maintained congruence with changes in the environment. Although telecommunications policies are different from country to country, there has been a general and accelerating trend around the world towards privatization that started in the US in reaction to the economic circumstances, forcing telecommunications carriers to enact environment adoptive strategies to respond to the emergence of new players and changing competitive environments and to maintain their market share.

Furthermore, regarding consistency between the internal managerial elements of corporate systems, companies executed new business, facility and technical strategies as environment creation strategies (developing various services with new telephone service architecture). In addition, to offer full customer service in highly competitive and burgeoning telephone service markets, telecommunications carriers must continually diversify the technical aspects of their telephone services (these are divergent among telecommunications carriers, and have been dependent on the softening of national regulations). At the same time, from the operations aspect, telecommunications carriers have to equip themselves with systems to rapidly provide highly customized services to meet local as well as national needs by introducing divisional systems and driving expansion through forming group companies and mergers and acquisitions, etc.

To deal with the ever-increasing amount of business that comes with the skyrocketing numbers of subscribers to telephone services, telecommunications carriers have also dramatically improved their internal business with ICT and computer technology. In addition to line organizations, such as flattened functional organizational systems driving regular business and divisional systems and project structures spanning divisions, typically cross-functional teams (CFTs) that were able to quickly solve problems and issues were required to optimize strategies, technologies and operations.

Here, in Phase 1, the telecommunications carrier leadership necessary for optimizing the various individual elements of strategy, organizations, technologies and operations did not just entail strong leadership centered on the CEO, but also required "middle-up-down management" centered on middle management (Nonaka, 1988). As well as that, strategic leadership was also important to present visions and provide guidance to stakeholders outside of the telecommunications carrier company, such as communications equipment manufacturers, facilities construction and maintenance services, etc., and lead them in vertically integrated value chains to create markets for diversified and high-quality telephone services.

(2) Internet Service and New Business Establishment and Expansion (Phase 2)

Phase 2, which began in the 1990s, was the step in which new markets were created, popularized and set in place with new services developed to respond with Internet technologies. This was a reaction to the danger posed by telephone service market saturation. The major difference from Phase 1 was that the telecommunications carriers redefined the vertical boundaries of their corporate systems as new vertical value chains centered on the telecommunications carrier that brought in new stakeholders, such as content and application providers.

For example, NTT DOCOMO of Japan, the world's first mobile communications provider to offer Internet services through mobile telephones, had to optimize its vertical boundaries for the mobile Internet market, and engaged in the dynamic maintenance of congruence in the changing competitive environment that came later. Furthermore, regarding the congruence of the managerial elements within corporate systems, what are particularly noticeable differences with Phase 1 are both the environment creation strategies needed to achieve various technical elements for market creation (new product architecture/service architecture/Internet platforms), and the environment adaptive strategies needed to respond to competitors in the competitive environment.

At the same time, in Phase 2, the defining of horizontal boundaries to get a footing in new business territory is also a significant difference from Phase 1. Certainly, mobile service providers such as DOCOMO have achieved a secure footing in the finance business with their electronic money and credit enterprises brought about by converging ICT with finance businesses. The convergence of broadcasting with communications, automotive and telematics businesses, ubiquitous businesses, and ICT with medical, welfare and health services have opened up horizontal boundaries with mobile communications providers and have triggered the formation of new business models through environment creation strategies.

At the same time, to develop new businesses along these horizontal boundaries, congruence between the internal managerial elements of corporate systems involves the simultaneous execution of environment adaptive strategies to respond to the competition and environment creation strategies to bring about the new technical factors on the vertical and horizontal boundaries required to create new markets (new product architecture/application service platforms). Compared to Phase 1, telecommunication carriers around the world have put more emphasis on strategic diversification. Strategic diversification is also illustrated by Figure 2.6 in Chapter 2.

The most important issue with setting down and executing these new business strategies was the organizational system used. This entailed setting up individual business domains and specialist organizations—business domains that were broken down for planning and developing individual business models and products and services (these vary from corporation to corporation, new service planning departments or new business development departments, organizations not only with R and D functions, but that are specifically set up to commercialize products and services). These organizations are characteristically configured as multiple project-based organizations within them.

These project-based organizations then engaged in close-knit partnering with existing infrastructure and sales business functional organizations such as sales, facilities, maintenance and so forth, and engaged in both environment creation strategies and environment adaptive strategies. Compared to Phase 1, there was more focus on the formation of exploratory networks as networks between telecommunications carriers and external partners. Telecommunications carriers also focused on the formation of exploratory networks as networks with external partners to expand horizontal boundaries and drive new business.

From the operations aspect, compared to Phase 1, to drive business efficiency, new company systems were developed and deployed using ICT to enable real-time management (enabling the access and understanding of management information any time in real time), business reforms, enhanced management accounting and a speedy response to legal financial accounting, which were common transformative features of telecommunications carriers. With greater business efficiency through the deployment of ICT in companies, operations data such as consolidated legal financial accounting data indicating business conditions for the telecommunications carrier and all of its group companies, management accounting data indicating performance for individual businesses and organizations as well as operation data including sales and communications traffic information could be accessed in real time, which made it possible to compare performance with business plans and take actions much quicker than before.

In optimizing the various elements of strategy, organizations, technology and operations in Phase 2, not only did the CEO have to demonstrate the strong leadership needed to run a telecommunications carrier, but also, following from Phase 1, the "middle-up-down management" centered on middle management became an important aspect of telecommunications corporate culture. On the other hand, for external stakeholders, telecommunications carriers had to not only create new markets for Internet services and configure vertically integrated value chains, but also engage in dialectical leadership (Kodama, 2005) and present new visions to different businesses on horizontal boundaries to create win-win relationships.

As mentioned earlier, important to the achievement of these services created from wide-ranging Internet services and the convergence of ICT with different businesses in the medical, welfare and healthcare fields was the internal and external congruence of company systems; however, it became clear that of particular importance was the "dynamic organizational form." To create business ecosystems (including health support ecosystems) across different industries, the formation of triad networks centered on telecommunications carriers and spanning the internal and external aspects of companies is an important factor, as discussed below.

5.4 TRIAD NETWORKS—NEW NETWORK THINKING

5.4.1 Leader Teams as the Nodes of Hybrid Networks

In Phase 2, in the top and middle management layers of telecommunications carriers in developed countries, visions were shared to quickly establish the Internet market and set up communications environments that would enable citizens to enjoy Internet services. For this reason, based on the visions of their companies, the top and middle management proactively engaged in quick decision-making through thorough discussion and shared knowledge and information among management level leaders to build new infrastructure, rapidly expand the market for Internet services and expand those services (for example, the services converging medical, welfare and healthcare with ICT). Here, the author calls the small-world networks (e.g., Watts,

1998) formed of leaders and managers at all management levels across organizational boundaries "leader teams."

In Phase 2, as well as expanding the market for Internet services provided by telecommunications carriers and growing business (improving profits and increasing the scale of business), leader teams became divided into top management-centered teams and middle management-centered teams with the subsequent enlargement of organizations. To strengthen the links between top management leader teams and middle management leader teams, important proposals from middle management leader teams are thoroughly discussed in top management leader teams (groups whose members also include middle managers) to enable swift and precise final decision-making.

Major Japanese telecommunications carriers NTT and KDDI simultaneously maintained and developed the positive elements of their traditional capabilities (high-quality disciplined and rigid business systems, etc. in disciplined organizational cultures) in R and D, network design, construction, high-level network operations and technologies, nationwide sales and manpower, while in Phase 2, these companies conversely nurtured a youthful and creative corporate culture by forming project-based organizations to maximize the capabilities of all staff to develop diverse Internet services and converged services spanning different businesses.

In short, as a common feature of the organizational structures of telecommunications carriers in developed countries, project-based organizations with a new corporate culture that drives new marketing and innovation to develop Internet and converged services, etc., coexist with the functional organizations with their intangible assets of the past through the development and improvement of telephone service in Phase 1. Moreover, as small-world networks, these leader teams also function as the nodes in hybrid networks made up of exploratory and exploitative networks.

In this way, as discussed, the network structure that integrates the leader teams—the nodes of the hybrid networks of exploratory and exploitative networks—is the tertiary network form described in this book as "triad networks." In this research, it became clear that triad telecommunications carrier-centered network structures spanning the internal and external aspects of companies are commonplace. Networks that are embedded deeply in society are also communities. Thus, triad networks can also be interpreted as innovation communities operating as organizational platforms for simultaneously executing exploration and exploitation as corporate strategies. Accordingly, triad networks of innovation communities conform to the insight below, taken from Chapter 2.

[Insight 4]

The dynamic formation of innovation communities as business networks built around leader and major following companies lies at the core of the formation of business ecosystems.

5.4.2 Strategic Innovation with Triad Networks

Following, the author discusses how triad networks are deeply embedded between organizations and companies to bring about the strategic innovation capability needed to integrate the innovation dynamic capability (exploration) and the adaptive dynamic capability (exploitation) discussed in Chapter 2 in Figure 2.7, and how they can go together with the environment creation strategy and environment adaptive strategy.

In the business activities of the telecommunications carriers in developed countries in recent years, they have unwavering visions for pursuing absolute value over the long term by creating new communications cultures and achieving a new knowledge society in the broadband, ubiquitous and convergence era in the 21st century. These telecommunications carriers constantly engage in "knowledge convergence activities" (Kodama, 2014) to achieve corporate missions and business domains based on these visions. As mentioned, the formation of triad networks both inside and outside of companies centered on telecommunications carriers simultaneously reinforces existing business while aiming to achieve strategic innovation (Kodama and Shibata, 2014) for new business developments.

In this way, the objectives of such triad networks for telecommunications carriers are to continually execute strategic innovation by dialectically synthesizing functional organizations with knowledge assets as know-how accumulated over many years and project-based organizations with new and dissimilar knowledge assets.

Project-based organizations bring about concepts for new business models through trial and error (new products, services, business frameworks, etc.), and through imagination and creativity to achieve innovation in uncertain environments. Here, exploratory networks are formed with a number of strategic business partners outside the company, and environment creation strategies are set down and executed through intentional/contingent emergent and entrepreneurial strategies, as described by Figures 2.6 and 2.7 in Chapter 2. In short, project-based organizations demonstrate innovative dynamic capability.

Individual projects in project-based organizations are carried out autonomously as networked organizations, although organizational leaders constantly monitor business activities to control the direction and objectives for entire project-based organizations. Concepts and prototypes for new products and services are brought forth one after the other in these project-based organizations, and a number of them are incubated (e.g., Kodama, 2003).

Nevertheless, the business processes of facilities construction, sales, distribution and after support and so forth are crucial for efficiently introducing, popularizing and spreading these new products and services in a timely manner. It is the infrastructure of functional organizations that carry these business processes, and the bureaucratic and functional organizations form traditional and functional exploitative networks with strategic outsourcing partners and group companies, based on the knowledge assets accumulated over many years. As described by Figures 2.6 and 2.7 in Chapter 2, these organizations engage in practice and processes with environment adaptive strategies through deliberate/intentional emergent strategies. In functional organizations, disciplined, deliberate and planned strategies are adopted, and routines for business process efficiency, and incremental improvements and upgrades are carried out regularly with the adaptive dynamic capability. These organizations then take the innovative new products and service concepts brought about through the project-based organizations, and efficiently and quickly get them onto the market, popularize and expand upon them.

These two types of organizations (project-based and functional) and network types (exploratory and exploitative) have paradoxical elements in terms of pursuing creativity and autonomy as opposed to efficiency and control. Thus, there is always conflict and friction occurring between these organizations. These conflicts can inhibit the integration of the knowledge of practitioners in all organizations. However, leader teams as small-world networks, the tertiary networks, drive this integration.

All telecommunications carriers form leader teams in their own forms. They are commonly formed at the executive level (CEO, senior executives, senior managers, etc.) and at all management levels (project-based organizations alongside top management and middle management in functional organizations, management teams that contain mixtures of these, and informal cross-functional teams or task forces).

Leader teams have the strong network integration capabilities needed to assemble hybrid networks. Network integration capability is the ability to bring together networks that contain dissimilar qualities or knowledge. Leader teams then converge the knowledge in these hybrid networks, combine strategic methods that may seem conflicting in terms of creativity and planning, and bring about the network integration capability for entire telecommunications carriers (See Figure 5.2).

Leaders in leader teams must demonstrate dialectical leadership (Kodama, 2007b) to achieve the objective visions and corporate missions of the telecommunications carrier. At the same time, dialectic dialog to thoroughly understand and share problems and issues must be promoted through healthy discussion among leaders, and leaders must also mutually recognize their roles and value in the jobs they do through communication and collaboration. This enables leaders to transform a variety of conflicts that occur into healthy conflicts.

While he or she must demonstrate top-down leadership as the final decision manufacturer at the top of the leader team, the CEO himself (or herself) must also proactively make time for discussions with leader teams to strengthen communication with leaders, and maximize the coherence of the dialectical leadership of those leaders.

To achieve services that converge ICT with health, medical and welfare, project-based organizations play the central role, and bring forth new service concepts through collaborative innovation with facilities in the medical,

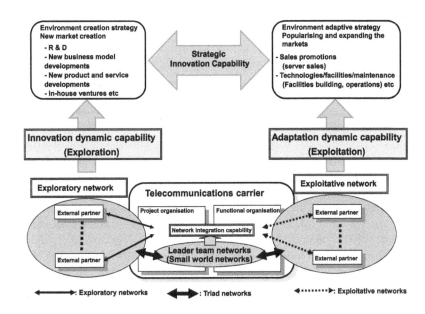

Figure 5.2   Strategic Innovation with "Triad Networks"

welfare and healthcare fields. They then execute strategies to create new and previously unseen markets by forming exploratory networks with their customer partners in the health, welfare and medical fields, the development partnerships required for technical and service development, and negotiate and coordinate with national and local governments.

Then, through the process of project-based concept making, marketing, prototyping and incubation, and once markets for new services are determined, functional organizations (facility, maintenance, sales departments and so forth) are brought to play in a timely manner to drive the spiraling popularization and embedding in the new market. In functional organizations, efficient and high-precision capital investment plans are set down for the predicted demand for the new services, network operations systems are deployed to maintain high-quality services, exploitation networks are formed with functional organizations through strategic alliances with group companies and dealerships or strategic outsourcing, and a series of efficient business process management cycles is promoted involving the establishment of sales systems, maintenance systems and after support systems.

Between the project-based organizations and functional organizations in telecommunications carriers, discussions are held and decisions are made about what sort of strategy mechanisms and resources to use, and about the timing of plans to respond with intentional emergent strategies or entrepreneurial strategies, through a variety of leader teams formed among the leaders in project and functional organizations involved in various businesses such as marketing, research, service development, sales, facilities, investments and maintenance services.

Thorough dialogue and discussion, the leaders on these leader teams select strategies and tactics that will enable the blossoming of genuine marketing innovations, and then move to the specific execution stage through their dialectical leadership. The synergies of dialectical leadership through the collaboration of management leaders, including the CEO and company executives, puts focus on dialectical dialogue, and drives deliberate and close-knit strategies for carefully selected intentional emergent strategies and entrepreneurial strategies, and integrates knowledge and strategies in diverse networks. This network integration capability brings about new markets (environments) and drives spiraling growth.

The creation of these triad networks with leader teams at their cores as tertiary networks enables telecommunications carriers to engage in combined, creative and planned paradoxical integrated strategies (Kodama, 2007a) from the perspective of the strategy-making processes mentioned earlier. From the capability theory perspective, this means the bringing about of the strategic innovation capability by integrating the dynamic adaptation capability (exploitation) and the dynamic innovation capability (exploration) brought about through the achievement of dynamic congruence both inside and outside of the company system, as described by Figure 2.7 in Chapter 2. Below, the author revisits the insights discussed in Chapter 2.

[Insight 6]

Consistency both within and outside of corporate systems ((1) strategy, (2) organizations, (3) technologies, (4) operations and (5) leadership) brings about the dynamic adaptation and dynamic innovation capabilities.

[Insight 7]

The integration (asynchronous and synchronous) of the dynamic adaptation and dynamic innovation capabilities brings about the strategic innovation capabilities of companies that execute both environment adaptive and environment creation strategies.

5.5 SUMMARY

This chapter has presented a strategic framework for configuring health support ecosystems through corporate strategies for collaborative innovation across different industries. As ICT businesses, this chapter discussed how collaborative innovation between telecommunications carriers and stakeholders such as healthcare institutions and medical equipment manufacturers, local and national governments, drives the configuration of health support ecosystems.

To succeed with collaborative innovation across different industries, tele-communications carriers must have a management innovation model that can drive congruence across the five managerial elements (strategy, organizations, technologies, operations and leadership) of corporate systems and can drive dynamic congruence between environments and corporate systems. For these reasons, it is important for telecommunications carriers to configure triad networks that span their internalities and externalities to acquire the strategic innovation capability. In this way, triad network configurations propel the embedding of the strategic innovation capability, and enable a company to create its management innovation models. Below, the author revisits the insight that dynamic strategic management achieves the creation, growth and development of ecosystems, which was discussed in Chapter 2.

[Insight 8]

Dynamic strategic management involving the strategic innovation capability embedded in a corporate management innovation model achieves the creation, growth and development of ecosystems.

COLUMN 5.1 NTT DOCOMO'S SERVICES CONVERGING ICT WITH THE MEDICAL, WELFARE AND HEALTHCARE FIELDS

In December of 2011, NTT DOCOMO commenced its "docomo Health-care" service, offering health management and disease prevention support to its customers via smartphones, etc. Currently, DOCOMO has partners in the healthcare and medical fields, and provides diet support programs to support actions for health management and disease prevention and support programs for child vaccination management. These services involve "self check" (simple questions that customers can ask themselves to determine 40 types of health conditions, including the level of danger of metabolic syndrome, menstrual disorders, swelling, insomnia, gastrointestinal troubles and so forth), "my record" (body information such as weight and blood pressure, and lifestyle information such as the amount of alcoholic beverage consumption, amount of sleep and amount of exercise), which also enables the results of the diagnosis and self check to be recorded and managed, "pharmaceuticals notebook" (dosage history records of prescribed medicines), and "information search" (searching for particular diseases and symptoms, local hospital information, the effects and side effects of pharmaceuticals).

Moreover, through its collaborative innovation with Omron Healthcare, DOCOMO uses the resources of both companies to plan, develop and provide its healthcare support services, and has established docomo Healthcare, Inc.[2], to enable the unified management and provision of health data to customers throughout their lives, and to provide a comprehensive health support service for lifestyles and different stages of life. This new company brings together the smartphone with Omron Healthcare's medical equipment (body weight and composition monitors, sphygmomanometers and sleep meters), and provides a cloud environment for the easy storage and management of the health data measured with this equipment (weight/BMI/amount of sleep, etc.). Furthermore, by partnering with companies that have health-related content and content providers, this company is driving the development of a wide range of services to deal with the stages of life of its customers and their lifestyles.

In August of 2014, DOCOMO began a cloud service to share patient image data and diagnostic results with a number of hospitals, deploying this service[3] in 15 well-known hospitals, such as the Jikei University School of Medicine Hospital, Tokyo. With its simpler deployment than the electronic chart system, this system makes it easy to check images with a smartphone, thus making it easier for doctors to coordinate with each other. Partnering in this way is useful for providing quick and accurate treatment beyond the boundaries of the hospital. Jointly developed with SkillUpJapan, DOCOMO's healthcare system development enables the cloud storage of patient magnetic resonance imaging (MRI) and computed tomography (CT) image data, test data and so forth, which can be accessed from a smartphone or PC by doctors and nurses, enabling them to exchange comments regarding diagnoses and healthcare policies, etc.

This service is expected to be useful in treating strokes, a condition that demands a swift response. Looking at the CT image and so on enables consultation about treatment policies between hospitals and specialists in other areas without the patient having to be in a particular specialist/treatment facility. There are also many cases where young doctors are on duty in university or large-scale hospitals at nighttime, and are calling a specialist up to come back to the hospital or asking for descriptions of symptoms by phone, which involves waiting and lengthens the time for the treatment to begin. Healthcare institutions such as Tokyo Medical and Dental University, Tokyo Saiseikai Central Hospital and Toranomon Hospital have also implemented the system. By enabling information sharing, hospitals and doctors can collect opinions from even more other doctors and hospitals, which means the patient will get the most suitable treatment available as quickly as possible. DOCOMO has also set up a special project organization in its corporate sales and marketing division to promote the deployment of the system in other hospitals. This is the first time DOCOMO has been involved in providing healthcare system services; however, because this strategy aims to strengthen the company's highly specialized corporate services, it is making DOCOMO a world leader in this area.

As a telecommunications carrier, DOCOMO is engaged in collaborative innovation with partners such as health and medical equipment manufacturers, medical institutions, content providers, associations and facilities involved in the health and medical fields. By collaborating with health and medical equipment manufacturers, DOCOMO enables the linking of smartphones with health and medical equipment, and provides an environment that enables customers to easily, conveniently and naturally record, store and manage their health and lifestyle data. By utilizing recorded and stored data, DOCOMO can provide rich health management and disease prevention support and services optimized for its customers by driving collaborative innovation between a range of application and content providers across different industries.

COLUMN 5.2 POPULARIZATION OF ICT APPLICATIONS IN HOME MEDICINE AND REMOTE TREATMENT, ETC.

ICT is spreading among various medical institutions, such as universities and hospitals, and medical institutions in Westernized, developed countries and Japan.

(1) Popularization of Home Medicine

The medical insurance system was amended to increase senior citizens' contribution to cost of their own medical care. It is thought that in the near future, we will begin to see cases of senior citizens selecting forms of medical treatment from home in place of expensive in-patient care.

It is important in home medical care to make regular assessments of the patient's condition, and for a doctor to respond quickly and appropriately if a sudden change occurs. Using video communications via a mobile terminal, a doctor can regularly "visit" and interview a patient at home. Thus, in an emergency, this system enables the doctor to more accurately determine the patient's condition and provide better patient care. Advanced clinics in developed countries have deployed an ICT application known as the "Home Visit Medical Examination Support System." Because this system enables interview-based examinations by video communications to be performed in addition to regular visits by the doctor, patients' confidence in their doctors increased along with the length of visits. The system also enables more a accurate assessment of patients during an emergency, thus enabling doctors to be dispatched more efficiently. Thus, the number of nighttime emergency visits by doctors decreased, and staff travel time was reduced through these regular consultations via video communications, resulting in reduced costs.

(2) Expansion of Emergency Medical Services

In a medical emergency, a small delay in treatment may have life-threatening consequences. Depending on the patient's symptoms, supporting physicians may be called in from other hospitals, and three or four physicians might handle the treatment of a patient with complicated injuries. An information network by which information about a patient's condition can be exchanged via real-time video communication is effective for providing the correct treatment. To accomplish this, universities in developed countries have built ICT that links university hospital emergency departments to hospitals across the nation, and that enables physicians to provide support while viewing a video of the conditions of patients who have been brought to other hospitals.

(3) Healthcare Consulting Uses

Both privately run and NPO healthcare consulting companies and facilities in developed countries have launched a smartphone, mobile and tablet PC-based, company-targeted healthcare consulting service. Many companies and facilities specialize in providing medical and healthcare consulting and advice via 24-hour telephone lines (including video communications). They receive a large number of consulting calls each month. The maximum potentials of the smartphone, mobile and tablet PC devices, which can be easily and inexpensively operated even by a family, are obtained in cases that are difficult to explain using words alone.

Healthcare consulting services utilizing smartphones, mobiles and tablet PCs can be used in a wide variety of fields. For example, property developers are offering options such as healthcare and safety measures that make use of the ICT and healthcare consultations services in condominiums.

This type of service can also be used in senior citizen facilities, where health is always a major concern. By combining this setup with home nursing equipment, it can also be used as a remote home nursing system. Smartphone, mobile and tablet PC-based healthcare consulting can provide solutions for both the aging of society and the health boom.

COLUMN 5.3 THE CREATION OF VIRTUAL LOCAL COMMUNITIES—COLLABORATIVE INNOVATION BETWEEN INDUSTRY, GOVERNMENT, AND ACADEMIA

In the 21st century, the medical, health and welfare fields in particular face the major social challenge of achieving "regional regeneration" through the effective use of ICT to create virtual communities and create new value within and between communities.

Created by a number of hospital and ICT businesses, with active participation from the national and local governments, the Multimedia Village Plan in Katsurao Village in Fukushima Prefecture, Japan, stands out as a grand technological project on a scale unlike any other (New York Times, 1999).

To reduce the burden that patients and families must face by traveling to the hospital, and to increase the efficiency of house calls, Katsurao Village has a system of TV phones in place that enables doctors to provide remote home treatment and health consultation.

This general medical and welfare support system enables carers to see elderly patients on the TV phone and thus provide more thorough care. The system also enables early detection for a faster response in case of emergency, and also enables exercise lessons to be delivered to the home from the local welfare center. These TV phones provide sign language support for the hearing impaired, and provide information about healthcare, insurance and welfare as video on demand (VOD) content viewable by patients in their homes.

The use of sensors and telemedicine to detect vital signs and provide medicine home delivery for patients with chronic illnesses after a clinical examination via videophone were revolutionary developments in Japan—they have enabled doctors to examine patients via videophone and prescribe medicines as required, and then send prescriptions via fax or e-mail to a pharmacy which then forwards the prescription to the patient. The pharmacy prepares the medicine according to the fax or e-mail prescription, and then a staff member goes to the patient's residence with the medicine and matches it with the original prescription. To receive the medicine, the patient then hands over the original prescription, payment and delivery fee for the medicine.

The candidates eligible for home delivery are patients with chronic illnesses, such as high blood pressure and rheumatism, whose condition is stable (the Japanese Ministry of Health granted permission for the home delivery of medicines following examinations via videophone in April 1999). Thus, beginning with Katsurao Village, the curtain was lifted on a brand-new era of residence-centered multimedia systems, opening frontiers of exploration into the ways these systems can contribute to advancing healthcare and a range of other developments.

Developments like the Multimedia Village Plan are poised to transform civilization and culture, and offer huge potential for developing multimedia businesses. With participation that includes villagers, hospitals and clinics, these face-to-face virtual medical communities also foster trust between doctors and patients by enabling physicians to diagnose patients and give them appropriate advice through personalized contact, while efficient medicine home delivery following these videophone examinations also provides patients suffering from chronic illnesses with peace of mind.

By extending these systems, virtual education communities that include village children and schools and universities outside the village could encourage interactive communication between teachers and villagers for face-to-face learning with a richer sharing of information, knowledge and content, while virtual communities could be created between villagers and government institutions to improve local living standards.

The basic concept behind these ICT systems is the easy-to-use videophone user interface that enables advanced linking between households, schools and the local community with multimedia services, regardless of skill. Such multimedia projects hold great promise as we explore new and modern forms of local communication and cultural paradigms towards building a society with genuinely free communications.

ICT almost completely dissolves the sense of distance between the town one lives in and other towns, between cities, and between countries. As people use diverse and interactive face-to-face communications across wider domains and access a greater variety of video content, more individuality will come to villagers and local communities alike, which will in turn encourage information, knowledge and content to be created and shared within and between these communities.

In rural areas all over Japan, where depopulation and aging continue, systems are in place for governments and the private sector to work hand-in-hand to transform and invigorate living environments through bidirectional voice and video with ICT and multimedia, using devices such as videophones that are easy even for the elderly to operate.

Following the development in Katsurao Village in Fukushima Prefecture, a second multimedia village was established in Nosegawa Village in

Nara Prefecture. Since then, the multimedia village model has been adopted throughout Japan in some 200 locations as of the end of FY 2011. Health support ecosystems such as these continue to be established nationwide.

For genuine local regeneration to occur, and new and unique local community value to be created, it is essential that each member of these societies has the opportunity to establish individuality and firmly define how they want to live. These established individuals can then use ICT to seamlessly and functionally connect with each other. In other words, as the individuals in local communities stimulate each other and grow together through ICT linking, they will be able to create new information, knowledge and content, and establish identities for regional regeneration. Thus, in the information era, these interactions are, and will continue to be, the driving force behind local development. The development of communities, including virtual ICT communities in which human beings can meet face-to-face, will underpin the information society and drive the expansion of health support ecosystems.

The creation of virtual local communities through close interaction between industry, government, and academia is another example of collaborative innovation. In forming the health support ecosystem, the core members of industry, government and academia engaged in trial and error to absorb, study and develop the knowledge of users. Collaborative innovation is characterized by the involvement of diverse stakeholders engaged in a specific dynamic context. Thus, by forming multi-tiered, dynamic "innovation communities," the innovation process accelerates as common values are shared, empathized and resonated.

NOTES

1. For example, to minimize the time lost when providing services, NTT, the largest telecommunications carrier in Japan, was forced to reshuffle its R and D organizations to make them more closely linked—organizations that had traditionally been set apart from other business organizations. In 1993, aiming for new services with Internet and multimedia technologies, NTT re-established its four headquarters—R and D HQ, Sales HQ, Corporate Sales HQ and Service Production HQ (an organization to which the Service Production and Planning Department that was the predecessor of the MBD organization belonged), and clarified the importance of its R and D functions with a focus on software development in the NTT Group. The reason NTT selected this management form was to achieve large corporate-group management with cutting-edge R and D capabilities at the highest global level focused on software development to meet the challenge of the even more intense global competition of the ICT era. Refer to Kodama (2011).
2. The objectives of the joint development considered by the companies are as follows: (1) to provide personalized physiological, health and medical treatment data management services, (2) to provide services linking various medical information with personalized physiological, health and medical treatment data, (3) to construct and provide a platform to enable these services, (4) to create a link between Omron Healthcare's health and medical equipment and

that platform, (5) to link with DOCOMO health support services and (6) to investigate future healthcare services (remote and home healthcare, etc.).

3. The initial cost burden on hospitals amounted to several million Japanese yen (JPY), while the monthly usage fee is about JPY 50,000. Separately, a fee of several hundred yen is applied per smartphone used by doctors. In the three years since the service began, the service aims for about one million doctor and nurse users, and sales of JPY 10 billion per year. There are examples of information systems to share electronic medical records via a server set up inside a hospital, but these systems cost upwards of JPY 10 million to deploy. Such high costs have been an impediment to the advancement of links between hospitals, but because cloud computing does not require specialized systems, the number of hospitals participating in information sharing can be expanded at any time. The range of information sharing is restricted within groups to prevent the leakage of the personal information of patients, but apart from that, this mechanism also enables participation by hospitals or doctors outside the group when required.

REFERENCES

Ackoff, R. (1981). *Creating the Corporate Future.* New York: Wiley.

Barley, R.S. (1986). Technology as an occasion for structuring: Evidence from observations of CT scanners and the social order of radiology departments. *Administrative Science Quarterly*, 31(1), 78–108.

Barley, R.S. & Tolbert, P.S. (1997). Institutionalization and structuration: Studying the links between action and institution. *Organization Studies*, 18(1), 93–117.

Burt, S. (1992). *Structural Holes: The Social Structure of Competition.* Cambridge, MA: Harvard University Press.

Chesbrough, H. (2003). *Open Innovation.* Boston, MA: Harvard Business School Press.

Dougherty, D. (1992). Interpretive barriers to successful product innovation in large firms. *Organization Science*, 3(2), 179–202.

Fleming, L., & Sorenson, O. (2004). Science as a map in technological search. *Strategic Management Journal*, 25(8–9), 909–928.

Giddens, A. (1984). *The Constitution of Society.* Berkeley: University of California Press.

Granovetter, M. (1985). Economic Action and Social Structure: The Problem of Embeddedness. *American Journal of Sociology*, 91(3), 481–510.

Gulati, R. (1998). Alliances and networks. *Strategic Management Journal*, 19(4), 293–317.

Hamel, G. & Prahalad, C.K. (1989). Strategic Intent. *Harvard Business Review*, 67(3), 63–76.

Hanna, M.T. & Freeman, J. (1989). *Organizational Ecology.* Cambridge, MA: Harvard University Press.

Haour, G. (2004). *Resolving the Innovation Paradox.* London, UK: Palgrave Macmillan.

Henderson, R. & Clark, K. (1990). Architectural innovation: The reconfiguration of existing product technologies and the failure of established firms. *Administrative Science Quarterly*, 35(1), 9–30.

Kodama, M. (2003). Strategic innovation in traditional big business. *Organization Studies*, 24(2), 235–268.

Kodama, M. (2005). Knowledge creation through networked strategic communities: case studies on new product development in Japanese companies. *Long Range Planning*, 38 (1), 27–49.

Kodama, M. (2007a). *The Strategic Community-Based Firm*. London, UK: Palgrave Macmillan.

Kodama, M. (2007b). *Knowledge Innovation—Strategic Management as Practice*. London, UK: Edward Elgar Publishing.

Kodama, M. (2009). Boundaries innovation and knowledge integration in the Japanese firm. *Long Range Planning*, 42(4), 463–494.

Kodama, M. (2011). *Knowledge Integration Dynamics—Developing Strategic Innovation Capability*. Singapore: World Scientific Publishing.

Kodama, M.(2014). Winning Through Boundaries Innovation–Communities of Boundaries Generate Convergence. Oxford: Peter Lang.

Kodama, M. & Shibata, T. (2014). Strategy transformation through strategic innovation capability—a case study of Fanuc. *R&D Management*, 44(1), 75–103.

Leonard-Barton, D. (1995). *Wellsprings of Knowledge: Building and Sustaining the Sources of Innovation*. Boston, MA: Harvard Business School Press.

Levitt, B. & March, J.B. (1988). Organization learning. In: W. R. Scott, J. Blake (eds.), *Annual Review of Sociology*. Palo Alto, CA: Annual Reviews, 319–340.

March, J. (1991). Exploration and exploitation in organizational learning. *Organization Science*, 2(1), 71–87.

Martines, L. & Kambil, A. (1999). Looking back and thinking ahead: Effects of prior success on managers' interpretations of new information technologies. *Academy of Management Journal*, 42(4), 652–661.

Nelson, R. & Winter, S. (1982). *An evolutionary theory of economic change*. US: Belknap Press.

New York Times (1999). Japan bets on a wired world to win back its global niche. August 30.

Nonaka, I. (1988). Toward middle-up-down management: Accelerating information creation. *Sloan Management Review*,29(3), 9–18.

Powell, W., Koput, K. & Smith-Doerr, L. (1996). Inter-organizational collaboration and the locus of innovation: Networks of learning in biotechnology. *Administrative Science Quarterly*, 41(1), 116–146.

Tushman, M.L. & Anderson, P. (1986). Technological discontinuities and organizational environments. *Administrative Science Quarterly*, 31, 439–465.

Watts, J. & Strogatz, S. (1998). Collective dynamics of "small-world" networks. *Nature*, 393(4), 440–442.

Weick, K.E. (1989). Theory construction as disciplined imagination. *Academy of Management Review*, 14(4), 516–31.

6 Building a Health Support Ecosystem That Utilizes Pharmacoeconomics

Makoto Shiragami

Due to the high costs of healthcare, etc., the effective use of healthcare resources has become a serious concern. Healthcare economics is an academic field of research that aims to economically assess healthcare actions. This field involves wide-ranging methods to analyze cost benefit and cost effectiveness, and to perform modeling and simulations, etc.

Healthcare economics is a new area of study. To date, there have been discussions on the economics of the pharmaceutical business from the hospital business and management perspectives; however, there has not been much scholarly analysis of the economics of pharmaceutical treatments themselves at the global level. Healthcare economics is an academic study that analyzes both the pharmacy and medicine and the economic aspects of healthcare, and is basically research that compares the costs and effectiveness of pharmaceuticals with suitable control treatments. For example, pharmaceutical companies use healthcare economics as an important strategic tool in a range of corporate activities, such as decision-making about developments, developmental planning, price setting and marketing planning, etc.

In addition, medical institutions also demand efficiency in terms of the adoption and use of pharmaceuticals from a business rationalization perspective. Therefore, in selecting pharmaceuticals to adopt or use, organizations need to rationally judge the price and performance of pharmaceuticals, which has led to a greater interest in healthcare economics worldwide.

This chapter looks at the existing research into healthcare economics, and discusses the vaccinations used in Japan as infectious disease countermeasures. Then, regarding the issue of routine vaccinations, this chapter identifies the importance of the healthcare economic analysis results and their diversity and appropriateness by carefully considering a range of assumptions, measurements and analyses based on the uncertain data arising from the unique premises of the analysis methods.

In addition, in view of the future usage of these healthcare economic analyses at the global level, this chapter offers ideas on enabling the creation of new value chains and business models by promoting collaborative innovation among stakeholders such as governments, the pharmaceutical industry and healthcare institutions, and an understanding of preventive medicine by citizens to promote the configuration of health support ecosystems.

6.1 VACCINATIONS AS COUNTERMEASURES TO INFECTIOUS DISEASES

Vaccinations are the most basic and effective countermeasures against infectious diseases[1]. Even if effective antibacterial and anti-viral agents are developed that enable the treatment of infectious diseases, it would be more desirable if nobody were ever afflicted by such illnesses, because illness usually has a significant impact on one's life.

Furthermore, drug therapies cannot completely eliminate pathogens. However, vaccines can eradicate contagion by entrapping it at its source. For example, smallpox has been brought under control, and there has not been a case of polio in Japan since 1980 due to the wild virus[2], which is close to being completely eradicated.

The World Health Organization (WHO) launched the Expanded Program on Immunization (EPI) in 1974 with the aim of vaccinating infants and children, and in 2012 launched the Global Vaccine Action Plan (GVAP)[3]. However, some vaccines that have already been deployed in other developed countries are not yet in use in Japan. Compared to the US, for example, Japan lags behind the US by 20 years for the Hib vaccine (for b-type influenza), 10 years for the 7-valent pneumococcal vaccine, six years for the rotavirus vaccine, and five years for the HPV vaccine (to prevent cervical cancer). To counter these problems, the vaccination law was amended in 2013[4].

For vaccines to be effective, a certain percentage of the whole of society must be immunized (Vaccination Guidelines Review Committee, 2012). Past cases show that when vaccination rates are low, the rates of infection rise (Tezuka, 2010a). Despite this fact, even if vaccines that are effective against pathogens are developed, there are a number of problems associated with popularization. The first of these is the uncertainty surrounding vaccines. For example, there are cases of infection even of people who have been vaccinated, while conversely, the lack of vaccination does not necessarily lead to infection (Tezuka, 2010b). In addition, there is a very small possibility of vaccines seriously damaging a person's health, even that of healthy individuals (children), and therefore, whether to vaccinate is a serious decision for an individual to make.

Governments that advise vaccination are also pressured by the same difficult decisions. For example, if a disease has reached epidemic proportions, citizens may willingly accept forced vaccinations. In actual fact, the vaccination laws enacted in Japan in 1948 have provisions for penalties for those who do not get vaccinated, although they have never been applied. However, while vaccines have effectively reduced the number of sufferers of infectious diseases, the potential damage to health from vaccines has become a social problem. Thus, the penalties for non-vaccination have been abolished, and there has been a retreat from recommendations for forced vaccinations towards making the effort to get vaccinated obligatory (Vaccination Guidelines Review Committee, 2012, p. 11).

Another factor in falling vaccination rates is the cost of vaccinations. Because vaccinations are not normally covered by health insurance, the cost of them must be borne by individuals (Shiragami, 2006). These costs are not negligible; for example, the pneumococcal vaccination requires a course of several injections, while the influenza vaccination must be done every year—factors that further increase the burden of cost. Falling vaccination rates also decrease vaccine production (Kurane, 2014), which affects the stability of the supply.

Right from the beginning of implementing vaccines in Japan, building a self-sufficient supply has been discussed. Even the vaccine industry vision announced by the Ministry of Health, Labour and Welfare in 2007 recognizes that "in the overseas vaccine industry, the manufacture and sales of vaccines is consolidated in corporations operating businesses internationally, and the American vaccine manufacturing system has moved from one of national self supply to one of mutual interdependence with European companies." However, the ministry also stated that "safeguarding the citizens of Japan from infections is an important role that should be played by the national government, and therefore it is of utmost importance to maintain the technological capability that enable[s] the development of new vaccines and vaccine manufacture within Japan from the perspectives of the safety and security of its citizens and national risk management"—thus indicating the ongoing necessity for a self-sufficient supply of vaccines within Japan.[5]

In spite of this, many Japanese vaccine manufacturers are only small-scale businesses, and because they rely on vaccine sales, they are unable to support their businesses if sales decrease due to a drop in the demand for vaccines. Thus, making vaccination optional, combined with the burden of costs on individuals, leads to a vicious cycle of falling vaccination rates and demand for vaccines, and hence instability in the vaccine supply. To break free from this vicious cycle, vaccinations must be made routine, and there must be a mechanism through which the majority of vaccination costs are publicly funded. For this reason, entities promoting vaccination, including the Ministry of Health, Labour and Welfare, have focused on healthcare economic analysis.

The appropriate operation and judgments of the healthcare economic analysis should promote a virtuous cycle in which vaccines are given routinely and the costs borne by individuals are reduced, thus raising the rate of vaccinations and the demand for vaccinations (also reducing their cost), leading to the stability of the supply. For this to happen collaborative innovation must be instigated among stakeholders; in other words, this means a deep understanding of the healthcare economic analysis in centralized government institutions, the appropriate decisions and actions taken based on its results, and close partnering between vaccine manufacturers and healthcare institutions.

Then, as the costs borne by individuals fall, and the vaccination of the populace is promoted, the potential to bring about a stable health support ecosystem to support the people's health will be raised. New value chain models enabled through this collaborative innovation will enable the creation of new services and business models in the vaccine industry. This discussion is supported by the insight below, cited in Chapter 1.

[Insight 1]

The value chain model arising from collaborative innovation promotes the creation of competitive new products and services as well as innovative business models.

6.2 VACCINATIONS AND COST EFFECTIVENESS

A healthcare economic analysis does not only look at the cost (burden) when it is identified as problematic, but also considers the benefits of assessing the appropriateness of costs by comparing the unit cost per benefit from among the choices to assess the appropriateness of costs. The WHO GVAP states that "[o]verwhelming evidence demonstrates the benefits of immunization as one of the most successful and cost-effective health interventions known"—thus, superior cost effectiveness is pivotal to the promotion of the program.

For example, regarding the elderly, when looking at the results of the analyses of the influenza vaccine, the costs of vaccines are nearly always reported to have been reduced, or good cost effectiveness is indicated (Nichol, 2003). Nichol et al. performed a cohort study on those who had received the influenza vaccine and those who had not over three seasons from 1990 on, from among residents who were members of the large Health Maintenance Organization (HMO) covering the suburbs of Minneapolis. As a result of analyzing the people who were over 65 in the various groups, which totaled more than 25,000 subjects, this study found that there were savings of $117 per vaccinated person, even including the cost of the vaccine, resulting in savings of roughly $5 million in total over the three-year period (Nichol, 1994). This study clarified that in the over 65 age group, there can be a concurrence of pneumonia or others ailments with influenza or worsening physiological condition due to an underlying disease that leads to increases in hospitalization and death rates. Conversely, hospitalization and death due to influenza among young, healthy people is quite rare, and therefore the analysis of the cost effectiveness reveals that it is not as great as that for the aged. For this reason, there have been attempts to show good cost effectiveness by performing analyses with a social perspective that also consider lost labor (Postma et al., 2002).

6.3 CIRCUMSTANCES LEADING TO ROUTINE PEDIATRIC PNEUMOCOCCAL VACCINATION

Routine pediatric pneumococcal vaccinations have been in place in Japan since March of 2013. Let us look at how the results of the healthcare economic analysis were handled in that process. The manufacture of the 7-valent pediatric pneumococcal vaccines was approved by the Minister of Health, Labour and Welfare in October of 2009, and went on sale in February of the following year[6]. Because this was not a routine vaccination, the cost of the vaccination is about JPY 10,000 per shot, with almost no municipal funding (in March of 2010, only 0.6% of all municipalities, or only 11 municipalities, had provided some funding to cover the cost of vaccination)[7]. The Ministry of Health, Labour and Welfare, 7th Health Science Council, Infectious Disease Subcommittee, Vaccination Subcommittee meeting held on April 21, 2010, approved the creation of a fact sheet and recommended the future deployment of the routine pneumococcal vaccination in light of the WHO recommendations on infectious diseases, etc.[8]. Then, a healthcare economics assessment was described at the eighth subcommittee meeting, held on May 19, 2010, and the fact sheet was submitted at the 11th subcommittee meeting, held on July 7, 2010[9]. This fact sheet described how pneumococcus could cause meningitis, particularly in infants, and that its prevalence is 2.6 people per 100,000 people under the age of five (2009), of which 2% had died from pneumococcal meningitis, and 10% had suffered from its aftereffects. In addition, the effect of the vaccine from the results of a double-blind study on 37,868 children done in California showed 89.1% effectiveness, including a serotype that is not in the vaccine. On the same day, the subcommittee was approved to set up a subcommittee and teams under it to study each vaccine[10].

In the second subcommittee meeting, held on October 8, 2010, a general method for estimating the cost effectiveness of vaccines that could be used by each vaccine team was presented (see Appendix)[11]. In the third subcommittee meeting, held on December 16, 2010, a healthcare economics assessment of the pneumococcal vaccine was presented. Research done by Kamiya (2009) found that compared to the JPY 29.6 billion cost of the vaccine, there was a JPY 68.7 billion saving in medical costs all the way through to middle ear infections, while a review of 16 medical economics assessments done in the previous 10 years internationally showed that there had not been good cost effectiveness for payers, although from a social perspective, good cost effectiveness was reported. In the assessments done by the vaccine teams analyzing the payers of health insurance costs, the cost of vaccines exceeded the medical insurance cost reductions due to vaccines, with the cost of acquiring one quality-adjusted life year (QALY) at JPY 45.546 million, while a single vaccine is reduced to JPY 6,090 (in basic analysis, JPY 11,109). Cost effectiveness fell to the general threshold of JPY 5 million/QALY. Thus, by performing an analysis from the social perspective that includes lost productivity, it was reported that the administration of vaccines promises cost reductions of JPY 14.84 billion, and could be even larger when considering herd immunity[12].

The subcommittee report was created in light of this data[13], which was approved at the sixth meeting on March 11, 2011[14], and the 16th meeting on May 26, 2011.[15] However, there was no negative data in these reports regarding the health economics assessments—the reports only stated that in analyzing the comparisons of costs, the cost of vaccines are outweighed by the savings in prevented medical costs related to dealing with disease and the value of lost productivity, thus promising an ongoing cost effectiveness of a savings of JPY 2.9 billion annually due to vaccination (however, these numbers are not visible on the fact sheet).

Regarding the burden of costs, to promote vaccinations to prevent cervical cancer and so forth, basic funding was provided to municipalities, and on November 26, 2010, budgetary provisions were made until the end of FY 2011 as special temporary grants for the emergency promotion of vaccinations against diseases such as cervical cancer (extended to the end of FY 2012); they also covered pediatric pneumococcal vaccines. Under this arrangement, the national government covered half the costs, with the other half being covered by municipalities. Pediatric pneumococcal vaccines are normally administered three times to children from zero to four years of age, beginning between two and seven months of age, with one additional dose administered at least 60 days after the initial three shots[16]. At the end of September 2011, the vaccination rate stood at 34.3%[17].

The meeting of the subcommittee on vaccinations for infectious diseases, held on May 23, 2012, summarized a review of the vaccination systems (second proposals), which was received by the Ministry of Health, Labour and Welfare and submitted to Parliament on March 1, 2013 as revisions to the vaccination law. These revisions were put into effect on March 29, 2013, and routine vaccinations against pediatric pneumococcal disease began on April 1 of the same year[18].

6.4 SUMMARY

To provide vaccines to the market, the approval to manufacture and sell them must be granted under the Pharmaceuticals and Medical Devices Act. The approval process involves the rigorous screening of a vaccine's safety, effectiveness and quality. They are also tested after release by the National Institute of Infectious Diseases, and there have not been many major issues regarding vaccine quality, effectiveness and safety with the introduction of the routine vaccinations.

Because of the issue of the burden of cost of routine vaccinations, the results of the healthcare economic analysis are critical. However, the discussions of those promoting routine vaccinations, including those of the Health, Labour and Welfare Ministry, only include the favorable aspects of the healthcare economic analysis results.

At the outset, the healthcare economic analysis is based on uncertain data and produces a range of results because it inevitably uses various assumptions and speculations. Thus, the failure to question the validity of the analysis and the diversity of results, and only including favorable results while ignoring negative ones, can only lead to doubt. For example, if savings are apparent when comparing vaccination with non-vaccination, only an analysis of the cost directly related to medical treatments is used. If the results do not indicate good cost effectiveness, analyses that also consider lost productivity are used.

In addition, the results of the healthcare economic analysis change when the infection rates fall when vaccines are introduced, and thus, cost effectiveness also falls. Even in the analysis we performed with the aim of implementing the 10-valent pediatric pneumococcal vaccine, because there was no immunological data available related to the serotype distribution after the introduction of the routine 7-valent pediatric pneumococcal vaccine, we did not compare it with non-vaccination, but compared it with the 13-valence pediatric pneumococcal vaccine to show good cost effectiveness (Shiragami, forthcoming).

On this point, even vaccination subcommittee members expressed the opinion that cost effectiveness would be easy to understand if illness were constant; however, if the rate of illness gradually falls, the cost effects reverse at some point. Therefore, discussions that place too much emphasis on cost effectiveness may be of little use, because as cost effectiveness disappears, objectives may become unreachable; but there were no further discussions about it[19].

Sometimes the numbers in the results of the healthcare economic analysis take on a life of their own. Because such erroneous results might be used, specialists in healthcare economics must have the courage to participate in discussions to correct these errors and lead public opinion.

APPENDIX VACCINE COST EFFECTIVENESS ESTIMATION METHOD

Expenses

1. Healthcare costs

   (1) Medical costs

   ① Medical expenses related to vaccine side effects and disease treatments, etc. adjusted to 2010 levels using the medical fee revision rate.
   ② Includes screening costs (for HPV).

③ Medical costs relating to life extension but unrelated to the disease not included.

(2) Vaccination costs

Vaccination cost assumes the cost of a single vaccination. The following totals include the 5% consumption tax.

① The desired retail vaccine price
② First visit fee JPY 2,700 (+ JPY 750 for children under 6)
③ Handling charge JPY 180
④ Biologics addition JPY 150

(3) Welfare facility costs

Includes healthcare costs.

2. Non-healthcare costs (costs incurred other than those related to healthcare)

Transportation costs to the facility where the vaccine is administered, or costs related to transportation to medical facilities for screening or treatment are not considered.

3. Loss of productivity

To calculate loss of productivity, the latest wage census, which was conducted in 2009, is used.

(1) Productivity lost by the patient

① Loss of productivity in the age range of 20–65 is calculated (lost income). However, the loss of productivity for child patients when they become adults is not considered if there are no ongoing adverse effects of disease.
② The cost-benefit analysis considers the loss of productivity due to morbidities and to early death.

(2) Loss of productivity due to family nursing and care

To avoid overestimation, the average (overall) women's monthly income of JPY 228,000 is used.

Analysis Period and Discount Rate

On principle, the analysis period should be a natural lifetime; however, if the effects on cost effectiveness are small, the analysis period may be shorter. Discounted rates are not considered with an analysis comparing single financial year costs. If the analysis period is greater than one year, the annual discount rate for costs and effects is 3%, with 0% and 5% sensitivity analyses performed.

Vaccination Rate

(1) Current vaccination rates
Current vaccination rate data understood to a certain degree for a vaccine is used.

If vaccination rates cannot be sufficiently understood because a vaccine has not been in use much since its introduction, for instance, 0% is used.

(2) Predicted vaccination rates following switch to routine vaccination

Rates for vaccines administered in childhood are set by referring to the 2008 measles vaccination rates. (1st period (one-year-olds) 94.3%, 2nd period (five-year-olds) 91.8%, 3rd period (7th graders) 85.1%, 4th period (12th graders) 77.3%)

100% is used for vaccination after childhood on principle.

Analysis method

A cost comparison analysis is done as a standard for vaccination in childhood, and cost benefit and cost effectiveness analyses are done if possible. A cost effectiveness analysis is done as a standard for vaccinations after childhood.

(1) Cost comparison analysis

Done from the social perspective, costs are compared before and after the implementation of routine vaccination. As well as medical costs, such as the cost of vaccination, the loss of productivity of nurses and caregivers is included. Loss of productivity (costs associated with morbidity and death) of the patients themselves is not included.

(2) Cost benefit analysis

Done from the social perspective, increased costs and increased benefits due to routine vaccination implementation are compared. Costs include cost of vaccination and the loss of productivity of companions during the administration of the vaccine. The benefits include reduced medical costs associated with vaccination, and reduced loss of the productivity of families due to nursing and care, as well as the loss of productivity of the patients themselves (costs associated with morbidities and death).

(3) Cost effectiveness analysis

Performed from the perspective of payers, the loss of productivity is not included in costs. On principle, the incremental cost effectiveness ratio (ICER) is calculated for one QALY, which is attained by calculating the costs and quality adjusted life year (QALY) associated with the vaccinated and control groups.

JPY 5 million is used as a measure of the ICER threshold for one QALY attained. If it is less than JPY 5 million, the cost effectiveness is judged as favorable.

NOTES

1. Ministry of Health, Labour and Welfare, Health Science Council, Infectious Disease Subcommittee, Vaccination Group. "Vaccination System Review (second proposals)," May 23, 2012, http://www.mhlw.go.jp/stf/shingi/2r985200

00033079-att/2r985200000330hg_1.pdf (accessed December 16, 2014) (In Japanese)

2. Ministry of Health, Labour and Welfare, "Fundamentals of polio and the polio vaccine," 2014, http://www.mhlw.go.jp/bunya/kenkou/polio/qa.html (accessed December 16, 2014) (In Japanese)

3. World Health Organization, "Global Vaccine Action Plan 2011–2020," 2011, http://www.who.int/immunization/global_vaccine_action_plan/GVAP_doc_2011_2020/en/ (accessed December 16, 2014) (In Japanese)

4. Ministry of Health, Labour and Welfare, Department of Health Tuberculosis Infection Division. 1st Health Science Council, Submission of the Vaccination and Vaccine Subcommittee, "Vaccination System (reference)," April 22, 2013, http://www.mhlw.go.jp/stf/shingi/2r98520000030o0g.html (accessed December 16, 2014) (In Japanese)

5. Ministry of Health, Labour and Welfare, "Vaccine Industry Vision: Supporting the fight against infectious diseases: Aiming for an image of the industry that meets social expectations," 2007, http://www.mhlw.go.jp/shingi/2007/03/dl/s0322–13d.pdf (accessed December 16, 2014) (In Japanese)

6. Ministry of Health, Labour and Welfare, Department of Health Tuberculosis Infection Division. 2nd Health Science Council, Submission of Vaccination Basic Policy Group of the Vaccination and Vaccines Subcommittee. "Study on the introduction schedule for 13-valent pediatric pneumococcal (PCV13)," 2013, http://www.mhlw.go.jp/stf/shingi/2r9852000003584p-att/2r98520000035rbk_1.pdf (accessed December 16, 2014) (In Japanese)

7. Ministry of Health, Labour and Welfare, Department of Health Tuberculosis Infection Division. 11th Health Science Council, Submission of Vaccination Group of the Infectious Disease Subcommittee. "Current state of expenses associated with vaccination," 2010, http://www.mhlw.go.jp/stf2/shingi2/2r9852000000bx23-att/2r9852000000bygx.pdf (accessed December 16, 2014) (In Japanese)

8. Ministry of Health, Labour and Welfare, 7th Health Science Council, Infectious Disease Subcommittee, "Vaccination group proceedings," 2010, http://www.mhlw.go.jp/shingi/2010/04/txt/s0421–8.txt (accessed December 16, 2014) (In Japanese)

9. National Institute of Infectious Diseases, "Fact Sheet on the pneumococcal conjugate vaccine (for children)," 2010, http://www.mhlw.go.jp/stf2/shingi2/2r9852000000bx23-att/2r9852000000bxqo.pdf (accessed December 16, 2014) (In Japanese)

10. Ministry of Health, Labour and Welfare, 11th Health Science Council, Infectious Disease Subcommittee, Vaccination Group Proceedings, 2010, http://www.mhlw.go.jp/stf/shingi/2r9852000000vxa6.html (accessed December 16, 2014) (In Japanese)

11. Ministry of Health, Labour and Welfare, Health Science Council, Infectious Disease Subcommittee, Vaccination Group, Subcommittee on Vaccine Evaluation. "Method of estimating cost effectiveness of vaccinations," 2011, http://www.mhlw.go.jp/stf/shingi/2r98520000014ryv-att/2r98520000014sdi.pdf (Accessed December 16, 2010) (In Japanese)

12. Ministry of Health, Labour and Welfare, Health Science Council, 3rd Infectious Disease Subcommittee, Vaccination Group, Submission of Subcommittee on Vaccine Evaluation, "Pneumococcal conjugate vaccine (for children)," 2010, http://www.mhlw.go.jp/stf/shingi/2r9852000000yw9d-att/2r9852000000ywig.pdf (Accessed December 16, 2014) (In Japanese)

13. Ministry of Health, Labour and Welfare, Health Science Council, Infectious Disease Subcommittee, Vaccination Group, Subcommittee on Vaccine Evaluation. "Report, March 11, 2011," http://www.mhlw.go.jp/stf/shi

ngi/2r9852000001e323-att/2r9852000001e3ff.pdf (accessed December 16, 2014) (In Japanese)
14. Ministry of Health, Labour and Welfare, Health Science Council, 6th Infectious Disease Subcommittee, Vaccination Group, Subcommittee on Vaccine Evaluation Proceedings, 2011, http://www.mhlw.go.jp/stf/shingi/2r98520 00003338n.html (accessed December 16, 2014) (In Japanese)
15. Ministry of Health, Labour and Welfare, 16th Health Science Council, Infectious Disease Subcommittee, Vaccination Group Proceedings, 2011, http:// www.mhlw.go.jp/stf/shingi/2r9852000001eq5c.html (accessed December 16, 2014) (In Japanese)
16. Ministry of Health, Labour and Welfare, Health Science Council, 3rd Infectious Disease Subcommittee, Vaccination Subcommittee, Submission of Subcommittee on Vaccine Evaluation. "Overview of extraordinary special grant for emergency promotion of cervical cancer vaccination," 2010, http:// www.mhlw.go.jp/stf/shingi/2r9852000000yw9d-att/2r9852000000ywjf.pdf (accessed December 16, 2014) (In Japanese)
17. Ministry of Health, Labour and Welfare, 20th Health Science Council, Submission of Vaccination Group of the Infectious Disease Subcommittee. "Extension of emergency promotion of cervical cancer vaccination past 2012," 2012, http://www.mhlw.go.jp/stf/shingi/2r98520000021b99-att/2r98520000021 bbt.pdf (accessed December 16, 2014) (In Japanese)
18. Ministry of Health, Labour and Welfare, Department of Health Tuberculosis Infection Division. 1st Health Science Council, Submission of the Vaccination and Vaccine Subcommittee. "Vaccination System, April 22, 2013," 2013, http://www.mhlw.go.jp/file.jsp?id=146395&name=2r985200000302v_1. pdf (accessed December 16, 2014) (In Japanese)
19. Ministry of Health, Labour and Welfare, 8th Health Science Council, Infectious Disease Subcommittee, Vaccination Group Proceedings, 2011, http:// www.mhlw.go.jp/stf/shingi/2r9852000000u6yr.html (accessed December 16, 2014) (In Japanese)

REFERENCES

Kamiya, T. (2009). Disease burden from pediatric pneumococcal infection and vaccine cost-effectiveness. *Journal of the Japanese Society for Pediatric Infectious Diseases*, 21(2), 142–148 (in Japanese).

Kurane, I. (2014). *Vaccines in Japan: Historical verification of development and quality management. Iyaku (Medical and Drug) Journal, Co., Ltd.*,126–127 (in Japanese).

Nichol, K.L. (2003). The efficacy, effectiveness and cost-effectiveness of inactivated influenza virus vaccines. *Vaccine*, 21, 1769–1775.

Nichol, K.L., Margolis, K.L., Wuorenma, J. & Von Sternberg, T. (1994). The efficacy and cost effectiveness of vaccination against influenza among elderly persons living in the community. *New England Journal of Medicine*, 331(12), 778–784.

Postma, M.J., Jansema, P., van Genugten, M.L., Heijnen, M.L., Jager, J.C. & de Jong-van den Berg, L.T. (2002). Pharmacoeconomics of influenza vaccination for healthy working adults. Reviewing the available evidence. *Drugs*, 62(7), 1769–1775.

Shiragami, M. (2006). Current state and issues of pharmaceutical prices. In: H. Endo, N. Ikegami (eds.), *Medical Insurance and Reimbursement System*, 166 (in Japanese).

Shiragami, M. Mizunuma, A., Leeuwenkamp, O., Mrkvan, T., Delgleize, E., Kurono, Y. & Iwata, S. Cost-effectiveness evaluation of the 10-valent pneumococcal non-typeable Haemophilus influenzae protein D conjugate vaccine and 13-valent pneumococcal vaccine in Japanese children. *Infectious Diseases and Therapy.* 2014 Dec 20. [Epub ahead of print])

Tezuka, Y. (2010a). *Structural Changes in Vaccinations, Post-War Administration Structures and Dilemmas* (in Japanese). Tokyo: Fujiwara-shoten, 207–208.

Tezuka, Y. (2010b). *Administrative Actions in Uncertainty, Post-War Administration Structures and Dilemmas* (in Japanese). Tokyo: Fujiwara-shoten, 37.

Vaccination Guidelines Review Committee. (2012). *Overview of Vaccination Systems* (in Japanese). Vaccination Companion, Foundation of Vaccination Research Center (public interest incorporated foundation), 8–11.

7 Achieving Health Support Innovation in a Smart City Concept

Nobuyuki Tokoro

The "smart city" is a new concept of urban infrastructure in which ICT, energy efficiency and electricity storage technologies are used to optimize the energy supply and demand while maximizing the use of renewables. For example, co-generation systems could use exhaust heat from food and plant production facilities to stimulate agricultural reform and other green innovations, while smart next-generation TVs and medical equipment at medical facilities and in people's homes could be linked over a network so that the elderly can receive services such as medical care, health checks and catering in their homes. These lifestyle innovations could take place both locally and nationwide.

Green and health support innovation creates new lifestyle value, but requires both the development of new technologies and structural reforms in social and economic systems—key elements of the smart city concept. In response to the challenges of health and medical care for aging societies, etc., smart cities will enable self-supporting lifestyles with health support ecosystems underpinned by energy independence attained with renewables.

In this chapter, the authors analyze and discuss the specific initiatives that individual countries have taken to build smart cities. Collaborative innovation involving alliances across different industries, including regional governments and independent bodies, is a special feature of the innovation process, and is needed to create the new knowledge required to build smart cities. Regarding the creation of innovation communities, I analyze and discuss the management and leadership models born from the collaborative innovation efforts to achieve health support ecosystems both locally and nationwide, and I identify the common factors of success.

7.1 SMART CITIES AND HEALTH SUPPORT

The construction of smart cities is gaining a lot of attention. Using ICT, smart cities aim to optimize the social infrastructure underpinning urban lifestyles, such as electricity, water, transportation and communications systems while aiming to be environmentally friendly by reducing energy consumption and carbon dioxide emissions. The construction of these cities also has the potential to solve a range of urban problems, such as population increase, the aging of society, traffic congestion and security issues.

This chapter looks at smart cities from the perspective of health support innovations. As described above, smart cities inherently offer solutions to a range of modern urban problems, and can bring about new value and innovation through their construction. Healthcare innovation is one of these aspects.

Briefly, using ICT in smart cities to network residences with medical institutions such as hospitals will enable services for the elderly, such as home treatment, health management and catering. Thus, these advances will bring about noticeably more comfortable lifestyles and higher-quality health services for the elderly, and will bring about health support innovations as the aging of society progresses.

This chapter presents the case of the Fujisawa Sustainable Smart Town (Fujisawa SST) in Fujisawa City in Kanagawa Prefecture, a project run by Japanese electronics major Panasonic that features health support innovations as new value created through the construction of the smart city, and considers the management models for creating these kinds of innovations.

7.2 THE CURRENT STATE OF SMART CITY
CONSTRUCTION PROJECTS

Before getting into the main discussion, the authors would like to briefly outline the state of smart city construction projects. There are many smart city projects ongoing all over the world, both in developed and developing countries. This fact tells us that there is a lot of hope that smart cities will offer solutions to the serious urban problems facing both developed and developing countries.

According to the existing research, there were 608 smart city construction projects around the world in 2013. Viewed in terms of countries and regions, China had the most projects with 225, followed by North America with 124 and Europe with 91, while there were 78 in Asia, 63 in Japan, 17 in Africa and 10 in South America.

Although these 608 projects are diverse, 315 of them, more than half, are projects that have the elements of urban development. Viewed in terms of developed and developing countries, 232 of these projects are in developing countries, which is two-thirds of the total of those urban developments. Most notably, 143 of these projects are in China, a country undergoing rapid urbanization, with about 12 million people moving into cities from rural areas every year. For these reasons, Chinese cities must solve a range of problems, such as population increase, air pollution and traffic congestion, although the underlying intention of these urban developments is nation building. Apart from China, new urban development projects have also started in regions such as Southeast Asia, Africa and the Middle East, where populations are also concentrated in large cities.

Many of these projects in developing countries feature cases of industrial zone development in conjunction with new urban development. In other words, as well as building new residential areas on land made available in wilderness or reclaimed areas, many of these projects are large-scale urban developments planned to attract industry by including industrial zones replete with infrastructure. Stimulating industry in this way is intended to ensure employment for the populations moving into these cities. For example, the Tianjin Eco-City on the salt field site on the coast of the Bohai Sea in China is a new urban project designed for a population of around 400,000. As well as the construction of residences, this project plans to attract industries involved in the environment, energy, research and development fields, as well as financing and outsourcing services. Another example is the Delhi-Mumbai Industrial Corridor, a wide area development plan between Delhi and Mumbai in India, which includes a 1500 km railroad designated for goods transport with residential and commercial zonings 150 km on either side that include industrial areas, distribution bases, power generation facilities, roadways and harbors.

In contrast, many projects in developed countries are characterized by stagnated industrial area development, and are projects that are intended to revitalize existing cities to solve the problems that mature cities face, such as carbon dioxide emissions, traffic congestion and worsening living environments.

There are many projects underway in the developed countries of North America and Europe and in Japan that include smart grids. In the US, the implementation of the smart grid is an ongoing national strategy to solve the problem of the country's aging power grid. These smart grid projects have been launched with subsidies from the American Recovery and Reinvestment Act (ARRA) established by President Obama in February, 2009—a political action intended to underpin smart grid development.

However, the situation in Japan and Europe is somewhat different. European and Japanese projects appear to place a greater focus on the implementation of smart grids as networked systems for distributing the unstable electricity produced by renewable energy sources as part of those countries' efforts to reduce greenhouse gases. Notably, the European Union has set down a renewable energy target of 20%, and its ongoing smart grid projects aim to achieve this target.

In contrast to Europe, the Japanese case has been heavily influenced by the Great East Japan Earthquake of March 11, 2011. Faced with rolling blackouts and the obligatory 15% reduction in power consumption, smart grid design and implementation is ongoing in Japan as part of the country's efforts to rethink its electricity supplies and energy planning.

While there are many cases of projects that demonstrate technical viability and deploy renewable energy in developed countries, there are also a number of large-scale projects in developing countries that warrant attention. One of these is the Masdar City project in Abu Dhabi in the United Arab Emirates. This project involves the construction of a planned city that is completely powered by renewable energy, such as solar power, and that accommodates 50,000 people in the desert near Abu Dhabi[1].

Compared to other projects, projects designed with a focus on coping with aging societies and providing health and welfare services are fewer in number, although these types of projects have enormous potential. Most of these projects are concentrated in developed countries—for example, of the 35 projects handling societal aging, 16 are in Japan, 11 are in Europe and eight are in North America. Nevertheless, demand for aged, healthcare and welfare projects in developing countries is also predicted to rise, which will also present business opportunities based on the experiences gained in developed countries.

7.3 A REVIEW OF THE EXISTING RESEARCH

While the social interest in smart cities is on the rise, their importance as a subject of research is also increasing, which has resulted in researchers making attempts at analysis from a wide range of perspectives. Here, the authors review some typical examples of this research.

The most common analytical approach to smart cities research involves the urban planning perspective. For example, Rassia and Pardalos (2014), who conducted broad surveys across construction, engineering and related areas, mainly analyzed smart cities from the urban engineering perspective with regard to the sustainable technologies, alternative energy sources and future energy systems needed to create a smart city, while Ercoskun (2012) cites the social and technical issues facing smart city planning and design, and focuses on "resilience" while discussing it in a range of eco-technology contexts.

In contrast to the urban planning perspective, there are also research approaches that focus on urban government. For example, Herrschel (2013) analyzes smart city construction from the "regionalism" perspective. Herrschel focuses on the mechanisms of policy and decision-making in the process of building smart cities, and considers the effects of the special circumstances of particular regions in the smart city building process while looking at the cases of Vancouver and Seattle. Similarly, Gibbs, Rob, and Gordon (2013) conduct their analysis on smart city construction from the urban government perspective. They argue that urban planning, as smart city construction, should be based on the three visions of economic growth, the integration of ecosystems, and social equality, and discuss the effects that spatial development will have on the existing urban social hierarchy, political culture and economic foundations.

Shaw (2013) cites the example of the redevelopment of the Melbourne Docklands, and through the analysis of a wide range of stories about the project spanning 20 years, favorably assesses the project for its sustainability.

In contrast, Tretter (2013) cites the case of Austin, Texas, and takes the negative view that in spite of being environmentally friendly, smart cities cannot solve a range of urban problems, such as homelessness.

Townsend (2013) looks at the rise of industrial society from the 19th century through to the present, and considers how much force town planning and design and the advent of information technology has had from a historical perspective. Townsend goes on to analyze to what degree rapid global urbanization and the spread of ubiquity are going to collide, and to analyze how much technology will impact the cities of the future. His analytical approach takes the "urban civilization theory" perspective.

From the perspectives of innovation and competitiveness, Deakin (2014) puts a focus on governments and modeling in the process of transforming intelligent cities into smart cities. Here, Deakin develops his assertion that a genuine smart city is not just simply a digital city or an intelligent city, but a city that has innovation networks and creative partnerships built in, and is a place where learning, knowledge transfer and skills development take place.

Furthermore, Campbell (2012) views smart cities as "cities that learn," and considers the relationship between the learning processes, innovation and competitiveness in cities. Campbell asserts that sustained learning and innovation must be enabled to build a truly 'smart' city, and analyzes the mechanisms, describing how networks in cities are formed and how learning and innovation breakthroughs occur through examples including Amman, Barcelona, Portland and Seattle.

However, none of this existing research thoroughly discusses the management that is necessary to build smart cities as "cities of learning" that will promote the formation of business ecosystems through sustained learning and innovation. However, as discussed in Chapter 2, although the execution of exploration and exploitation through the four spiral stages is necessary for the creation, growth and development of business ecosystems, these processes require collaboration (cooperation through strategic alliances, joint ventures, M&A, etc.) through the formation of business networks built around leader and major follower companies as the organizational infrastructure, which leads to the following insight.

[Insight 4]

The dynamic formation of innovation communities as business networks built around leader and major follower companies lies at the core of the formation of business ecosystems.

As described by [Insight 4], this chapter analyzes and considers managerial factors (e.g. leadership models) that are necessary for stakeholders, including leader corporations and major follower corporations, to dynamically form innovation communities as business networks that will make up the foundational business ecosystem elements of smart cities.

7.4 CASE STUDY: FUJISAWA SUSTAINABLE SMART TOWN (FUJISAWA SST)

This chapter analyzes the Fujisawa Sustainable Smart Town (Fujisawa SST) that is under construction in Fujisawa City in Kanagawa Prefecture, Japan. Beginning in 2011 and slated for completion by 2018, this ongoing project has participation from companies involved in a range of industries that are cooperating under the leadership of Panasonic to build the smart city. Thus, the project involves knowledge, technology and know-how exchange and integration between participating companies, and is gaining attention as a project that promises the creation of new value.

7.4.1 Fujisawa SST Overview

Fujisawa SST is an advanced town building project aimed at housing around 3,000 people in about 1,000 households, built on the site of the old Panasonic factory (approximately 19 hectares) in Fujisawa City in Kanagawa Prefecture. The project, which began in 2011, will cost around JPY 60 billion, and will be completed by 2018. The project has the following features.[2]

Firstly, Fujisawa SST will feature solar power generation systems and domestic power storage systems as standard to supply electricity to all residences, facilities and public zones throughout the town. All retail premises in the town will also be controlled for energy saving with equipment designed to work in the four areas of wind, light, heat and water to create, conserve and store energy.

Public spaces in the town will also implement "eco-cycle pack" equipment as the charging infrastructure for electric and plug-in hybrid vehicles, for power-assisted bicycles, and as car parks with solar power generation, etc. Moreover, the project will also feature eco-cars and electric vehicles, mobility-sharing services, optimized security services using lighting, sensors and security cameras, as well as healthcare services to ensure comfort for the aged and so forth.

As well as that, as a community platform supporting these mechanisms, the town will also provide terminals for a one-stop portal that provides the applications to access and use the services. Links with Smart Energy Gateway (SEG—an integrated networked domestic appliance control device) will the enable visualization of energy, the notification of time-limited sales in commercial facilities, facility bookings and so forth from the household living room. These measures aim to reduce the carbon dioxide emissions of the entire Fujisawa SST by 70% to that of the 1990 levels, and to reduce water consumption by 30%.

As a project under the guidance of Panasonic, Fujisawa SST strongly reflects the intentions of Panasonic in everything from the creation of the original vision through to planning and implementation. In other words, this project is being carried out under the Panasonic strategy of "comprehensive solutions for the entire house, entire building and entire town." As a new strategy, Panasonic wants to take the opportunity of Fujisawa SST to transform itself from a company that manufactures white goods and electronic devices to one that creates new urban spaces for the 21st century. Thus, Panasonic will take the knowledge it gains from the Fujisawa SST project to create business models with which it will be able to pioneer new markets around the world, and thus create a pillar for new business. Accordingly, companies other than Panasonic that are participating in Fujisawa SST understand this Panasonic strategy, and are following the intention of it by fulfilling the range of roles required. These eight other participating companies are businesses involved in residential construction, real estate, gas distribution, finances and commercial enterprises, etc. The roles of each of these companies in the project are described as follows (see Table 7.1).

The 19-hectare block of Fujisawa SST is partitioned into areas for the construction of housing, commercial facilities, health, welfare and education facilities as well as community centers, etc. For example, there is a strong emphasis on creating the commercial facilities (Shonan T-SITE) as a base for showcasing the new lifestyles born in Fujisawa SST to the world—in other

Table 7.1 Roles in Fujisawa SST

Accenture	• Smart town conceptualization, service model planning and promotion • Smart town platform support in light of global trends
Orix	• Service planning for increased overall town value, and comfortable, ecological, safe and secure lifestyles
Nihon Sekkei	• Space design and optimal planning for deploying new energy devices, etc.
Sumitomo Trust and Banking	• Smart town evaluation index design (environment and real estate value) • Product planning for environmentally friendly housing loans designed for Fujisawa SST
Tokyo Gas	• Installing the latest "ene-farm" home fuel cell equipment • Proposals for comfortable and ecological living using ene-farm
PanaHome	• Basic land readjustment project arrangements • Residential land and housing sales
Mitsui Fudosan	• Basic land readjustment project arrangements • Residential land and housing sales
Mitsui & Co.	• City block, infrastructure and real estate development, also applicable for global expansion • Energy management services that take into account global smart city trends

Source: Created from Materials on Fujisawa SST

words, these will not be facilities for simply selling goods, but will only feature products selected to resonate richly with the sensibilities of human beings. The town community center, called "Fujisawa SST Site" (F-SITE) will provide the welcoming, town management and community functions while playing the role of the town landmark. The welcoming function of the F-SITE is aimed at general information reception and dissemination, guest reception, PR, business consultation, residential sales promotion and support for social studies field trips, etc., while the town management function aims to enable people to create new voluntary lifestyles by themselves by setting up residential workshops in which residents can actually build the things they want or require. The community function will provide an opportunity for site residents, the residents of surrounding towns and visitors to engage in exchanges in the cafe lounge and community shop, etc. The facility will also provide environmental education and function as a venue for events held in the smart city.

Fujisawa SST is a project intended to raise the value of the entire town by creating the diversity of value. Although this project is aligned with Panasonic's strategy, it is not intended to create value for Panasonic alone—the diversity of the value created will come about through the collaboration between Panasonic and the eight other participating companies.

7.4.2 Health Support Innovation

The problems of the aging society are some of the most serious problems facing cities, and are problems that can be found in developed countries all over the world. As mentioned, there is an overwhelming trend in smart city construction in developed countries around the world towards projects for handling societal aging and providing health and welfare services. Particularly in Japan, a country whose population is aging faster than anywhere else, solutions to the problems of societal aging are a matter of urgency.

Thus, one of the main themes of the Fujisawa SST project is to create a town in which the elderly can live with ease. Put differently, this is about how to create value as healthcare. On this point, the authors discuss the reasons behind citing the Fujisawa SST project.

What sort of a town is it in which all residents, from children through to the elderly, can live healthily in their own way? The authors believe Fujisawa SST answers this question with the idea of "connection." With this key concept, Fujisawa SST has created a general base called the "Well SITE," which incorporates the latest healthcare, welfare and education services by linking special nursing homes for the aged, serviced residences designed for the elderly, and range of clinics, pharmacies, daycare centers and preparatory schools, etc. This seamless linking will transcend the boundaries between all of these services and thus enable the provision of services that are optimized to individual residents. To achieve this vision, Fujisawa SST is implementing a comprehensive local care system to link and provide these medical, nursing, care and pharmaceutical services efficiently.

As described, this system is designed to provide seamlessly linked combinations of services in place of individual and disconnected services. For example, medicine and nursing care were previously thought of as separate fields. This meant that the medical services received in a hospital and the care services received in a nursing care facility were thought of as being different services, and not many services that combined both of these were available. However, if these services are seamlessly linked, they can provide solutions to the problems of the unavailability of appropriate home care due to distance once a patient goes home after hospitalization, as well as the unavailability of sufficient information about the patient once he or she has gone home. By tackling these problems through information sharing, the Fujisawa SST local care system will enable effective and efficient service deployment, and it is information and communications technology (ICT) that will enable this information sharing. Through ICT and a central server, the local care system will provide access to resident healthcare information by the main hospitals, clinics, pharmacies, specialist aged care homes, service accommodations for the aged, the residents themselves, home nursing stations and sports clubs, etc. in the area. All resident data is managed uniformly in the central server so that concerned parties can provide services appropriately when required.

Nevertheless, Fujisawa SST is not just a town being built for old people. The town is designed for 1,000 households with 3,000 residents in all age groups, from children and young people through to those who are middle aged and older. Of course, because the needs of the individual residents will change according to their age, the services provided by the town to the residents must also change.

Because it is anticipated that Fujisawa SST will house people of all ages from infancy through 90 years old, the town is designed to provide services to meet the needs of the individual age groups. These services are being developed under the key concepts of "using living energy" and "securing living energy." For example, under the concept of using living energy, services are provided that include parent-child science classrooms, a child raising salon and field crop planting (for zero to 13-year-olds), baby weaning courses, health and preventive medicine courses, all kinds of volunteering (for 18 to 40-year-olds), general consultation, dementia prevention programs, and restaurants to invigorate both the mind and the body (for 50 to 90-year-olds). Under the concept of securing living energy, services will be provided that include self-study areas, a day care center and experimental classrooms (for zero to 13-year-olds), pharmacies, health management data sharing using ICT and clinics (for 18 to 40-year-olds) as well as the local healthcare system (for 50 to 90-year-olds).

In this way, the Fujisawa SST concept of resident connections enables the mechanisms through which the right services can be provided to meet the diverse needs of residents across a wide range of age groups. This is one of the defining characteristics of Fujisawa SST, and is directly aimed at tackling the well-known problem of the rarefaction of human relationships in urban settings.

For example, large international cities such as Tokyo, New York and London are places where people, goods, money and information collect, but while these places bring about an extremely dynamic energy, human relations tend to become more rarefied and characterized by indifference, and thus create discomfort in living environments. Tragic incidents such as the child abuse due to parents or guardians becoming neurotic and solitary death among the elderly are also chronic issues. In facing these modern-day urban problems, Fujisawa SST aims to offer solutions under its key concept of "connection" using ICT.

Based only on existing technology, the systems used at Fujisawa SST will not be particularly special or new. In other words, the project does not involve the development of revolutionary technology or destructive innovations that could impact entire societies. However, in spite of that, the authors believe the efforts made at Fujisawa SST are a kind of innovation. This is because innovation does not only mean technical innovation, but can also be thought of as actions that create new value through collaboration between participating agents (e.g., Prahalad and Ramaswamy, 2003). Fujisawa SST cannot be perceived as simply urban infrastructure and living space, but must be considered to be a dynamically creative project that creates new value as people living in the town collaborate and resonate with each other and the urban infrastructure. This idea is expressed in the Fujisawa SST slogan of "a town where living energy is born."

So, rather than a divided approach to creating living spaces for children through to the elderly, the project aims to provide appropriate and effective services to meet the needs of various people by creating connected living spaces using ICT.

New value will be born as residents share their needs and resonate with each other in the diverse "Ba" created. For example, a "Ba" like the general consultation area will create opportunities for the elderly and youths to interact, and enable their experiential and practical knowledge to reverberate and create new value (e.g., the elderly conveying their life experiences to the young, or the young instructing the elderly with their knowledge of IT).

Shared experiences through volunteer activities can also enable the resonance of the tacit knowledge of people to bring about new ideas and services. As these processes accumulate, the new value of "a town where living energy is born" will be spread through the entire town. Of course, these kinds of services are not limited to Fujisawa SST, but are also offered in existing cities, although they might not necessarily entail this kind of comprehensive deployment through "connection" with children through to the elderly. This is because in many cities, these services have been added as they have become necessary, and are thus individualized and fragmented.

Fujisawa SST has been designed to solve these urban problems as an artificially constructed town that will enable the creation of new value across its entirety through these types of health support innovations.

7.4.3 Creating Innovation by Forming Innovation Communities

As discussed, a range of new values is going to be created through the construction of the new urban space in Fujisawa SST. The Fujisawa SST is itself an example of innovative urban construction, as it features aspects not seen in conventional town building. Therefore, what kind of processes and mechanisms create this innovation in Fujisawa SST?

As a project under the guidance of Panasonic, Fujisawa SST certainly reflects the intentions of Panasonic in everything from the creation of the original vision through to planning and implementation. However, the innovation in the Fujisawa SST will not be brought about just by Panasonic alone, but also through the exquisite processes set up to enable co-creation with its partner companies, the autonomous resident organizations and the contributions of the local Fujisawa government. This co-creation becomes evident when considering the approaches and processes active during the time it took to design and construct Fujisawa SST.

The Fujisawa SST site is on the site of an old Panasonic factory that began production in 1961 of such goods as black-and-white televisions, refrigerators and ventilation fans. When the factory closed in 2007, it presented a problem of what to do with the site. Panasonic engaged in ongoing discussions with the local Fujisawa government about using the land and announced the joint policy on the Fujisawa SST urban development in 2010. This policy forms the basis for the Fujisawa SST construction.

Following, the parties formed a town building committee centered on this urban development policy. In addition to participation by Panasonic, its partner companies and the local Fujisawa government, the town building committee engaged in discussions to set down concepts, overall objectives and guidelines for the urban development. It was through these actions that the Fujisawa SST concept of "a town where living energy is born" came to be. This concept specifically expresses the value that will be created in Fujisawa SST, and is pivotal in its meaning. Based on the fundamental factors of combining comfort with ecology, and safety and security, the Fujisawa SST urban development committee extracted the factors that make up living environments—connections, people gathering together, work, study, child raising, health, eating and recreation, etc.—and created the two slogans of "a town that brings about energy essential for living," and "a town in which energy that activates people is born" from these factors.

In addition, the committee also set down three overall objectives in the forms of environmental targets, energy targets and safety and security targets. They used specific numeric targets to reduce carbon dioxide emissions by 70% (to the 1990 levels), to reduce water consumption by 30% (to the ordinary facility levels in 2006), to introduce more than 30% renewable energy, and to insure at least three days of emergency supplies. The committee also created three guidelines to achieve these overall objectives. These included project design guidelines related to processes, town design guidelines related to urban design and development, and community design guidelines for the sustainable operation of the town. All of these came about through discussions in the town building committee.

The final process in designing and constructing the town was the establishment of the town management company and autonomous resident's organization, called the Fujisawa SST Committee. Fujisawa SST aims to be a town that can sustain itself for at least 100 years into the future, and therefore requires an organization that enables residents to take action, and a company that can reflect the needs of the residents in the town's services and systems.

In addition to the conventional role of a residence organization, the Fujisawa SST Committee also takes on the important roles of maintaining and managing a range of activities and assets involved with the environment, energy, safety and security. This committee is the central residential body involved in creating a resident-driven town, and brings about specific ideas and actions. In contrast, the town management company, Fujisawa SST Management, takes up the opinions of residents through the Fujisawa SST Committee to reflect them in the town's services and systems.

With Panasonic as its major shareholder, Fujisawa SST Management also received capital from eight partner companies to be established in March of 2013 (see Figure 7.1).

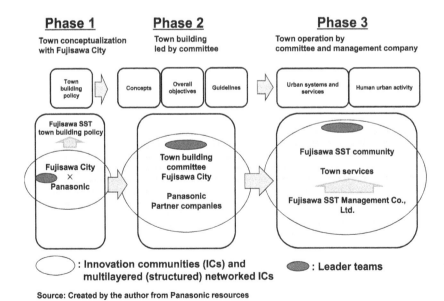

Source: Created by the author from Panasonic resources

Figure 7.1   Approaches during the Planning and Construction of Fujisawa SST

As described by Figure 7.1, the planning and construction of Fujisawa SST is divided into three phases. Of these phases, Phase 1 involved the formation of the town building policy set down through discussions, Phase 2 involved the formation of the town building committee to discuss and bring about the Fujisawa SST concepts, overall objectives and guidelines, and Phase 3 involved the establishment of the residence organization and town management company to promote the operation of the town.

Through these three phases, Fujisawa SST has aimed to bring about new value and create new innovation. Common to these three phases is the formation of diverse and multilayered (and structured) innovation communities formed through the generation of "Ba" to create new value through co-creation between the different entities involved.

As "Ba" enable different bodies to interact with each other, they are conceptually important part of the processes that create value and bring about innovation.

The concept of "Ba" was first put forth in research done by Japanese philosopher Kitaro Nishida in 1965. Then, in their knowledge creation theory, Nonaka and Takeuchi (1995) defined "Ba" as an important factor in the creation of new knowledge, and were the first to introduce the concept of "Ba" into the areas of business and management. Moreover, the creation of "Ba" leads to the creation of innovation communities—organizations that create new knowledge. Kodama (2007d) describes innovation communities (ICs) as having the following four characteristics.[3]

An IC is based on four basic concepts. The first is the element of "Ba"—a constantly changing shared context that enables corporations to dynamically respond to changes in markets and technologies (or to create new ones) (Nonaka and Konno, 1998; Nonaka, Toyama, and Konno, 2000).

Knowledge needs a context to be created, and is thus context-specific. Contexts define the participants and the nature of their participation. Contexts are social, cultural and even historical, and provide a basis for interpretation, thereby enabling the creation of meaning, which becomes knowledge.

Therefore, "Ba" are not necessarily just physical spaces or even a geographical locations or virtual spaces connected through ICT, but linkages in time and space as well as shared mental spaces. Because "Ba" transcend formal business structures, any form of new knowledge can be created regardless of the structure. Participating in a "Ba" means transcending one's own limited perspective or boundaries and contributing to the dynamic process of knowledge creation. In an IC, the participants, including customers, who have different values and knowledge, consciously and strategically create a "Ba" in their shared and constantly changing context, and continually create new knowledge and competencies as new "Ba" by merging and integrating a single "Ba" or multiple numbers of "Ba" both organically and from multiple points of view.

The second concept is that the IC is a community of practice (Wenger, 2000) rooted in the resonance of values (Kodama, 2001) among the participants in the IC. This aspect promotes mutual learning within the community by enabling the resonating of values and the mutual understanding of contexts among members, and thus continually generates new knowledge. The participation and leadership of the IC gradually comes into being, dynamically producing the context to work toward fulfilling the community mission. This involves the development of new products and services while community members create new knowledge by learning from one another and sharing.

The third concept is that the IC provides pragmatic boundaries that enable participants with different contexts to transform existing knowledge (Carlile, 2004). These concepts of "Ba" and communities of practice create shared meanings and transform knowledge along these boundaries (Dougherty, 1992; Nonaka and Takeuchi, 1995) and foster organizational learning and best practices. However with innovation (for example, new cases of previously unheard of innovation, like those described in this chapter) where high levels of novelty occur on organizational boundaries (or pragmatic boundaries), there are demands on participants for new knowledge creation and the transformation of existing knowledge that transcends organizational learning.

Thus, as the level of novelty increases on the semantic boundaries between participants, driving the creation of shared meaning and the translation of knowledge, the boundaries between participants change into pragmatic boundaries (Carlile, 2004).

However, a variety of problems occur on these pragmatic boundaries, challenging participants to create new knowledge and come up with solutions. For this reason, participants have to engage in practical yet creative confrontation and conflict (Leonard-Barton, 1992), which also requires them to have political negotiation skills (Brown and Duguid, 2001).

The fourth concept is that in which the participants, as the hubs or connectors in an organization, dynamically bridge multiple ICs (or span boundaries) to form networks (or links) between them. Participants who are committed to more than one IC play a central role in linking ICs and integrating their knowledge. To integrate different knowledge, participants must thoroughly understand and share the tacit and explicit knowledge of each IC, and they must then make this shared knowledge fully accessible over the network connecting the IC boundaries. In sharing tacit knowledge, it is particularly important for the ICs to be well connected, so that context can be thoroughly shared over the network. In the product and service development in this case study, as soon as the company decided to form strategic ties, strong links between the ICs were formed to enable access to different types of knowledge and to enable new knowledge to be created as technical integration that came to be embodied in new products and services.

When multiple ICs (or boundaries) become integrated in this way, they enable corporations to create new knowledge. Thus, to build a new product development or business model, participants must consciously network ICs (pragmatic boundaries) among the various organizations in the corporation and integrate multiple organizational boundaries. If needed, the participants also form ICs through strategic alliances with external entities, including customers, and embed them into the ICs within the corporation (e.g., Kodama, 1999a, 2001, 2002).

Here, as pragmatic boundaries, the authors would like to discuss the existing literature on ICs and the integration of them (networked ICs) (Kodama, 2007d). Clark and Fujimoto (1991) call the function of an organization that provides products and services to meet market needs "external integrity," and call the functions needed to coordinate between functional divisions in an organization and bring about consistent products "internal integrity." Thus, according to Clark and Fujimoto (1991), the participants driving both external and internal integrity must act as bridges between organizations, and gather the information required by the organization from external sources and analyze and interpret it (to give it new meaning), and spread it within their organizations. Thus, these participants are special participants that take coordinator roles, and are sometimes called gatekeepers or boundary spanners (Adams, 1980; Allen, 1977; Hargadon and Sutton, 1997; Tushman, 1977).

The basic role of these boundary spanners or gatekeepers is to process a wide range of information and knowledge both within and outside of their organizations, and to carry out project management that involves driving communications and coordinating and integrating business between organizations. Accordingly, the actions of boundary spanners and gatekeepers on the boundaries between organizations can be interpreted as the information processing approach or the interpretive approach described by Carlile (2004).

In contrast, the participants on pragmatic boundaries do not only engage in the information and knowledge processes of information and knowledge gathering, analysis, interpretation and transfer, but also play a role that takes on the pragmatic task of transcending these processes to transform knowledge and achieve new goals. However, the integration of ICs (organizational boundaries) differs from the organizational information processing approach typical of contingency theory, and is an interpretive approach or organizational learning approach by which common meanings are developed to create shared meaning by enabling the assessment and sharing of knowledge across boundaries.

For example, theories such as Lawrence and Lorsch's "differentiation and integration" (Lawrence and Lorsch, 1967) or Galbraith's "adequate information processing capacity" (Galbraith, 1973) are based on the information processing model, and are used to describe more efficient product development and business processes in which participants in formal organizations within corporations and in other corporations coordinate and communicate. The central concepts of these theories focus on functions such as the efficient processing, transfer, storage and retrieval of large quantities of information or knowledge.

These processes are thus examples of the syntactic boundaries described by Carlile (2004). In contrast, communities of practice that drive organizational learning and best practices entail a focus on the translation processes mainly relating to new knowledge. These processes create shared meanings between participants and new agreements between participants on boundaries. These processes are examples of the semantic boundaries described by Carlile (2004). Innovation or creativity, however, emerge on the boundaries between the disciplines and specializations of different organizations (Leonard-Barton, 1995). Thus, the information processing approach, with its focus on information or knowledge processing efficiency, or the interpretive approach, with its focus on the translation of knowledge (organizational learning), alone cannot by themselves sufficiently describe the innovation process on boundaries (Carlile, 2004).

The smart city project described in this chapter is a case of business innovation in the high-tech field in which a high level of novelty occurs on the boundaries between organizations. Thus, the participants in this project must face the practical challenges of developing new business models and technologies, and in so doing face the contradictions, frictions and conflicts that arise from the differences in the interests of individuals and the political aspects of organizations. In other words, these types of projects involve processes that go beyond the smoothing of communications and the coordinating of business between departments and organizations on pragmatic boundaries. Thus, how to overcome the variety of hurdles, contradictions and conflicts that arise in the process of bringing about new knowledge (or transforming existing knowledge) on pragmatic boundaries is a serious issue for participants.

As described in this chapter, the case of Fujisawa SST requires its participants to engage in practical, political and pragmatic methods that transcend the information processing and interpretive approaches (organizational learning) to transform existing knowledge (Carlile, 2004). Thus, the networking of ICs also offers a practical method for participants to bridge and integrate ICs that exist on the many pragmatic boundaries within and between corporations.

In the interpretation of ICs above, the multilayered (and multi-structured) participation of Panasonic, its partner companies, Fujisawa City and its residents in the Fujisawa SST urban planning and development processes can be seen as an IC formed from integrating and networking those ICs described earlier. The participating entities in ICs bring with them different knowledge, values and interests, which clash along the pragmatic boundaries described earlier, but bring about new ideas and knowledge as they converge.

The building of the Fujisawa SST smart town on the site of an old Panasonic factory is an example of this—an IC was formed between Panasonic and Fujisawa City to discuss the nature of the target urban development. As a major electronics manufacturer, Panasonic has embodied its new "comprehensive solutions for the entire house, entire building and entire town" business strategy in Fujisawa SST and wanted to verify the strategy for future global business, while Fujisawa City was thinking first about residential services and wanted to solve the problems that the city faced through this project. Thus, it can be seen that Panasonic and Fujisawa City's interests were not completely in agreement.

Nevertheless, the two parties engaged in discussions about the new urban development policy from 2007 onwards, and produced an urban development policy in 2010. The Fujisawa SST slogans about a sustainable town offering comfortable, environmentally friendly, safe and secure and ecologically smart lifestyles that include the blessings of nature do not only reflect the strategies of Panasonic as the project leader, but reflect the intention of Fujisawa City to appeal to the city's charms, such as the natural environment of the Shonan area, the high environmental awareness of its local residents and the strengthened local disaster prevention bodies, while highlighting the city's efforts to find solutions, such as relieving its chronic traffic congestion problems. In short, the Fujisawa SST urban development policy came about as a result of the co-creation of value through a "Ba" formed around Panasonic and Fujisawa City, two dissimilar entities.

However, there are a number of problems in the co-creation of value between the two dissimilar entities through the formation of an IC. For example, ICs that have pragmatic boundary characteristics are places where the interests of different entities come into conflict, and therefore, the story of how new value is created through convergence on those boundaries will always be unfolding. What if, for argument's sake, conflicts of interests become more serious and recovery between the entities becomes impossible, and the continuance of the IC itself, supposedly the place for value co-creation, becomes threatened? Or, what if dissimilar entities participate in an IC but fail to engage in creative dialogue to bring about a higher level of value, although the entities have agreed to coordinate their interests?

These scenarios should be viewed as the problems of IC management and leadership. In other words, even if an IC is formed with participation from dissimilar entities, it does not necessarily mean that value co-creation will always occur—in actual fact, the existing research that analyzes the collaborations between organizations points out this difficulty.

For example, Vangen and Huxham (2003) assert that although many organizations hope to obtain superiority by collaborating with other organizations to create value, managing such an endeavor is highly problematic in reality. Nevertheless, they also assert that fostering trust between organizations is the key to success. Research done by Kanter (1994), Dacin, Hitt, and Levitas (1997), Gray (1985), Wistow and Hardy (1991) and others also points out the importance of value born through collaboration between organizations while emphasizing the difficulties of managing the collaboration process. In other words, the existing research suggests that there are many hurdles to overcome to achieve collaborative innovation.

Therefore, what processes are required for the suitable management of an IC? What kind of leadership is required, and what kind of thinking and actions are required of the organizational participants that carry out these tasks?

7.4.4 Leadership for Creating Innovation Communities

Kodama (2004, 2005) states the following about leaders, managers and leadership in corporate organizations: Presented as theoretical frameworks and practical knowledge needed to achieve diverse business innovations, innovative leadership that can combine integrated and centralized leadership with autonomous, decentralized leadership, or the dialectical leadership that can combine directive control (strategic leadership and forceful leadership) and participative control (creative leadership and servant leadership), are critical aspects of the leadership of organizational leaders and managers.

Presented as new knowledge in Kodama (2004, 2005), the leadership exercised by the leaders and managers of organizations has the following three characteristics. The first characteristic is a characteristic that leadership needs for the rules and regulations of formal organizations, and needs for strategic planning and to achieve visions such as integrated, centralized leadership, or directive control (strategic leadership and forceful leadership). The second characteristic is autonomous and dispersed, and is the creative and supportive leadership that is born through the informal human networks created in innovation communities, such as autonomous, decentralized leadership (or distributed leadership), or participative control (creative leadership and servant leadership). The third characteristic is the mental ability of the practitioners themselves to perceive and recognize a range of paradoxes, and combine these various leadership factors as dialectical leadership.

According to Kodama (2004, 2005), enacting IC management through the thinking and actions of dialectical leadership in this way invigorates ICs and enables the creation of new value through ICs. Thus, it is the role of the leaders and managers participating in the ICs to manage the ICs. If we attempt to apply the thinking of Kodama (2004, 2005) to the various ICs set up for the process of planning and building Fujisawa SST, we can see that the various stakeholder organizations, such as the project leader Panasonic and its partner companies, play the roles of the leaders and managers to execute the management of the ICs involved in the project.

Figure 2.2 in Chapter 2 (management innovation model data structures) describes the importance of community systems established as innovation communities for the creation, growth and development of the ecosystem, as a driving factor in establishing a business ecosystem (in this case, the creation of a new business model through the establishment of a smart city). It also highlights the importance of stakeholders companies (organizations) in establishing community systems while they aim for dynamic consistency and suitability through their interactions with the environment (the structure) as the ecosystem.

This work also describes the necessity of executing dynamic and appropriate consistency ((8) corporate system consistency) between the internal corporate managerial elements of (3) strategy, (4) organization, (5) technology, (6) operations and (7) leadership, and presents the framework for a new management innovation model (see Figure 2.2).

Observing the factors of leadership therein, as linkages between top-down and bottom-up, reinforced top strategic leadership and the driving of autonomous and dispersed middle and lower management leads to the aspects of centralized and distributed leadership. In short, this work emphasizes the importance of the dialectical leadership needed to combine centralized and distributed leadership.

In this case study, as leaders and managers exercise strategic and centralized leadership, Panasonic has been able to verify its new business strategy of "solutions for the entire house, the entire building, the entire town" in the picture of Fujisawa SST that it has painted. At the same time, the productive, creative and distributed leadership centered on the leaders and managers of the innovation communities reflects Fujisawa City's intentions to appeal to the attractiveness of the natural environment of the Shonan area, the high environmental awareness of the local residents and the strength of the local disaster prevention entities while highlighting the city's intentions to solve problems, such as its chronic traffic congestion, has been demonstrated.

Therefore, the authors believe that it is the dialectical leadership exercised by leaders and managers to combine strategic and centralized leadership and creative and distributed leadership that will create value for the entire town. However, ICs are formed from many participants, and in reality have a multilayered structure. What sorts of dynamic organizational formations and abilities do leaders and managers need to demonstrate effective dialectical leadership in these types of complex ICs? The authors would like to discuss this in the next section.

7.4.5 The Integrity of the Competencies of Leader Teams

Realistically, in business, there is always a tug of war or conflicts occurring on the structural and multilayered pragmatic boundaries in ICs. These are inhibiting factors to the integration of the diverse knowledge in an IC. However, it is the leader teams created from the organization's leaders and managers participating in the IC that drives this integration.

Leader teams bring about integrative competencies (also called synthesizing capability) as network power across the entire IC. To achieve integrative competencies, leader teams play the role of combining a range of paradoxical factors and issues in the multilayered ICs. The leaders and managers on leader teams consciously demonstrate dialectical leadership, and must engage in constructive dialogue to resolve a range of frictions and conflicts through interactive learning (Kodama, 2004). As a result, the leader teams actively work to analyze problems and come up with solutions to them, and bring about high-level knowledge creation through the formation of "Ba" to resonate new values.

Dialectical leadership is based on Hegelian ideas, and is a practical way to solve conflicts and frictions both within and between organizations. The first point about combining paradoxical elements or problems is to mutually synthesize the ideas of the organization's members that spring from different organizational cultures, while the second point is to synthesize conflicting business issues (management such as different procedures, technologies or business models, etc.). In the creation of the smart city business model, the leader teams synthesized a range of paradoxical elements and problems involving human aspects, the aspects of living environments and technology development and business considerations. The new ways of coming up with ideas and taking action that the leaders and managers obtain by including the methodology of dialectical leadership to synthesize paradoxical elements and problems are examples of the creation of knowledge and innovation.

At the same time, the leaders and managers on leader teams must promote dialogue to thoroughly understand and share problems and issues, and they must also mutually recognize their roles and value in the jobs they do through communication and collaboration (through collaborative innovation). This enables leaders and managers to convert conflicts that occur between individual people into constructive conflicts (e.g., Kodama, 2007a, 2007b, 2007c).

To achieve an objective mission, this requires that leaders and managers engage in patterns of thinking and action upon asking the question, "With my own thinking and visions, what specific strategic and tactical actions can I take to contribute to our objective business innovation and business concepts?" Thus, to achieve innovation in business, dialectical leadership that enables leaders and managers to demonstrate leadership with integrative synergy will bring about high levels of integrative competencies (synthesizing capability) as leaders and managers in leader teams promote the sharing and resonating of values. It is these processes that have enabled the creation of the new smart city business model.

However, in a different interpretation, it can also be seen that the formation of leader teams through leadership synergies and resonances of values between leaders and managers, and the acquisition of high levels of integrative competencies (synthesizing capabilities) has brought about the establishment of solid ICs.

7.5 CONCLUSIONS AND IMPLICATIONS

Finally, the authors would like to discuss the implications gained from the matters considered in this chapter. The purpose of this chapter was to consider the managerial factors needed for the creation of innovation through the analysis of the case study of Fujisawa SST, an urban construction led by Panasonic in Fujisawa City, Kanagawa Prefecture. Designed to connect people with people, and to connect people with the town, the Fujisawa SST infrastructure drives the creation of value for the entire town by bringing about diverse value, and as the mechanism to enable this creation of diversity of value, a variety of ICs were created for Fujisawa SST.

The key point here is the role of IC management in driving co-creation between participating entities by the creation of ICs and the invigoration of them. If this IC management had failed to function, the ICs themselves would have become worthless and their existence meaningless. The problem then is what kind of entities has management that is capable of steering the IC to a position of worth.

It is no simple task for management to drive co-creation between participating entities through the formation and operation of ICs in which the entities with different interests and backgrounds participate. This kind of management does not only require conventional organizational management—the leaders and managers on IC leader teams must also demonstrate dialectical leadership.

While dialectical leadership entails centralized top-down management through strategic and centralized leadership, the leaders and managers practicing dialectical leadership must also demonstrate creative and distributed leadership to manage phenomena that emerge from the workplace in the process of executing strategy, as emphasized by Mintzberg (1973,1978,1994). In the Fujisawa SST project, Panasonic has taken on the leadership role to manage the ICs. However, at the same time, the other participants in the IC, Panasonic's partner companies, Fujisawa City and its autonomous residents groups, act while they share Panasonic's visions and strategies. In this regard, the ICs in Fujisawa SST exhibit the characteristics of strategic and centralized leadership.

However, there is a certain degree of flexibility and autonomy ensured with Fujisawa SST ICs, meaning that Panasonic does not have complete control. This means that the dialectical leadership of the project also exhibits the characteristics of creative and distributed leadership that drives collaborative innovation between the participants as they build their ICs with an awareness of co-creation with the other participants. As discussed, Panasonic created a "Ba" with Fujisawa City, the local government involved, to discuss and produce basic policies on which to base the construction of the town, a process reflected in the joint discussions that were ongoing for over three years.

The Fujisawa SST case clearly illustrates the leadership role of Panasonic in IC management and the participation of its partner companies and the autonomous residents groups of Fujisawa City, and can be interpreted as a case in which the leader corporation was tirelessly aware of the need for co-creation with other entities as it formed and managed the ICs. The dialectical leadership of the leader teams enabled the exchange and convergence of the knowledge to bring about the reactions needed to create new value.

NOTES

1. The Masdar City project is one model case of a smart city construction project in a developing country, and has caught the interest of corporations from developed countries. Participating companies include Siemens of Germany, GE of the US and Mitsubishi Heavy Industries of Japan.
2. Data on the Fujisawa SST was obtained from a hearing that the authors attended in the Panasonic Tokyo Shiodome Building on February 26, 2014, from materials obtained from Panasonic staff at the event and from materials available publicly on the Panasonic website.
3. Kodama (2007d) cites innovation communities (ICs) as strategic communities (SCs); however, in this the context of chapter, they are similar in meaning and are both referred to as ICs.

REFERENCES

Adams, J.S. (1980). Interorganizational processes and organization boundary roles. In: B. Staw, L. Cummings (eds.), *Research in Organization Behavior* (Vol. 2). Greenwich, CT: JAI Press, 321–355.

Allen, T.J. (1977). *Managing the Flow of Technology*. Cambridge, MA: MIT Press.

Brown, J.S. & Duguid, P. (2001). Knowledge and organization: A social-practice perspective. *Organization Science*, 12(6), 198–213.

Campbell, T. (2012). *Beyond Smart Cities: How Cities Network, Learn and Innovative*. Abingdon: Earthscan.

Carlile, P. (2004). Transferring, translating, and transforming: An integrative framework for managing knowledge across boundaries. *Organization Science*, 15(5), 555–568.

Clark, K.B. & Fujimoto, T. (1991). *Product Development Performance*. Boston, MA: Harvard Business School Press.

Dacin,T., Hitt,M. & Levitas, E.(1997). Selecting partners for successful international alliances: Examinations of U.S. and Korean firms. *Journal of World Business*, 32(1), 3–16.

Deakin, M. (ed.). (2014). *Smart Cities: Governing, Modelling and Analyzing the Transition*. New York: Routledge.

Dougherty, D. (1992). Interpretive barriers to successful product innovation in large firms. *Organization Science*, 3(2), 179–202.

Ercoskun, Y.O. (ed.). (2012). *Green and Ecological Technologies for Urban Planning: Creating Smart Cities*. Hershey, PA: Information Science Reference.

Galbraith, J.R. (1973). *Designing Complex Organizations*. Reading, MA: Addison-Wesley.

Gibbs, D., Rob, K. & Gordon, M. (2013). Grappling with smart city politics in an era of market triumphalism. *Urban Studies*, 50(11), 2151–2157.

Gray, B. (1985). Conditions facilitating interorganizational collaboration. *Human Relations*, 38, 911–936.

Hargadon, A. & Sutton, R. (1997). Technology brokering and innovation in a product development firm. *Administrative Science Quarterly*, 42(3), 716–714.

Herrschel, T. (2013). Competitive and sustainability: Can 'smart city regionalism' square the circle? *Urban Studies*, 50(11), 2332–2348.

Kanter, R. (1994). Collaborative advantage: Successful partnerships manage the relationships, not just the deal. *Harvard Business Review*, 72(4), 96–108.

Kodama, M. (1999). Strategic innovation at large companies through strategic community management: An NTT multimedia revolution case study. *European Journal of Innovation Management*, 2(3), 95–108.

Kodama, M. (2001). Creating new business through strategic community management. *International Journal of Human Resource Management*, 11(6), 1062–1084.

Kodama, M. (2002). Transforming an old economy company through strategic communities. *Long Range Planning*, 35(4), 349–365.

Kodama, M. (2004). Strategic community-based theory of firms: Case study of dialectical management at NTT DoCoMo. *Systems Research and Behavioral Science*, 21(6), 603–34.

Kodama, M. (2005). Knowledge creation through networked strategic communities: Case studies in new product development. *Long Range Planning*, 38(1), 27–49.

Kodama, M. (2007a). *The Strategic Community-Based Firm*. London, UK: Palgrave Macmillan.

Kodama, M. (2007b). *Knowledge Innovation—Strategic Management as Practice*. London, UK: Edward Elgar Publishing.

Kodama, M. (2007c). *Project-Based Organization in the Knowledge-Based Society*. London, UK: Imperial College Press.

Kodama, M. (2007d). Innovation and knowledge creation through leadership-based strategic community: Case study on high-tech company in Japan. *Technovation*, 27(3), 115–132.

Lawrence, P. & Lorsch, J. (1967). *Organization and Environments: Managing Differentiation and Integration*. Cambridge, MA: Harvard Business School Press.

Leonard-Barton, D (1992). Core capabilities and core rigidities: a paradox in managing new product development. *Strategic Management Journal*, 13(8), 111–125.

Leonard-Barton, D. (1995). *Wellsprings of Knowledge: Building and Sustaining the Sources of Innovation*. Boston, MA: Harvard Business School Press.

Mintzberg, H. (1973). Strategy-making in three modes. *California Management Review*, 16(2), 44–53.

Mintzberg, H. (1978). Patterns in strategy formulation. *Management Science*, 24(9), 934–948.

Mintzberg, H. (1994). *The Rise and Fall of Strategic Planning*. New York: The Free Press.

Nonaka, I. & Takeuchi, H. (1995). *The Knowledge Creating Company*. New York: Oxford University Press.

Nonaka, I. & Konno, N. (1998). The concept of "Ba": Building a foundation for knowledge creation. *California Management Review*, 40(1), 40–54.

Nonaka, I., Toyama, R. & Konno, N. (2000). '"Ba" and leadership: A unified model of dynamic knowledge creation. *Long Range Planning*, 33(1), 5–34.

Prahalad, C.K. & Ramaswamy, V. (2003). The new frontier of experience innovation. *MIT Sloan Management Review*, 44(4), 12–18.

Rassia, S.Th. & Pardalos, P.M. (eds.). (2014). *Cities for Smart Environmental and Energy Future: Impacts on Architecture and Technology*. Heidelberg: Springer.

Shaw, K. (2013). Docklands dreamings: Illusions of sustainability in Melbourne Docks redevelopment. *Urban Studies*, 50(11), 2158–2177.

Townsend, M.A. (2013). *Smart Cities: Big Data, Civic Hackers, and the Quest for a New Utopia*. New York: W.W. Norton & Company.

Tretter, E. (2013). Sustainability and neoliberal urban development: The environment, crime and the remaking of Austin's downtown. *Urban Studies*, 50(11), 2222–2237.

Tushman, M.L. (1977). Special boundary roles in the innovation process. *Administrative Science Quarterly*, 22, 587–605.

Vangen, S. & Huxham, C. (2003). Nurturing collaborative relations: Building trust in international collaboration. *The Journal of Applied Behavioral Science*, 39(1), 5–31.

Wenger, E.C. (2000). Communities of practice: The organizational frontier. *Harvard Business Review*, 78(1), 139–145.

Wistow, G. & Hardy, B.(1991). Joint management in community care. *Journal of Management in Medicine*, 5(1), 40–48.

8 A Health Support Innovation Model for Generating a Business Ecosystem

Mitsuru Kodama

In this chapter, regarding the interaction of the medical, welfare and healthcare fields with technology (in particular, with ICT), the author analyzes and discuss an innovation model to establish business ecosystems in the medical, welfare and healthcare fields, from the historical perspective of societies, economies and markets.

With the advancement of the Internet and computer technologies since the 1990s, new application markets, user innovations and business ecosystems have come into being that have had major transformative effects on societies and economies (that continue to this day), including the medical, welfare and healthcare fields.

In this chapter, the author discusses how the proactive use of video-based information networks (VIN tools hereinafter) across different industries and with customers is an enabler that drives the creation of new health support innovation models that transcend space and time. The first new insight offered by VIN tools is the emergence of collaborative innovation through diverse communications and collaboration using VIN tools for B2B communications within companies and between companies. The combination of VIN tools' video, audio and data functions offers modified real-time communications and collaborations, and has brought about new business structures as unique and autonomous usage patterns in B2B (and in B2C and C2C) communications.

The second insight is how technical modularization has driven the formation of new business networks and ecosystems. These business networks entail new community formations across different businesses and industries. Specifically, modularized VIN tools technologies (hardware and software) drive a technology transfer across different product families and industries (e.g., technology transfer of individual functions to smartphones, tablets and PCs, etc.), and through the use of VIN tools, new medical, welfare and healthcare communities are formed as ecosystems.

8.1 INTRODUCTION

Video communication through PCs, smartphones like the iPhone, tablet PCs like the iPad, mobile videophones, and SNS (e.g., Facebook, Google+)

undescores the possibilities of creating new cultures with new work and life-styles, and daily habits that together make up the "image culture." Thanks to the expansion of broadband and ubiquity, the means of communication, which range from voice and data to still images and video, are currently developing rapidly alongside the diversification of person-to-person communications and collaboration. This chapter systematically surveys the changes in the video communications market and the relationship between technological innovation and new communities in the medical and welfare sectors and other business fields over the past two decades, and clarifies new insights into the impact of these ICT "video-based information network (VIN) tools"[1] on corporate ICT and collaborative innovation in this age of ubiquitous broadband.

Previously in the world of information communications, "video" communications were generally thought of as being high priced, of poor quality and difficult to use, and were often specialized for corporate applications. Recently, however, the remarkable development of the broadband and mobile multimedia infrastructure, along with video and voice encoding technologies, have led to high functionality, lower cost, compactness and user-friendly interfaces. VIN tools have also become available for video and web conferencing, mobile videophone, smartphones, videochat and IP multimedia phones, and are accompanied by unified communications integrating a range of functions.

Thus, VIN tools have become more diverse and available for both business and consumer uses. In addition to those technological drivers, market drivers such as collaboration tools that have come to assist corporate global management, strategic outsourcing and off-shoring, and the distributed models of product development project teams have become key factors in accelerating penetration and market expansion. Moreover, multimedia communication needs are soaring, not only among business users, but also in such areas as small office/home office (SOHO), education, medical treatment and welfare.

Based on a survey analysis of the usage patterns in various business fields (such as manufacturing, IT, finance, retail, education, medical treatment and welfare) and in public institutions in Asia, including Japan, the US, and Europe, this chapter describes how VIN tools have become enablers that transcend space and time, promote the creation of new knowledge and bring about new research and managerial implications for the practitioners and academics who specialize in business and management. The chapter presents two new insights based on a decade of field research (including participant observation, ethnography and interviews).

The first new insight into VIN tools reveals the diverse communication and collaboration effects that these tools provide. The combination of VIN tools' video, audio and data functions offers modified, real-time communications and collaborations, and has brought about new business structures as unique and autonomous usage patterns (enactment of new business structures). The use of VIN tools brings about the emergence of collaborative innovation through diverse communications and collaborations in B2B communications within companies and between companies [Insight 1].

The second insight is how the technical modularization of VIN tools (e.g., Baldwin and Clark, 2000; Fine, 1998) has driven the formation of new business networks and ecosystems. These business networks also entail new community network formations across different businesses and industries (Kodama, 2007a). Modularized VIN tools technologies (hardware and software) drive technology transfer across different industries (e.g., the technology transfer of individual functions to smartphones and tablet PCs, etc.), and through the use of VIN tools, new medical, welfare and healthcare communities have formed as ecosystems [Insight 2].

8.2 ICT CAPABILITY THROUGH COLLABORATIVE INNOVATION

The true significance of broadband ICT lies in the management and virtual business innovations that have come about through the formation of "Communities of Practice (CoP)" (e.g., Wenger, 1998) that are enabled by the overwhelming sense of realism that transcends time and distance. In the broadband environment, however, the way many corporate ICT collaboration tools, such as VIN tools, have been used and their effects on business have often been unclear—very few academic studies have addressed the relationship between companies (organizations) and VIN tools.

A small amount of literature that discusses the relationship between VIN tools and corporate management claims that VIN tools, in contrast to e-mail and groupware, not only promote the sharing and utilization of knowledge and competencies within and between organizations, but also are strategic network tools that enable rapid decision-making. However, this literature does not clarify how the organizations or their actors master the use of this type of ICT or the factors of actor capability (or organizational capability).

On the other hand, there is a certain amount of existing literature on the relationship of ICT and organizational capability. In reviewing this literature, the author investigated the existing research into the organizational capabilities of companies using ICT, and presents the results and significance of new research.

Recent studies have reported that ICT has already become commoditized and cannot by itself be the source of a company's competitiveness (Carr, 2003, 2004). Also, from the positioning-based and resource-based views in the field of academic research, scholars have indicated that while ICT has the potential to raise operational efficiency, the fact that it is easy to copy means that ICT alone cannot be a source of competitiveness, and is thus unlikely bring about differentiation from rivals or to sustain competitiveness

(Barney, Wright and Ketchen, 2001; Clemons and Row, 1991; Mata, Fuerst, and Barney, 1995; Porter, 2001).

Moreover, the scholars researching the relationship between organizational capability and company performance with ICT point out the various factors that underpin the acquisition of high-value, copy-resistant ICT capability. These factors first of all include the interaction of a physical ICT infrastructure (hardware and software) with staff skilled in ICT and the intangible assets that enable ICT (Bharadwai, 2000). Second is the need to acquire ICT capabilities to build trust, coordinate and negotiate through communication and collaboration with business unit managers using in-house ICT (Ross, Beath, and Goodfue, 1996).

As a third factor, these scholars point to the relationship between an organization and ICT, and the effect it can have of integrating human, ICT and business resources to redesign business processes and create ICT capability with a sustainable competitive edge (Powell and Dent-Micallef, 1997). They also suggest that organizational learning (Huber, 1991) can be developed through a company's new knowledge and competences, and that ICT capability to enhance company performance can be enabled through hands-on organizational learning within a company (Tippens and Sohi, 2003).

Therefore, with this thinking, acquiring and sustaining ICT capability is not just a matter of setting up the ICT infrastructure and hiring world-class ICT managers. Rather, ICT capability is the enabling of effective interaction and cooperation (between people and organizations) in company-specific contexts (such as changing circumstances, corporate culture, strategy formulation and implementation processes) both inside and outside of the company to enhance company performance.

Generally speaking, strategic contexts (strategy formulation and implementation) and organizational contexts (business processes, decision-making, organizational structure, in-house political power, corporate culture) differ from company to company. Thus, the ICT embedded in a company has the potential to create a copy-resistant organizational capability and sustainable competitive edge to differentiate a company from its rivals (Clemons, 1991a, 1991b; Clemons and Row, 1991; Weill and Broadbent, 1998; Weill and Ross, 2004), as well as to provide advantageous interactions between a company's inherent strategic and organizational contexts. Also, systematic research into ICT and productivity (Brynjolfsson and Hitt, 1995, 1996) has suggested that supplementary investment in intangible assets, such as the organizational resources within a company, must take place simultaneously with business process innovation to enhance productivity through ICT. The research also suggested that ICT investment enables companies to demonstrate its effects on productivity when linked with investments in personal and organizational intangible assets. The research clarified that the same amount of ICT investment can bring about high productivity gains in one company and low gains in another (Brynjolfsson, 2000).

Thus, the above discussion suggests that combining intangible assets, such as human resources and competencies, with ICT resources has the potential to raise the quality of ICT capability, to contribute to an improved company performance, and thus to bring about a competitive advantage. Therefore, academically, the insights gained through the research mentioned above imply that ICT alone cannot be a source of a company's competitive excellence (Carr, 2003, 2004).

Much of the existing research findings into the connection between ICT capability and company performance have been derived by the statistical analysis of large-scale samples, and its content focuses on the static experimental study of the structural elements of the ICT capability in a fixed competitive environment. Much of the existing research does not take into account the formulation and implementation of ever-changing ICT strategies in dynamic and competitive environments, nor does it analyze ICT capability in such contexts. In other words, this research lacks a dynamic analysis.

Many talented business practitioners face a range of problems and issues on a daily basis. They ask such questions as, "How can we structure our ICT capability to give us a competitive edge?," "How can we reconfigure our existing business processes using ICT to raise operational efficiency and productivity?" and "How come other companies have had success with this ICT system, and we haven't?" From the perspective of practical strategic management (Kodama, 2007b), answering the "who," what," "why," "when," "with whom," and "how" questions about these many issues and ICT strategies is an important concern of many practitioners. For this reason, the construction, adoption, planning, development, installation and operation of a dynamic "ICT capability" theory and the results that stem from it will be an important theme in future academic research, while the pursuit of this ICT capability may offer benefits to practitioners.

Nevertheless, ICT uses must be closely linked to collaborative innovation between people, between organizations and between companies to reinforce and promote the ICT capabilities of people, organizations and companies. Collaborative innovation using ICT drives new usage patterns in the areas of B2B, B2C and C2C, and brings about new business structures, as discussed in the next section.

8.3 ANALYSIS AND DISCUSSION

8.3.1 The Formation of New Business Structures through Collaborative Innovation with VIN Tools [Insight 1]

Examples of how VIN tools are used are shown in Table 8.1 below; they are taken from the findings obtained through the interviews and surveys of users in various industries and types of operations. Currently, it is clear that

Table 8.1   VIN Tool Application Domains

Business formation		Communication and collaboration		
		Peer-to-peer	Multiple people (two-way)	Multiple people (broadcasting)
B2B		★Monitoring applications • Monitoring system operations • Construction sites • Monitoring stores • Monitoring unattended facilities • Disaster prevention and monitoring systems, etc.	★Building supply chains through virtual integration • In-house and inter-corporate meetings • Virtual project teams • Teleworking, etc.	★Knowledge transfer • In-house lectures • In-house training • e-learning for the public, etc.
B2C			★Customer services • Remote medical treatment • Care support • Various consulting services, etc. / ★Building supply chains, including customers	
C2C			★Community and private applications	★Private broadcasters • Broadcasting, etc.

the use of these tools is expanding well beyond simple videoconferencing, and in addition to the interpersonal communication that goes on in education, medical, welfare, training and discussions, they are actively being used to transmit images between people and machines for monitoring or relaying purposes. Further expansion of ubiquitous image networking among machines is also conceivable.

In addition, a look at matters from the agency perspective (Barley, 1986; Olikowski, 2000; Olikowski and Barley, 2001; Robey and Sahay, 1996) shows that because actors in different companies and industries have different strategic and organizational contexts, their methods of use will differ even with the same VIN tools. Thus, the resultant business structures (such as the business behaviors and forms that stem from the actors' training in VIN application methods and ICT tools) will also differ (Orlikowski, 2000).

Table 8.1 classifies VIN tool business (B2B, B2C and C2C) and communications patterns. No longer limited to the business field (B2B), VIN tools are driving the creation of consumer-oriented e-business (B2C) and new patterns of use (C2C). These VIN tool uses are important factors that drive collaborative innovation between people and organizations as a result of the communications and collaboration in and between companies, including their customers.

Businesses are improving VIN tool functionality in response to market and social demands, and are creating differentiated usage patterns and business models with a range of types and conditions. Put another way, if the structuration theory (Giddens, 1984) and the agency theory (Emirbayer and Mische, 1998) were integrated, when the definition of human agency is limited to the physical structure of ICT, people will transform their thoughts and actions through their ICT capability with collaborative innovation while interacting with ICT (the physical functions and application methods of the human agency and ICT). They will then create new business structures, including usage patterns, habits and new business models, as ecosystems.

In the author's view, the "knowledge community" structures trigger the introduction and application of VIN tools. VIN tool usage patterns obtained from the data are shown in Table 8.2, and are classified as CoP (Wenger, 1998)—"knowledge community" formations. One aspect that became clear

Table 8.2 Creating Knowledge Communities with VIN Tools

Communities integrated withVIN tools	Knowledge communities
• *Business*	1. Businesses (meetings)
1. Communities in large organizations where frequent meetings are required to exchange opinions and make reports	2. Entrepreneur communities
2. Hierarchical communities where the communication of complex or troublesome data is required between management and staff	3. Industry groups
3. Large organizations where a means of office substitution is required	4. Multiple store (franchise) communities
• *Regional government*	5. Non-store business communities
Communities where flexible communication, such as the provision of information to citizens and welfare services, is required	6. City, town and village communities
• *Education, medical and welfare issues*	7. Remote education
Communities where interactive, remote lectures, telemedicine and care or training while staying put is required	8. Telemedicine and healthcare
• *Mass model*	9. Volunteer groups
Conventional communities where face-to-face communication is required	10. Event relaying
VIN Tool features	1. Interactive image communication functions
	2. Meeting functions
	3. Portability and portable sign language possibilities, smartphones, etc.

Ecosystems

from this classification was that business communities are configured for the purpose of sharing a range of information and knowledge, and thus for promoting collaborative innovation. For example, these are equivalent not just to business meetings within a company, but also to CoP formed from entrepreneurial, industry group, franchise, NPO and volunteer group communities.

Another aspect is the formation of local authority communities centered on municipalities, or CoP formed to deliver information flexibly to the public and welfare sectors. A third aspect are CoP as knowledge-based businesses (Kodama, 1999) that deliver new value to customers, including private-sector company medical, welfare, and education services. VIN tools support the CoP structures described above, and contribute to those structures so that value and trust can be shared.

The formation of CoP (knowledge communities) through these diverse VIN tool uses leads to the formation of networks at the application level as individual usage patterns, and forms ecosystems across different domains, including B2B, B2C and C2C (See Table 8.2).

Significant to the use of VIN tools are the dynamic changes through collaborative innovation in individual cultures and entire organizational landscapes, and the dynamic adoption of VIN tool-based information networks. It is important for companies exploiting VIN tool activity to drive dynamic business through collaborative innovation that combines actual face-to-face communications with video communications in virtual space.

8.3.2   Technical Modularization Driving the Formation of New Business Networks and Ecosystems [Insight 2]

Modularized VIN tools technologies (hardware and software) drive the technology transfer across different product families and industries (e.g., the technology transfer of individual functions to smartphones and tablet PCs, etc.). Through the use of VIN tools, new medical, welfare and healthcare communities have formed. Firstly, the author discusses the modularization seen with the evolution of the architecture of VIN tools, and how this modularization has driven the formation of new usage patterns for customers in diverse ecosystems that include the medical, healthcare and welfare communities, through the technology transfer across different product families and industries.

(1) Evolution of VIN Tools Product Architecture

At the beginning of 1990, VIN tool developers and manufacturers focused on the technical theme of encoding for high-quality audiovisual (AV) compression based on switching circuit technology for VIN tools using designated lines and integrated services digital network (ISDN). These systems had to be developed to meet the constant demands for reliability and stability. It was also necessary to continuously pursue compression technologies to transfer high-quality multimedia efficiently on narrow bandwidths. Specialized large-scale integrated (LSI) circuits were used as the hardware to achieve the encoding for this high-quality compressed audio and video (Step 1 in Figure 8.1).

Then, as engineers lowered the power consumption and increased the processing capabilities of these specialized LSI devices (calculations/sec), manufacturers also aimed for unique high-performance hardware architecture. The achievement of specialized LSI devices in the 1980s involved the adoption of hardware architecture with specialized logic circuitry designed as the functional blocks needed to achieve AV encoding.

However, in the latter half of the 1980s and at the beginning of the 1990s, mixed types (so-called system LSIs) were adopted. These consisted of multiple processors to achieve the functional blocks and multiple specialized hardware blocks. With this shift from specialized LSIs hardware to system LSIs with built-in CPUs, software elements began to be added to the architecture.

Following, low-cost VIN tools advanced (this period the author calls Step 2, see Figure 8.1). Then, US companies in particular began to produce new product architecture that did not use specialized LSIs. A classic example of this technology is the "Desktop Conference" (DTC), a Windows 3.1-based video conferencing product released by PictureTel in 1992

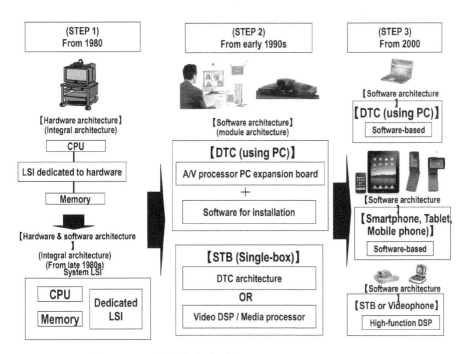

Figure 8.1   Advances in VIN Tools Architecture

(PictureTel was later bought up by Polycom). Following that, Intel released its "ProShare" product for under JPY 300,000. Then, NTT of Japan released its "Phoenix" product for under JPY 200,000. At a stroke, these developments expanded the DTC market beyond large corporations to small and mid-sized companies and individual users. PictureTel also took up this PC architecture, developed unified specialized VIN tools that did not require a PC, and developed a low-cost set-top box (STB) that was cheaper than the specialized devices that were using the older types of special-purpose LSIs.

These DTC and STB developments came about through modular innovation (Henderson and Clark, 1990) with software-based architecture. Modularization is enabled by well-defined individual interfaces between parts, and entails less interdependency between structural elements. Modular architecture is advantageous because it enables product upgrades and product lineup diversifications and thus offers strategic flexibility (Sanchez & Mahoney, 1996; Worren, Moore, and Cardona, 2002).

In this way, the product architecture shifted from the old-type hardware-based architecture to modular software-based architecture that used general-purpose processors. Even though there was no huge architectural change from Step 1 to Step 2 in terms of the audiovisual signal processing and communications processing functions of teleconferencing systems (linkage changes in structural elements), there was a massive change in the core concept of the structural elements needed to produce the architecture. For this reason, DTC and STB can be said to be examples of modular innovation. This technical shift enabled the US company Polycom (which bought PictureTel) and Sony to quickly dominate the global market by successfully downsizing their costly, specialized systems with low-cost DTC and STB technologies.

Now, as we move into the broadband era, we break through to Step 3 (See Figure 8.1). Thus, with the disruptive technology of Internet Protocol (IP) (Christensen, 1997), and the enhanced performance of PC central processing units (CPUs) compared to the older video conferencing systems, VIN tools that cost even less are emerging. As CPU performance advances according to Moore's Law, it has become possible to encode both audio and video in real time, and has become possible to videoconference using only a commercially available camera and software to process audio and video with the CPU in the PC (technologies such as Skype or video chat associated with social networking services).

In particular, Skype (owned first by eBay, then Microsoft), a no-cost client TV phone application, does not conform to the ITU-T international standard but is becoming rapidly popular in the C2C domain. Furthermore, software processing web conferencing systems such as WebEx (bought by Cisco Systems) that enable multipoint connection and are Software as a Service (the SaaS model) products are also becoming increasingly popular. In general, between 2000 and 2008, this low-cost, software-based product architecture (an example of destructive technology) overtook hardware-based products (an example of sustainable technology) due to the advances in microprocessor technology, bringing improved performance and the global shift from ISDN to IP products. In other words, the teleconferencing market for the old type of VIN tools using ISDN or the dedicated lines sustainable technology has been eroded by gradual increases in the performance of destructive technology; namely, IP-based VIN tools.

Smartphones, tablets and the latest generation of mobile devices that has emerged in recent years have become generic hardware devices, and have spurned the emergence of new VIN tools (See Figure 8.1). Video communications are bundled functions in these products, and are software-based applications brought about mainly by system on chip (SoC) technologies. Taken to the extreme, a smartphone or tablet enables good-quality video communications any time, any place and with anybody, and enables users to completely bypass TV conferencing systems, STB or TV phone devices. And all of these new products, including those that connect by radio, work on broadband IP networks.

This transition from Step 1 to Step 3 over the last 20 years has greatly reduced the price of VIN tools. Changes to the core technologies and technological architecture have accelerated product miniaturization and cost reduction while bringing about new markets. Moreover, multipoint connection units (MCUs) that enable conferencing in many different locations are gradually being replaced by the software architecture products that use high-performance servers and PCs, and these replacements are driving costs down even further. These software-based, low-priced MCUs promote use in user companies, while corporate users that need the reliability and high quality of IP networks engage in outsourcing with multiple point connections with application service providers (ASPs).

As described above, technological advances—the rapid development of core technologies such as semiconductors and broadband—have brought about changes to core components and technological architecture that defined the competitiveness of products (Henderson and Clark, 1990). Although investments of business resources in product development with software architecture based on general-purpose hardware devices involves prudent selection, the main issue facing companies is how to respond to the fierce, low-priced competition with many competing players. Although Skype and SNS are not products that are mutually inter-connectable with any other manufacturers' products, because they are free of charge, their existence is one that vendors cannot ignore.

Also, most interestingly, in recent years, the merging of the iPad with robot technologies has brought about the development and release of the "tele-present robot (double)". A double is a VIN tool designed for a new communication style that enables users to create a sense of their own presence—the double—in any place (e.g., an office), anywhere in the world as long as there is a network environment available, thus enabling users to communicate with other members of staff as if they are moving around the same office. The iPad can thus be said to be a new product created by converging video communications and robot technologies. These technologies also hold promise for use as remote care robots in the future.

Another new architecture that has emerged is unified communications. Not only do unified communications flexibly join together different communication methods, but they also merge the technologies of different product families, such as the IP phones, PCs, mobile telephones, smartphones and tablets mentioned earlier, enabling seamless communications between terminals. Linking together multiple different communication methods gives companies the advantages of better business efficiency and greater productivity, and currently, companies are making use of unified communications using cloud computing as a strategic tool for better business efficiency and staff creativity.

Modern companies and organizations use a wide range of communications methods for a range of applications. These methods involve different individual devices, terminals, applications and software, etc. Unified communications enable flexible intercommunication by integrating different families of communications on IP networks.

Many companies have taken up various types of groupware and enterprise resource planning (ERP) tools to drive information sharing and communications between organizations to promote their best practices. However, issues have surfaced; notably, companies that have already transformed their corporate culture by implementing these tools have been unable to achieve quicker decision-making and reinforced communications both within and between organizations using only e-mail and groupware. This is because e-mail and groupware do not sufficiently convey the nuanced thoughts and intentions of individuals, and leave users with a sense of being shut out. Thus, cloud-based VIN tools could be one form of unified communications that overcomes this problem—these are extremely practical ICT tools that lead to corporate transformation.

In short, VIN tools enable discussions replete with content and enable swift decision-making. From the viewpoint of the knowledge creating processes, as the core of activities to transform business, e-mail, groupware, application sharing and databases are powerful tools used to link up and bring efficiency to explicit knowledge (i.e., knowledge that has already been documented). However, in contrast, unified communications converging video, voice and text data through the world of dialogue and collaboration in real and cyberspace have the potential to induce new ideas, thoughts, perceptions and emotions between people at the tacit knowledge level (for instance, knowledge that cannot be put into words, such as people's beliefs and thoughts, perceptions and imagery). Thus, unified communications in this cloud era could bring about an age of 'creation' in which the unevenly distributed and diverse knowledge around the world is collected, analyzed and merged to create new knowledge and value (in which rich tacit knowledge emerges and is transformed into explicit knowledge). Not limited to businesses, these types of unified communications also hold promise for medical, welfare and healthcare applications.

(2) Building New Business Networks and Ecosystems

Looking at the evolution of VIN tool product architecture, as discussed earlier, the shift from Step 1 to Step 2 in Figure 8.1 is mainly characterized by changes to the product architecture of TV conferencing systems (integral architecture → modular architecture). Most of the cases of usage were B2B within or between companies, but because the dynamism of the evolution of the product architecture in Step 1 and Step 2 was brought about by a transformation in technical elements, it can be interpreted as evolution in the vertical direction.

Conversely, because core technical modularization (hardware and software) was brought about through the product architecture advances of TV conferencing systems in Step 3 (the so-called modular innovation), and core technologies were transferred to diverse product families (e.g., PCs, application software, smartphones and tablets, etc.), these processes have arrived at the evolution of a new product architecture, which means that product architecture modularization is bringing with it dynamism in the horizontal direction. This is a dynamism that has effects that span and transcend the different classes of products and industries. It is causing technical transfer at the modular level between many different products and industries, and is a phenomenon that is redefining product architecture.

In the VIN tools case, this modularized technical transfer has given birth to new markets by expanding usage to include not only B2B uses, but also C2C users. In other words, as illustrated by Table 8.2, the knowledge communities in "Creating knowledge communities with VIN tools" indicate the establishment of ecosystems through the formation of networks of new communities that include customers and consumers.

Behind the achievement of these networks and communities in new markets lie the businesses and industries that arrived at modularization (for example, the TV conferencing, PC, mobile telephone, smartphone, business application and robot industries), and that have played the leading role in bringing about changes to product architecture. Horizontal dynamism that transcends businesses and industries comes about in businesses and industries that are developing product families based on modularization, because transferring technical knowledge at the modular level lowers costs without affecting the architecture for entire completed products.

Moreover, technical transfer at the modular level enables the low-cost diversification of current product value, because it enables functions developed by different businesses and industries to be added to products (e.g., Baldwin and Clark, 2000). Video communications functions that were limited to B2B uses within and between companies are now available at the consumer level, and, as shown in Table 8.1, have brought about new product value with a range of new usage patterns. Put differently, the spiraling of VIN tools with people and organizations has brought about the creation of new business structures.

The technical transfer at the modular level described above has effects between different modularized industries and businesses. These effects are horizontal dynamism. In contrast, the dynamism accompanying the technical elements advances of the B2B video conferencing product architecture described from Step 1 to Step 2 is dynamism with its effects in the vertical direction. Thus, vertical dynamism and horizontal dynamism have different driving forces—no two cases are necessarily alike. These two types of dynamism have brought about product architectures that have changed the boundaries of company product systems, which in turn have changed the boundaries of company systems and have affected entire business and industry classes (Shibata and Kodama, 2009), thus bringing dynamic change to markets.

As described above, the modularization of VIN tool technology (hardware and software) has driven a technological transfer across different families of products and industries. As a result, diverse B2B, B2C and C2C knowledge communities and business networks have formed. These networks have brought about new customer usage patterns, and have spawned the formation of ecosystems as medical, welfare and healthcare communities, described as the "health support innovation model."

8.4 CONCLUSION

This chapter has described how collaborative innovation through the use of VIN tools across different industries and between companies, including their customers, has driven the formation of business networks as new knowledge communities that transcend time and space. These networks have brought about new customer usage patterns, and have spawned the formation of ecosystems as medical, welfare and healthcare communities.

The first new insight into the characteristics of the uses of VIN tools uncovers the emergence of collaborative innovation through diverse communications and collaborations by using VIN tools for B2B communications within and between companies. VIN tools' video, audio and data functions combined offer modified real-time communications and collaborations, and have brought unique and autonomous usage patterns to B2B communications (or to B2C or C2C).

The second insight is how modularized technology has driven the formation of new business networks and ecosystems. The modularization of VIN tool technologies has driven a technology transfer across different families of products and industries, while the use of VIN tools has brought about new medical, welfare and healthcare communities that form ecosystems. These developments have brought about the health support innovation model.

NOTE

1. The market for the multimedia videoconferencing systems, videophones, web meetings, mobile videophones and smartphones (video terminals) is growing worldwide as broadband continues to develop.

   Thanks to the development of Internet Protocol (IP), mobile videophones, smartphones, videoconferencing systems and software-based products (disruptive technologies) (Christensen, 1997) have appeared that are still faster, cheaper (flat rate systems with always-on connections) and of better quality than the high-functioning, high-priced systems that had preceded them. Moreover, in terms of speed and functionality, software-based products have caught up with the hardware-based product groups of the ISDN era.

   The development of IP for video terminals has enabled systems to offer much more than the conventional full-scale, meeting room-based videoconferencing. To meet user demands, the range of systems that use this technology has diversified to include PC videoconferencing systems for groupware, collaboration, chat and integrated videophones. Multipoint connection units based on low-priced software have promoted independent use by companies, while companies that prioritize the reliability and quality of their IP networks have made use of multipoint connectability by outsourcing services to application service providers (ASPs), thus driving the growth of the ASP market worldwide.

   Using video terminals, networked VIN tools are faster than various text-based communication and collaboration methods such as email and groupware, and enable interactive communication and collaboration combining images, voice and text. VIN tools are already playing a central role in the development of broadband technology and innovations in a wide range of network devices.

REFERENCES

Baldwin, C. & Clark, K. (2000). *Design Rules: The Power of Modularity*. Boston, MA: The MIT Press.

Barley, S. (1986). Technology as an occasion for structuring' evidence from observations of CT scanners and the social order of radiology departments. *Administrative Science Quarterly*, 31(1), 78–108.

Barney, J., Wright, M. & Ketchen, D. (2001). The resource-based view of the firm: Ten years after 1991. *Journal of Management*, 27(3), 625–641.

Bharadwai, S. (2000). A resource-based perspective on information technology capability and firm performance: An empirical investigation. *MIS Quarterly*, 24(1), 169–196.

Brynjolfsson, E. (2000).*Understanding the Digital Economy: Data, Tools, and Research*. Boston: MIT Press.

Brynjolfsson, E. & Hitt, L. (1995). Computers as factors of production: The role of differences among firms. *Economics of Innovation and New Technology*, 2 May, 183–199.

Brynjolfsson, E. & Hitt, L. (1996). Paradox lost? Firm-level evidence of high returns to information systems spending. *Management Science*, 42(4), 541–558.

Carr, G. (2003). IT Doesn't Matter. *Harvard Business Review*, May, 41–49.

Carr, G. (2004). *Dose IT Matter?* Boston: Harvard Business School Press.

Christensen, C. (1997). *The Innovator's Dilemma: When New Technologies Cause Great Firms to Fail*. Boston: Harvard Business School Press.

Clemons, K. (1991a). Corporate strategies for information technology: A resource-based approach. *Computer*, 24(11), 23–32.

Clemons, K. (1991b). Evaluation of strategic investments in information technology. *Communications of the ACM*, 34(1), 22–36.

Clemons, K. & Row, C. (1991). Sustaining IT advantage: The role of structural differences. *MIS Quarterly*, 15(3), 275–292.

Emirbayer, M. & Mische, A. (1998). What is agency? *American Journal of Sociology*, 103, 962–1023.

Fine, H. (1998). *Clockspeed: Winning Industry Control in the Age of Temporary Advantage*. New York: Perseus Books.

Giddens, A. (1984). *The Constitution of Society*. Berkeley, CA: University of California Press.

Henderson, R. & Clark, K. (1990). Architectural innovation: The reconfiguration of existing product technologies and the failure of established firms. *Administrative Science Quarterly*, 35(1), 9–30.

Huber, G. (1991). Organizational learning: The contributing processes and the literature. *Organization Science*, 2(1), 88–115.

Kodama, M. (1999). Customer value creation through community-based information networks. *International Journal of Information Management*, 19(6) 495–508.

Kodama, M. (2007a). *The Strategic Community-Based Firm*. London, UK: Palgrave Macmillan.

Kodama, M. (2007b). *Knowledge Innovation—Strategic Management as Practice*. London, UK: Edward Elgar Publishing.

Mata, J., Fuerst, J. & Barney, J. (1995). Information technology and sustained competitive advantage: A resource-based analysis. *MIS Quarterly*, 19(4), 487–505.

Olikowski, W. (2000). Using technology and constituting structures: A practice lens for studying technology in organizations. *Organization Science*, 11(4), 404–428.

Olikowski, W. J. and Barley, S. R. (2001). Technology and Institutions: What can research on information technology and research on organizations learn from each other? *MIS Quarterly*, 25, 145-165.

Porter, M. (2001). Strategy and the Internet. *Harvard Business Review*, March, 63–78.

Powell, C. & Dent-Micallef, A. (1997). Information technology as competitive advantage: The role of human, business, and technology resources. *Strategic Management Journal*, 18(5), 375–405.

Robey, D. & Sahay, S. (1996). Transforming work through information technology: A comparative case study of geographic information systems in county government. *Information Systems Research*, 7, 93–110.

Ross, W., Beath, M. & Goodfue, L. (1996). Building long-term competitiveness through IT assets. *Sloan Management Review*, 38(1), 31–45.

Sanchez, R. & Mahoney, T. (1996). Modularity, flexibility, and knowledge management in product and organizational design. *Strategic Management Journal*, 17(winter special issue), 63–76.

Shibata, T. & Kodama, M. (2009). *Management Architecture* (in Japanese).Tokyo: Ohom Publishing.

Tippens, J. & Sohi, S. (2003). IT competency and firm performance: Is organizational learning a missing link?. *Strategic Management Journal*, 24(8), 745–761.

Weill, P. & Broadbent, M. (1998). *Leveraging the New Infrastructure: How Market Leaders Capitalize on Information Technology*. Boston, MA: Harvard Business School Press.

Weill, P. & Ross, W. (2004). *It Governance: How Top Performers Manage It Decision Rights for Superior Results*. Boston, MA: Harvard Business School Press.

Wenger, E. (1998). *Community of Practice: Learning, Meaning and Identity*. Cambridge: Cambridge University Press.

Worren, N., Moore, K. & Cardona, P. (2002). Modularity, strategic flexibility, and firm performance: A study of the home appliance industry. *Strategic Management Journal*, 23(12), 1123–1140.

Part III

Results and Discussion

9 Comparative Case Studies and New Implications

Mitsuru Kodama

In Part 3, the authors derive common theoretical and practical knowledge through a number of in-depth case studies in Part 2. In particular, in achieving the strategic innovation capabilities needed to promote the creation, development and growth of the ecosystems discussed in Chapter 2, there needs to be "dynamic boundary consistency" both within and outside of corporate systems, while optimized organizational models must be created through collaborative innovation between stakeholders such as leader and follower companies to achieve this. As highlighted by [Insight 4] in Chapter 2, the formation of innovation communities as business networks is key to the configuration of an ecosystem. In other words, this means there have to be dynamic "community systems" formed through collaboration among stakeholders.

In this chapter, through the previous research of the authors and the case studies in Part 2, the authors present the key logical framework and characteristics of the innovation communities that promote collaborative innovation. The authors also observe and analyze the theoretical frameworks of the dynamic community systems that bring about the sustainable strategic innovation capability through a management innovation model to optimize corporate systems.

9.1 THE INNOVATION COMMUNITY CONCEPT

Improving decision-making was discussed as an important strategy in the Canadian Blood Services (CBS) case discussed in Chapter 3. Before the implementation of BSC, decision-making in this organization was slow and extremely hard to handle. To counter this, CBS achieved organizational reform and improved decision-making by driving collaborative innovation through the formation of innovation communities. Similarly, University Health Network (UHN) also created, developed and grew a health support ecosystem by achieving a spiral of exploration and exploitation centered on the UHN leader organizations, through collaborative innovation in innovation communities formed across the various departments of the organization.

These innovation communities, as issue-driven communities, are dynamically formed by actors who have different specialties as informal networks for dealing with urgent issues. Thus, these communities are characterized by the urgency of the context, the diversity of expertise and as dynamic human networks in which collaboration takes place. Innovation communities are informal organizations created for the integration of different kinds of knowledge (knowledge integration), and therefore have different characteristics than the so-called "communities of practice" (Brown and Duguid, 1991; Wenger, 2000).

R.H. Buckman, the former CEO of Buckman Laboratories, had the following to say about communities of practice (Buckman, 2003, p. 163): "Given that definition, what I'm calling an Issue-Driven Community would be considered a Community of Practice. I prefer to differentiate between the two, however, because of the significant difference in the sense of urgency and the diverse population required to create the dynamic character I regard as the essential feature of an issue-driven community. Generally speaking, Communities of Practice contain fewer members and do not have the same sense of urgency as issue-driven communities usually do. They take a longer, slower look at developments in their field, which can also be valuable to an organization but on a different basis."

As practitioners, the authors completely agree with Buckman's views. The "issue-driven community" at Buckman Laboratories is precisely the sort of "innovation community" that I discuss here—a community that seeks out solutions to various issues and strategic goals on organizational and knowledge boundaries on which actors with diverse knowledge are active.

In this interpretation, an innovation community (IC) is a community in which the members share common values and strategic objectives, and has the following two characteristics: The first characteristic is the generation of new meaning from learning and innovation—the characteristic of a learning community working towards incremental innovation. The second characteristic of these communities is the generation of never-before-seen new knowledge and radical innovations—Chapter 7 presented the innovation community observed in Fujisawa SST, an innovation community characterized by its roots as a community of practice (Wenger, 2000). This is because daily learning processes are also an important basic generator of innovative actions.

Learning has often implied the accumulation or improvement and upgrade of existing knowledge, although in the cognitive science sense, learning is a process that will introduce new information into existing knowledge networks and make the network more prosperous. On the other hand, the creative process of innovation involves processes of creating new networks spanning existing and dissimilar networks (e.g., Gardner, 1985, 1982).

In other words, learning involves information spreading across new networks passively from external sources (e.g., single loop learning), while the spontaneous occurrence of information is creativity (innovation). Thus, learning comes from externalities such as teachers or teaching materials, while creativity (innovation) is a process that requires voluntarily searching for new knowledge and networks in the process of obtaining self-realization. Opportunities for creativity may come from external sources, although the discovery of solutions is voluntary and generative. Argyris (1978) discussed double loop learning as a complement to single loop learning, meaning voluntarily motivated actions with a sense of responsibility that are conducive to transformation and innovation. Therefore, in achieving innovation by integrating different kinds of knowledge, many cases can be seen that acquire wide-ranging existing knowledge (or in cases of facing such necessities), and the characteristics of communities of practice can also be found within innovation communities.

Such characteristics can be found in the health support ecosystems configured by the telecommunications carriers described in Chapter 5. This is a case of collaborative innovation across different industries that has different aspects than the cases of CBS and UHN described in Chapter 3 in terms of the knowledge sharing and integration in dissimilar contexts. However, in the case of telecommunications carriers, networked ICs are formed across the boundaries between different industries, which means that the further networked factors of ICs as issue-driven communities are included. The cases discussed in Chapter 5 of the formations of innovation communities between the innovative customers and companies across different industries and business classes (the healthcare and telecommunications fields) are also similar examples.

In these cases, the innovation community formed by the telecommunications carrier plays the role of the hub or node that networks multiple innovation communities outside of the company (Barabasi, 2002; Kodama, 2009; Watts, 2003). These networked innovation communities formed from dissimilar contexts and knowledge bring about even newer knowledge. In the processes of urban development in the Fujisawa SST development discussed in Chapter 7, networked ICs were created through the integration of multilayered (and multi-structured) and diverse innovation communities that involved the participation of Panasonic, its partner companies, Fujisawa City and its local residents. The actors who participate in innovation communities have a wide range of different knowledge, values and interests, which collide in the ICs' pragmatic boundaries, as discussed in Chapter 7. Nevertheless, the integration of these brings about new ideas and knowledge.

Regarding IC and networked IC characteristics, the following describes the differences between communities of practice and projects from the perspectives of strategy, boundaries, networks, personnel, capital provision and organizations. A comparison between the IC, networked IC and other organizational structures is shown in Table 9.1.

Although there are commonalities with ICs, networked ICs and projects in real-life businesses, the choice of organizational structure for each case is

Table 9.1 Comparison of Innovation Communities with other Organizational Forms

Organization Structure	Main Patterns of Strategy	Boundaries	Networks	Personnel	Capital Provision	Organization Lifetime
Innovation Communities and Networked Innovation Communities (ICs and Networked ICs)	• Strategies under difficult to predict business environments • Innovation community forms business concepts and ideas as they emerge. • Valid strategies must be searched through repeated trial and error. (Promotion of incubation) • Executing deliberate strategies towards achieving strategic objectives • Execution of strategic outsourcing or strategic group management	• Sharing contexts in dissimilar "ba" • Creative abrasion and productive friction among actors • Pursuit of innovation beyond learning • Pragmatic boundaries	• Building vertical boundaries network & horizontal boundaries network • Flexible reconfiguration of ICs and networked ICs • Networking modular structures	Community leaders encourage community members to resonate values based on clear visions and concepts, and to form innovation communities for uniform missions.	Innovation community activities are authorized within the corporation (at top or senior management level), and securing capital required for daily operations is possible.	As long as there is necessity to maintain the innovation community

Projects	• Strategies under management environments where analyses and forecasts are possible • Business strategies formed at top or senior management level. • Daily operations based on established strategies (Clear milestones and goals)	• Precise information dissemination • Coordination • Information processing approach • Syntactic boundaries	• Networking mainly project team members	Employees assigned by top management and senior management	Project activities are authorized with the corporation (at top or senior management level), and securing capital required for daily operations is possible.	Until the project is complete
Communities of Practice	• Improvements in routine tasks at the workplace resulting from voluntary behavior of employees. • Improvements in the daily process of supplying products and services. (Improvements in total quality management (TQM), customer service, etc.)	• Generating and sharing meaning • learning organization • Semantic boundaries	• Networking mainly actors with similar jobs or specializations	Members who select themselves	Community activities are not disclosed within the corporation and many cases are not authorized. Securing capital required for activities is difficult. (Operated mostly on voluntary basis)	As long as there is interest in maintaining the community

dependent on the particular business environment that the enterprise is in, and on the strategy that the enterprise might take. In business achievements that have relied on company-wide corporate stratcgics involving the promotion of ties between strategic enterprises and large-scale businesses, projects are set down as formal organizations with clear milestones and goals within companies, and are based on clearly established strategies and the assignment of top and senior-level management. To execute these strategies, appropriate personnel are assigned to the project from within the company (and sometimes are sourced from outside). These projects follow deliberate strategies (Ansoff et al., 1965; Hofer, 1978; Mintzberg, 1978) as so-called traditional management strategies that promote business operation to realize strategic objectives within a fixed period, be it short- or long-term. Projects are thus notably effective as organizational structures.

On the other hand, ICs and networked ICs are adopted when companies need to find effective strategies in difficult-to-predict environments or when there are many uncertainties.

Realistically, as a method that is adopted to solve new business challenges or create new businesses, the concept of an innovation community also covers gatherings of specialists in various fields of expertise in companies in formal organizations as closed, cross-functional teams or taskforces.

However, as illustrated by the telecommunications carrier case discussed in Chapter 5, the importance of the meaning of "innovation community" is illustrated by the actors voluntarily, intentionally and dynamically forming ICs and networked ICs (including restructuring) across different industries both within and between companies, and that include customers, because concrete business concepts and ideas emerge and are implemented through these ICs and networked ICs.

Moreover, through the formation of ICs and networked ICs, actors seek to uncover changes in markets by "scanning the periphery" (Day and Schoemaker, 2005), or using "boundary vision" (Kodama, 2011b, 2014) between different businesses and industries to bring about new business models that influence industries other than those of their own companies.

Trial and error methods such as incubation are necessary; however, strategies will emerge from the actions in ICs and networked ICs. For the most part, (senior) middle management plays the central role in ICs and networked ICs as they form virtual teams both inside and outside of the company that include customers, and actively generate intentional emergent strategies, entrepreneur strategies and contingent emergent strategies (see Figure 2.6 in Chapter 2). They then produce new and previously unseen demand and create new markets. In other words, the ICs and networked ICs are like engines that enable enactment (Weick, 1979).

To position ICs and networked ICs in strategy-making processes, the aspects of emergent and entrepreneurial strategies are emphasized; however, there are IC and networked IC factors that companies execute as deliberate strategies to fully achieve target strategic and market positions. As transaction costs in and out of companies are rigorously scrutinized, efficiency through strategic outsourcing is pursued, or, at the same time, the economies of scope and scale are pursued to raise strategic synergies with group companies.

Furthermore, ICs and networked ICs are fundamentally different from projects in that project members are assigned mainly by the upper strata of enterprises, while in ICs and networked ICs, the community leaders, who are the executive and middle managers, form virtual teams that contain members from both inside and outside of the company through spontaneous and emergent thinking and action.

For example, many of these cases include new ICs formed as modular structures by actors on the business frontline aiming to develop new products and services through architectural innovation (Eisenhardt and Brown, 1998; Henderson and Clark, 1990; Sanchez and Mahoney, 1996) or radical innovation (Kodama, 2007b), as well as dynamically configuring vertical and horizontal boundaries networks to achieve the desired architecture for the new product or service (entire systems). As discussed in Chapter 7, the organization of the Fujisawa SST town building committee and Fujisawa SST Committee involved the formation of vertically and horizontally multi-layered (and multi-structured) innovation communities.

These have in common IC and networked IC activities, while projects are authorized by the upper levels of management, and are able to obtain operating capital. Conversely, "communities of practice" (Wenger, 2000) are informal, self-organizing organizations formed virtually that promote improvements in daily business processes, although in reality, these have difficulty obtaining personnel or capital support from within the company.

Furthermore, members in ICs share the time and space of "Ba" (shared context in motion) (Nonaka and Konno, 1998), and engage in trust building (Vangen and Huxham, 2003) and the resonance of values (Kodama, 2001) by bringing about new meaning among themselves for changing contexts. Thus, these communities engage in dialogue and accumulate practice to face the challenges of new problems and tackling the unknown. Actors in these communities face and overcome friction and discord between themselves to engage in learning in the pursuit of innovation.

A decisive difference between an IC and a community of practice is that a community of practice generally is a learning community that consists of members of the same specialty (Brown and Duguid, 1991; Lave and Wenger, 1990; Orr, 1996), whereas an IC consists of members who have dissimilar and diverse backgrounds. As mentioned, there are elements of learning among different specialists in ICs, but ICs are characterized by creative and innovative aspects that go beyond the routines of learning and best practice, as well as friction, conflicts and discord among the members of the IC (Carlile, 2002, 2004). However, these vicissitudes can be transformed into creative abrasion (Leonard-Barton, 1992, 1995) and productive friction (Hagel III and Brown,

2005) to drive collaborative innovation among community members through dialectics and occasional trade-offs and so forth.

In addition, from the crucial strategic management perspective, there is a relationship between the content of strategy and process in the formation of ICs and networked ICs. Creating new knowledge by forming ICs and networked ICs is intrinsically linked to corporate strategy formulation and implementation. In selecting and pioneering new markets (or by increasing existing market share), from the positioning-based view (Porter, 1980, 1985), actors are inspired towards the implementation of the formation of ICs and networked ICs as a strategy-making process. Thus, as a result of these activities, new resources (knowledge and capabilities) are accumulated by people and organizations. On the other hand, from the perspective of the resource-based view (e.g., Wernerfelt, 1984), the accumulated resources (knowledge) embedded in people and organizations (or across entire companies) that result from the formation of ICs and networked ICs affect strategy making processes in terms of strengthening the existing positions of companies, or in terms of the acquisition of new market positions.

Then again, to create the flexible and dynamic capabilities (Teece, Pisano, and Shuen, 1997) needed to respond to changing environments, actors need to refine or replace existing resources, and to acquire new knowledge by reconfiguring their ICs and networked ICs. Accordingly, as positioning IC and networked IC in strategy, the first point includes the perspective that dichotomies must be integrated in strategic theory in terms of positioning and resources. The second point is characterized by the perspective on bridging strategic contents, context and process in micro-strategies (e.g., Pettigrew, 1977; Johnson, 1987), as the formations of ICs and networked ICs change over time.

9.2 COMMUNITY SYSTEM MECHANISMS FROM THE NETWORK THEORY

This section discusses the basic concepts of community systems in terms of the co-evolution models used for sustainably creating, developing and growing the business ecosystems illustrated in Figure 2.1 in Chapter 2, from the perspective of the network theory (e.g., Motter, 2004; Watts, 2003; Barabasi, 2002). According to the existing research, the networks linking people, associations and organizations are important platforms for facilitating information and knowledge-based activities, in that the formation of organizations and networks has a major impact on the dissemination of knowledge and information (e.g., Lin and Kulatilaka, 2006; Owen-Smitsh and Powell, 2004). Also, as illustrated by Figure 2.1 in Chapter 2, the formation of networks is indispensable for acquiring sustainable strategic innovation capabilities and continuously creating, developing and growing ecosystems, whereas the dynamic reconfiguration of networks is necessary to respond to changes in environments or strategic activities.

In recent times, the proactive use of ICT has driven coordination and collaboration among practitioners in organizations beyond the businesses with which formal organizations are concerned (Kodama, 2013). Moreover, to efficiently integrate various businesses within the corporation, these approaches bring about organizational formations such as cross-functional teams in real and virtual space within companies (e.g., Ahuja and Carley, 1999; Fulk and DeSanctis, 1995; Kraut, Steinfield, Chan, Butler, and Hoag, 1999; Kodama, 2013).

In applying these organizational formations, ICT is indispensable to driving global business beyond the boundaries of organizations or companies (e.g., Fulk and DeSanctis, 1995; Jarvenpaa, Knoll, and Leidner, 1998; Zwass and Veroy, 1988). The network theories of nodes (e.g., individuals, groups of people, organizations of groups), network ties or several network topologies (e.g., small-world structures, scale-free structures, etc.) (e.g., Barabasi, 2002; Motter, 2004; Watts, 2003) provide important knowledge and insight into not only the behaviors of practitioners and organizations in the real and virtual space that transcends companies, but also into the relationships between these.

Network formations are generally classed as being either centralized or decentralized (Ahuja and Carley, 1999; Albert and Barabasi, 2000). Recently, several network formations that vary from the two extremes (e.g., highly centralized or decentralized) have been applied extensively in analyzing the patterns in organizational information and knowledge processing.

Centralized networks are mainly adopted for the vertical and efficient execution of routine information and knowledge flows and interactions (e.g., information and knowledge sent from central nodes to peripheral nodes) (e.g., Albert and Barabasi, 2000; Tushman, 1979), whereas decentralized networks are generally applied in uncertain conditions or in conditions when there are new challenges to be directly faced (e.g., smaller hubs) (e.g., Watts, 2003). Following, the authors discuss these two network formations.

9.2.1 Decentralized Networks

It is important that decentralized network formations feature the tight clustering and autonomy of work groups. This design enhances the information and knowledge exchange and interaction at the work group level, and effectively facilitates mutual adjustments among peripheral local nodes (Tushman, 1979). Such local cluster coordination and collaboration reduces the information processing load assigned to the central node, as the peripheral nodes do not need to communicate directly with the central authority every time a decision needs to be made (e.g., Watts, 2003).

Small-world networks, in which a high degree of local clustering and only a small number of links between any two nodes exist, was found to enhance mutual dependence among cluster nodes and facilitate communications, coordination and collaboration among practitioners, especially when tight collaboration is necessary for connecting value chains between organizations (e.g., Newman, 2004). The availability of such short paths between nodes enhances the coordination and collaboration of the network, particularly with interaction between organizations (e.g., Watts, 2003; Baum, Rowley and Shipilov, 2004). Moreover, such network properties are effective when creating new ideas and innovations in complex and dissimilar organizations (e.g., Braha and Bar-Yam, 2004).

Small-world networks provide organizations with robust network formations that can deal with sudden environmental changes, such as concentrated information traffic, overloads, bottlenecks or unexpected accidents, or environmental destruction (Newman, 2004; Shah, 2000).

Thus, because ICs are formed cross-functionally by practitioners in different organizations and companies, the ICs themselves are small-world networks (see Figure 9.1). From a social network theory perspective, ICs correspond to clusters and cliques of people as the smallest nodes (e.g., Roethlisberger, 1977; Roethlisberger and Dickson, 1939)—assemblies where practitioners share and exchange information, contexts and knowledge. They

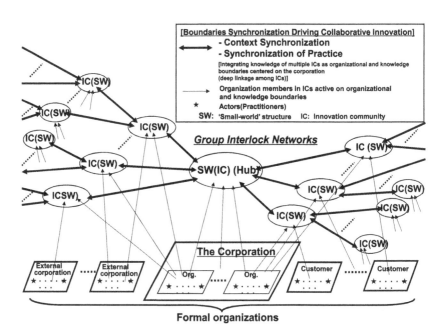

Figure 9.1   Boundaries Synchronization Driving Collaborative Innovation to Build Ecosystems

are teams that enable information exchange among actors, and also enable new dynamic contexts and knowledge in response to environmental changes.

ICs are small-world networks consisting of groups of practitioners with diverse specialties who discover new tasks, implement creative strategies and achieve new innovations to solve the problems they face. Small-world networks feature short connections between the nodes (with people being the smallest node units) and local clustering. Short paths among the practitioners acting as the nodes linking dissimilar organizations enable practitioners operating within the company and those in other companies to connect, including with their customers. Each node in a small-world network is embedded in a local cluster. These local clusters enhance the potential for reliable accessibility (White and Houseman, 2003). A small-world network can be formed either by randomly reconfiguring sections of an existing regular network or by attaching new nodes to a "neighborhood" that already exists (Watts and Strogatz, 1998).

Figure 9.1 corresponds to what is known in social network theory as a two-mode (bipartite) and affiliation network (e.g., Faust, 1997; Wasserman, and Faust, 1994; Watts, 2003). The authors would like to focus on the dynamically changing ICs and networked ICs formations that Watts (2003) termed "group interlock networks." Watts (2003) used this term based on the actors connected in specific contexts, but in the real business world, actors (practitioners) subjectively and independently form specific-context groups and embed other actors (practitioners) in these groups by extending links to other actors. Accordingly, these IC groups change dynamically in response to context while dynamically forming and transforming their networked IC formations.

Practitioners dynamically rebuild ICs on a daily basis. Practitioners also participate in multiple ICs—they share information, context and knowledge, transfer them to the other ICs in which they operate, where they continue to share, which forms the group-interlock type of networked IC. Within the framework of this network, ICs correspond to the nodes and hubs. Practitioners in node or hub ICs both inside and outside of the company dynamically bridge the multiple and diverse ICs and create or link networks among ICs. As a result, multiple ICs become integrated into the network to create new contexts and knowledge. Practitioners deliberately create networks of multiple ICs among the various organizations inside and outside of their companies, and link them closely to develop new products and build new business processes (see Figure 9.1).

The creation of ICs across different organizations and specialties within internal divisions such as consumer electronics, communications equipment, semiconductor and machine tool manufacturers integrates the knowledge in these organizations, and also creates the vertically integrated business models unique to Japanese and Korean companies. The building of these networked ICs also leads to the absorption of external knowledge (of specialist partners in horizontal business layers). Networked ICs are thus the basis of the "knowledge integration model" (Kodama, 2009), in which knowledge is integrated internally and externally.

For example, in the case of collaborative innovation across the different industries centered on the telecommunications carrier that drive the configuration of the health support ecosystem discussed in Chapter 5, to share and integrate dissimilar contexts and knowledge, not only were ICs formed within companies as small-world networks, but ICs were also formed as multiple small-world networks with external partner companies and certain customers. Furthermore, the formation of networked ICs across the boundaries of different industries further reinforced this networking. The case cited in Chapter 5 is also a case of the formation of ICs that include companies and innovative customers, as ICs formed across different industries (across the healthcare and ICT industries). The urban development described in the Fujisawa SST case in Chapter 7 is also a case of networked ICs that were created through the integration of wide-ranging multilayered (and multi-structured) and diverse ICs that involved the participation of Panasonic, its partner companies, Fujisawa City and the local residents.

Moreover, the research done by the authors illustrates not only the case of the ICs formed as small-world networks within Apple that lie behind the successful development of the iPhone, a device that caused a major revolution in the smartphone world, but also the multiple small-world networks formed as ICs between Apple and its partner companies that included certain customers. Configurations like those seen at Apple can also be seen behind the NTT DOCOMO i-mode development, the world's first mobile phone Internet service, as well as the success of the Sony PlayStation released by Sony Computer Entertainment (SCE) (Kodama, 2007b), which shook up the computer game industry.

Thus, the way the leader companies (Apple, NTT DOCOMO, SCE) in ecosystems formed ICs as small-world networks by linking follower and partner companies in clusters and cliques was key to their success. The birth of the iPhone, i-mode and PlayStation business models entailed the configuration of ecosystems as new business models that were enabled by the collaborative innovation between the leader and follower companies that were enabled by the configuration of small-world networks within and between companies, and with certain customers. Thus, the formation of small-world network structures both internally and externally in companies (ICs and networked ICs) is an important factor in creating business models (ecosystems).

From these considerations of small-world networks, the following insight may be drawn:

[Insight 9]

Small-world networks enable leader and follower companies to integrate the knowledge necessary for creating, developing and growing an ecosystem.

9.2.2 Centralized Networks

When comparing small-world networks with random networks (Erdos and Renyi, 1960), the degree of the centralization of the practitioners, who are the smallest nodes of the network, is large, while a comparison with centralized networks reveals a lower degree of centralization. The topologies of centralized networks are typically characterized by the "scale-free network" pattern described by Barabasi (2002).

Unlike decentralized networks, such as "small-world networks," "random networks" and "scale-free networks" form a stratified structure in which the node connections are unevenly distributed and concentrated on certain key nodes. In contrast to decentralized networks, in which each node has a similar degree of importance, these hub nodes serve as primary information conduits that are of much higher importance to the network than other nodes.

Moreover, scale-free networks promote a cumulative advantage through which key nodes attract new nodes in large numbers (Cole, and Cole, 1973). In terms of organizational or corporate formations, scale-free networks are typical of entrepreneurial organizations and so forth that are under the control of a strong leader who engages in direct supervision.

Considering ICs and networked ICs from the perspective of scale-free networks, the Apple, NTT DOCOMO and SCE company-internal ICs involved in the iPhone, i-mode and PlayStation developments acted as the nodes (hubs), with multiple links to the ICs, which consisted of external partner companies and certain customers, and were centralized network structures similar to scale-free networks (Barabasi and Albert, 1999). In addition, company-external partner companies formed ICs with subcontractors, and thus configured stratified structures centered on the ICs at Apple, NTT DOCOMO and SCE.

Also, in considering the smartphone, mobile telephone and game business developments through time (from starting up a service through to the process of growing it), as the ICs with external partner companies and certain customers increase, cumulative links are forged from these ICs to Apple, NTT DOCOMO and SCE. Thus, the creation of these networks enabled these smartphone, mobile telephone and game businesses to experience rapid growth.

The "preferential attachment effect" (also called the "Matthew effect") (Merton, 1968) characteristic of scale-free networks enables new nodes (new ICs) to connect with particular center nodes (hubs such as the ICs in Apple, NTT DOCOMO or SCE). Thus, there is tendency at Apple, NTT DOCOMO or SCE to experience phenomena such as "success breeds success" or "the rich get richer" (Barabasi, 2002; Watts, 2003). While the iPhone continues to enjoy success, the success of NTT DOCOMO's i-mode and SCE's PlayStation developments can also be qualitatively described as being enabled by the formation of scale-free networks between these companies[1].

The explosive growth of smartphones, mobile phones and games is due to the creation of win-win business models through the knowledge integration process enabled by collaborative innovation among players across different industries. As discussed, the ICs as small-world networks in companies that play the central role of large-scale hubs (the ICs within organizations at Apple, NTT DOCOMO and SCE) also entailed vast amounts of linking with the small-world networks consisting of external partners and customers. External partner companies then formed ICs with subcontractors, and thus configured stratified structures as scale-free networks centered on the ICs at Apple, NTT DOCOMO and SCE. Therefore, these scale-free networks enable the configurations of ecosystems as new value chains in the smartphone, mobile telephone and game businesses (See Figure 9.1). The following new insight can be drawn regarding these scale-free networks.

[Insight 10]

Scale-free networks enable leader and follower companies to integrate the knowledge necessary for creating, developing and growing an ecosystem.

According to Steven's power law, scale-free networks are characterized by self-organization (Barabasi, 2002; Watts, 2003). In the world of physics, self organization implies a phase transition from disorder to order, in which atoms are vibrating on the boundaries between chaos and order, and in which criticality occurs when the spin of the atoms become aligned with each other and they behave as a community. Thus, the focus here is not on individual atoms, but on groups of atoms in several boxes, for example, and in which the atoms in each of those boxes are behaving exactly the same as one another (Barabasi, 2002). Behind the self-organizational shift from disorder to order lies these scale-free network formations. So then why did the scale-free networks occur between companies in the real-world smartphone, mobile phone and game business developments? These organizational phenomena were caused by "boundaries synchronization," as discussed in the next section.

9.2.3 Boundaries Synchronization Driving Collaborative Innovation

In the case of the business innovation model and the forging of new businesses in the healthcare field, and in the birth of the iPhone, i-mode and PlayStation business models that the authors have researched, small-world structures are formed within and between companies, and new practices are brought into being through collaborative innovation between the leader company (ies) and follower company (ies) arranged in these "small worlds." Behind these developments, a number of boundaries synchronizations occur between the small-world clusters between companies (including customer companies) and the small-world clusters that act as hubs on which new business models are centered (for example, Apple, NTT DOCOMO and SCE company-internal ICs). Boundaries synchronization promotes collaborative innovation, and has two main elements. The first of these elements is "context synchronization," and the second of these elements is the "synchronization of practice."

(1) Context Synchronization
By synchronizing business-related contexts between different small worlds, practitioners are able to dynamically and concurrently share knowledge about problems and issues with strategic objectives and the achievement of strategy. Strategic contexts that begin in the small-world hubs are disseminated to the small worlds of external partners and certain customers, and even on to small worlds further down, so that the information is shared dynamically across the entire scale-free network.

Knowledge in between small worlds does not just simply entail the information processing model as syntactic boundaries (Carlile, 2004), but also entails the interactive and concurrent sharing of strategic co-creation contexts between stakeholders for the creation of new business models. Even after the co-creation of a new business model, issues and problems that occur in response to changing situations are also shared dynamically in small-world networks. As practitioners co-create and co-evolve new business models in this way, they also inspire the element of "synchronization of practice" between each of the small worlds, as will be discussed.

To achieve a new business model, practitioners in diverse organizations and companies must discuss specifically what needs to be done. Thus, the huge number of action items that comprise the overall tactics and strategy related to the business model must be broken down into items to be executed by each of the many organizations involved, such as the leader companies that play the central role (for example Apple, NTT DOCOMO, SCE), the external partner and customer companies, subcontractors and so forth. Most importantly, these large numbers of action items include action items that cannot be completed within the scope of the business of a single organization. For instance, there are items that need to be executed through coordination and partnering with other organizations and companies, or items that need to be executed by one's own organization or company based on the output of other organizations.

Thus, all of the action items that cannot be completed entirely within a single company or organization are executed through the formation of small worlds that span organizational and knowledge boundaries. The strategic contexts disseminated in small worlds are given meanings and agreed upon through practitioner discussions about specific objectives, meanings, timeframes and methods, such as the "who," "what," (action items that should be executed), "why," "when," "with whom" and "how." Specifically formulating and implementing these strategies and tactics is performed at the micro level by the "micro strategy, strategizing and organizing" of practitioners (e.g., Kodama, 2007a; Whittington, 1996, 2003).

Moreover, for practitioners who engage in "strategy as practice," trial and error through time is also an element of their dynamism. These practitioners always have a "dynamic view of strategy" (Kodama, 2006), and not only do they engage in deliberate strategies, but they also execute intentional emergent, entrepreneurial and contingent emergent strategies flexibly, as illustrated in Figure 2.6 in Chapter 2. Practitioners also improvise when situations suddenly change.

Practitioners thoroughly share context and knowledge through collaboration and dialogue in each of their small worlds, and execute action items through strong mutual interdependence with other organizations and companies. Practitioners specifically execute items of strategy as practices decided upon in small worlds, and the level of achievement in these practical processes is always monitored among practitioners. These individual "strategy as practice" action items in each of the small worlds are interdependent between the small worlds. In other words, the items of "when," "with whom" and "how" require coordination and collaboration between practitioners in different organizations and companies.

(2) Synchronization of Practice

As strategy as practice, practitioners who commit to strategic activity and plan in multiple small worlds need to align themselves chronologically with the pitch and rhythm of the achievement of the business objectives in each of the individual small-world ICs to achieve the target business models. In executing business in each of these small worlds, practitioners have to align their thoughts and actions, and carry out strategy as practice in each of the small worlds with a certain pitch and rhythm; in other words, they must engage in the "synchronization of practice"—a mechanism for achieving business objectives concurrently.

Practitioners in small-world networks engage in dynamic context synchronization and the synchronization of practice to bring about new knowledge; thus, these small-world networks are aspects of the organizational platforms for achieving knowledge integration. These aspects are also characteristics of practical, semantic and pragmatic small-world networks operating in time and space that are enabled through the creation, discussion and sharing of high-quality tacit and explicit knowledge. Even through the healthcare case analysis discussed in this book and the existing research into the smartphone, mobile phone and game businesses, the new perspective that emerges is the constant existence of diverse small-world structures and of "stratified network structures" of small-world structures with dissimilar contexts and knowledge. These structures are created and linked by the practitioners playing the leading roles in their own circumstances (customers, etc.) or organizations and bringing about effects on others.

(3) Promoting Collaborative Innovation through
Boundaries Synchronization

Context synchronization and the synchronization of practice enable the formation of small-world clusters of all of the ICs that form scale-free networks. Then, the increase in the number of small-world clusters due to the "preferential attachment effect (the Matthew effect)" (Merton, 1968) and the increase in links to central hubs amplify these boundaries synchronization factors.

As discussed, practitioners who inspire context synchronization and the synchronization of practice across multiple small-world clusters are crucial for the achievement of boundaries synchronization. The overlapping or interlocking of small-worlds centered on certain practitioners is brought about, and a phenomenon analogous to a physical phase transition in which atoms resonate together occurs.

This results in the growth of business models that increase customer, partner and follower companies centered on leader companies; in other words, increases in the number of small-world clusters and the emergence of large-scale central hubs of the main player companies (for example, the leading telecommunications carrier described in Chapter 5, Panasonic described in Chapter 7, or Apple, NTT DOCOMO and SCE). Large-scale boundaries synchronization of this sort brings about new markets as ecosystems in which all players co-evolve to mutually grow their businesses, which leads to the following new insight:

[Insight 11]

Boundaries synchronization as context synchronization and the synchronization of practice integrates the knowledge necessary for creating, developing and growing a business ecosystem.

In observing how new businesses are created and grown by integrating contexts and knowledge dynamically in this way, it is necessary to analyze and consider the dynamic formations of community systems of practitioners. However, as small-world networks, ICs and networked ICs are not formed randomly (i.e., they are not random networks). This is because these "community systems" are formed of practitioners that have subjective intentions.

9.3 BOUNDARIES CONSISTENCY BY KNOWLEDGE INTEGRATION THROUGH COLLABORATIVE INNOVATION

Encouraging the consistency of boundaries is part of the knowledge integration process enabled through collaborative innovation inside and outside of companies, including their environments. In other words, the important factor in enabling dynamic consistency in the boundaries between environments and corporate systems, and the boundaries between the individual internal managerial elements of corporate systems, is the ability to integrate knowledge (i.e., capabilities) both within and between companies across a diverse range of boundaries.

Factors of consistency in boundaries between environments and corporate systems include the knowledge integration processes for optimizing vertical and horizontal boundaries, as well as the knowledge integration processes to build new value chains. On the other hand, factors of consistency in boundaries between individual managerial elements within the company systems include the knowledge integration processes to optimize strategy, technologies, organizations, operations and leadership to respond to changing situations (See Figure 9.2).

Small-world structures, as community system-based business networks, are required to achieve knowledge integration in this way, while collaborative innovation driven through the formation of ICs and networked ICs is required to build ecosystems and to sustain the growth of companies (See Figure 9.2).

As illustrated by Figure 2.3 in Chapter 2, the management innovation model consists of the managerial factors of strategy, organizations, technologies, operations and leadership, although there has to be the suitable integration of knowledge (including capabilities) required in each managerial

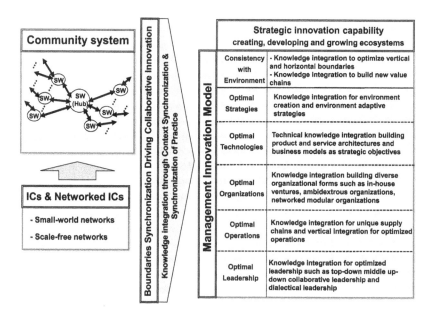

Figure 9.2 Integrating Knowledge and Building Ecosystems by Setting up Community Systems

factor to appropriately bring about consistency between these elements and the environment. To achieve this knowledge integration, the processes of collaborative innovation through context synchronization and the synchronization of practice by practitioners forming centralized ICs and networked ICs is critical.

Thus, context synchronization and the synchronization of practice are crucial factors in promoting collaborative innovation. For example, in terms of strategy, knowledge integration is key to suitably setting down and executing environment creation strategies and environment adaptive strategies to respond to environmental change. In consideration of not only the short-term profits, but also the diversity of potentials that lie ahead in the future, companies must integrate different strategies with different objectives and execute them.

To achieve an environment creation strategy, new business developments and technological innovations enabled through the formation of ICs and networked ICs are critical, as can be seen in the examples of the business transformations of CBS and UHN described in Chapter 3, or the ecosystem strategy in the healthcare field carried out by the telecommunications carrier described in Chapter 5, or in the case of Apple, NTT DOCOMO and SCE in the previous researches. Also, as illustrated by Figure 2.7 in Chapter 2, the strategic innovation capability that combines both environmental adaptive strategies that tend towards short-term profits in existing businesses and environmental creation strategies for long-term innovation are crucial for these corporate enterprise structures.

Furthermore, regarding the core business models of these environment creation and environment adaptive strategies, or the technical elements of the products and services that achieve these, unique product architecture and process architecture, technological innovation elements with competitiveness and differentiation from other companies (modular innovation/architecture innovation/radical innovation, etc.) (Henderson and Clark, 1990), and the technical knowledge integration process to achieve marketing-centered business model innovation (Kodama, 2007b) are also critical.

For example, the technological innovation of product architecture was an important factor in acquiring sustainable competitiveness in the case of Fanuc, a global leader in the machine tool field (Kodama and Shibata, 2014). In addition, convergence between the IT and distribution systems was an essential mechanism for the growth of new distribution innovators such as Yamato Transport in Japan (Kodama, 2014). Another example is TSMC of Taiwan, whose virtual integration mechanisms and the creation of a standardized semiconductor production platform tied with the process architecture evolution in the semiconductor industry were critical to its success (Kodama, 2011b). Such business model transformations were also crucial for Apple, NTT DOCOMO and SEC—transformations that not only entailed technical innovation in the smartphone, mobile phone and game device businesses, but also entailed innovations in sales and distribution systems.

The knowledge integration process is also a requisite for suitably designing organizations to achieve these strategies and technologies. For example, in order to grow its semiconductor foundry business, TSMC formed modularized and networked organizations between all its stakeholders, and configured an ecosystem for the production of semiconductors through collaborative innovation between these modularized organizations (Kodama, 2011b). To establish its game business, as the parent company, Sony set up and invested in its SCE subsidiary through a joint venture, and succeeded with the development of the PlayStation through collaborative innovation between Sony and SCE (Kodama, 2007b).

NTT DOCOMO succeeded in its mobile phone businesses by setting up new project-based organizations within the company to continuously establish new businesses such as the i-mode, and by driving collaborative innovation between its new and existing organizations. Another example is that of the "ambidextrous organization" (Tushman and O'Reilly, 1997) seen at Fujitsu, in which an autonomous venture organization was set up within the company to grow a new business (Kodama and Shibata, 2014). The new organization then split off from Fujitsu as Fanuc, an ambidextrous organization that combined both existing and new organizations in charge of new technologies to enable a technical transformation to develop new products through the adoption of new technologies (Kodama and Shibata, 2014).

Existing organizations focus on costs and short-term profits and aim for gradual innovation in the execution of their businesses. Here, organizational forms are dictated through firm top-down management, and organizational operations are regulated and run in pursuit of better productivity through business efficiency. In contrast, new organizations face challenging new issues as they work towards new innovation and growth. Although there are many organizational forms observable, in many large companies where top and middle management, including senior executives, vice presidents, etc., play the central roles, there are also many cases of autonomous and distributed leadership (Kodama, 2005) that has achieved new innovation.

Companies must adopt the most optimal way of operating these strategies, technologies and organizations (for example, through new supply chains or by executing business with ICT), and build unique core competencies, such as a knowledge integration process for unique supply chains and virtual integration for optimized operations. Apple and TSMC are companies that have virtually integrated unique supply chains using ICT (Kodama, 2011b). SCE is also a company that configured new sales and distribution systems for its game business. NTT DOCOMO engaged in locally distributed operations to respond to competitive environments and real-time management with ICT (Kodama, 2011b). Fanuc developed and implemented a production system to correspond to new product architecture.

Company top and middle management steer these strategies, organizations, technologies and operations, and use the right leadership style to respond to circumstantial changes. There are commonalities in the research done on the cases of the CBS and UHN business transformations discussed in Chapter 3 and the healthcare ecosystem strategy carried out by the telecommunications carrier discussed in Chapter 5 that include the execution of top-down, middle-up-down and collaborative leadership (Kodama, 2005) through the formation of multitier small-world networks as ICs and networked ICs within and outside of organizations.

Knowledge integration is also required to optimize leadership, such as dialectical leadership, to focus on the relationships between stakeholders outside of the company (Kodama, 2005). As discussed in the Fujisawa SST case in Chapter 7, dialectical leadership of leaders and managers that combinined strategic and centralized leadership and creative and distributed leadership to create value for the entire town were observed. As described above, consistency in strategy, organizations, technologies, operations and leadership with environments is the wellspring that achieves optimized management innovation models and the strategic innovation capability for corporate growth, and brings about corporate competitiveness to create, develop and grow ecosystems (see Figure 9.2).

However, as described by Section 2.3.4 in Chapter 2, the management innovation model is also perceived as constantly changing over time and dynamically advancing through configuration and reconfiguration. In other words, the management innovation model is never fixed, but is always changing to achieve consistency with changing environments. The process of altering this management innovation model enables companies to bring about new corporate competitiveness and achieve the sustainable strategic innovation capability (see Figure 2.7 in Chapter 2).

Dynamic strategic management entails continuous and ongoing activity to create new value. Therefore, the evolution of this management innovation model is a dynamic process that leads to the sustainable corporate competitiveness needed to create, develop and grow ecosystems.

NOTE

1. Barabasi (2002) also observes a similar trend, in which 80% of all World Wide Web connections are "occupied" by only 20% of "hub" Web sites. However, in reality, there are limitations to the number of partners a business can have, and companies made up of practitioners with subjective intentions at the macro level must consider the merits and demerits of a partner relationship and transaction costs. Networked IC formations are somewhat dissimilar to the highly centralized scale-free networks (Barabasi and Albert, 1999; Cole and Cole, 1973) observed on the Internet (Watts, 2003).

REFERENCES

Ahuja, M. & Carley, K. (1999). Network structure in virtual organizations. *Organization Science*, 10(6), 741–757.

Albert, R. & Barabasi, A. (2000). Topology of evolving networks: Local events and universality. *Physical Review Letter*, 85(24), 5234–5237.

Ansoff, H.I. (1965). *Corporate Strategy*. New York: McGraw Hill.

Argyris, C. & Schon, D. (1978). *Organizational learning: A theory of action approach*. Reading, MA: Addison Wesley.

Barabasi, A.-L. (2002). *Linked: The New Science of Networks*. Cambridge, MA: Perseus Books Group.

Barabasi, A.-L. & Albert, R. (1999). Emergence of scaling in random networks. *Science*, 286, October, 509–512.

Baum, J.A.C., Rowley, T.J. & Shipilov, A.V. (2004). The small world of Canadian capital markets: Statistical mechanics of investment bank syndicate networks. *Canadian Journal of Administrative Sciences*, 21(4), 307–325.

Braha, D. & Bar-Yam, Y. (2004). Information flow structure in large-scale product development organizational networks. *Journal of Information Technology*, 19(4), 234–244.

Brown, J.S. & Duguid, P. (1991). Organizational learning and communities-of-practice. *Organization Science*, 2(3), 40–57.

Buckman, R. (2003). *Building a Knowledge-Driven Organization*. New York: McGraw Hill.

Carlile, P. (2002). A pragmatic view of knowledge and boundaries: Boundary objects in new product development. *Organization Science*, 13(4), 442–455.

Carlile, P. (2004). Transferring, translating, and transforming: An integrative framework for managing knowledge across boundaries. *Organization Science*, 15(5), 555–568.

Cole, R. & Cole, S. (1973). *Social Stratification in Science*. Chicago, IL: University of Chicago Press.

Day, G. & Schoemaker, P.J. (2005). Scanning the periphery. *Harvard Business Review*, 83, 135–148.

Eisenhardt, K.M. & Brown, S.L. (1998). Time pacing: Competing in markets that won't stand still. *Harvard Business Review*, March–April, 59–69.

Erdos, P., and Renyi, A. (1960). On the evolution of random graphs. *Publications of the Mathematical Institute of the Hungarian Academy of Sciences*, 5, A, 17–61.

Faust, K. (1997). Centrality in affiliation networks. *Social Networks*, 19, 157–191.

Fulk, J. & DeSanctis, G. (1995). Electronic communication and changing organizational forms. *Organization Science*, 6(4), 337–349.

Gardner, H. (1982). *Art, Mind, and Brain: A Cognitive Approach to Creativity*. New York: Basic Books.

Gardner, H. (1985). *The Mind's New Science*. New York: Basic Books.

Hagel, J., III & Brown, J.S. (2005). Productive friction. *Harvard Business Review*, 83(2), 139–145.

Henderson, R. & Clark, K. (1990). Architectural innovation: The reconfiguration of existing product technologies and the failure of established firms. *Administrative Science Quarterly*, 35, 9–30.

Hofer, C.W. & Schendel, D. (1978). *Strategy Formulation*. St. Paul, MN: West Publishing.

Jarvenpaa, S.L., Knoll, K. & Leidner, D.E. (1998). Is anybody out there? Antecedents of trust in global virtual teams. *Journal of Management Information Systems*, 14(4), 29–64.

Johnson, G. (1987). *Strategic Change and the Management Process*. Oxford: Blackwell.

Kodama, M. (2001). Creating new business through strategic community management. *International Journal of Human Resource Management*, 11(6), 1062–1084.

Kodama, M. (2005). Knowledge creation through networked strategic communities: Case studies in new product development. *Long Range Planning*, 38(1), 27–49.

Kodama, M. (2006). Knowledge-based view of corporate strategy. *Technovation*, 26(8), 1390–1406.

Kodama, M. (2007a). *Knowledge Innovation—Strategic Management as Practice*. London: Edward Elgar Publishing.

Kodama, M. (2007b). *Project-Based Organization in the Knowledge-Based Society*. London: Imperial College Press.

Kodama, M.(2009). Boundaries Innovation and Knowledge Integration in the Japanese Firm. *Long Range Planning*, 42(4), 463–494.

Kodama, M. (2011a). *Knowledge Integration Dynamics—Developing Strategic Innovation Capability*. Singapore: World Scientific Publishing.

Kodama, M. (2011b). *Interactive Business Communities-Accelerating Corporate Innovation through Boundary Networks*. London: Gower Publishing.

Kodama, M.(2013). *Competing Through ICT Capability*. London: Palgrave Macmillan.

Kodama, M. (2014). *Winning Through Boundaries Innovation—Communities of Boundaries Generate Convergence*. Oxford: Peter Lang.

Kodama, M. & Shibata, T. (2014). Strategy transformation through strategic innovation capability—a case study of Fanuc. *R&D Management*, 44(1), 75–103.

Kraut, R., Steinfield, C., Chan, A., Butler, B. & Hoag, A. (1999). Coordination and virtualization: The role of electronic networks and personal relationships. *Organization Science*, 10(6), 722–740.

Lave, J. & Wenger, E. (1990). *Situated Learning: Legitimate Peripheral Participation*. Cambridge, UK: Cambridge University Press.

Leonard-Barton, D. (1992). Core capabilities and core rigidities: A paradox in managing new product development. *Strategic Management Journal*, 13(2), 111–125.

Leonard-Barton, D. (1995). *Wellsprings of Knowledge: Building and Sustaining the Sources of Innovation*. Boston, MA: Harvard Business School Press.

Lin, L. & Kulatilaka, N. (2006). Network effects and technology licensing with fixed fee, royalty, and hybrid contracts. *Journal of Management Information Systems*, 23(2), 91–118.

Merton, R. (1968). *Social Theory and Social Structure*. New York: Free Press.

Mintzberg, H. (1978). Patterns in Strategy Formation. *Management Science*, 24, 934–948.

Motter, A.E. (2004). Cascade control and defense in complex networks. *Physical Review Letter*, 93. doi:10.1103/PhysRevLett.93.098701

Newman, M.E.J. (2004). Fast algorithm for detecting community structure in networks. *Physical Review E*, 69(6), 1–5.

Nonaka, I. & Konno, N. (1998). The concept of "Ba": Building a foundation for knowledge creation. *California Management Review*, 40, 40–54.

Orr, J. (1996). *Talking about Machines: An Ethnography of a Modern Job*. Ithaca, NY: ILP Press.

Owen-Smith, J., and Powell, W.W. (2004). Knowledge networks as channels and conduits: The effects of spillovers in the Boston biotechnology community. *Organization Science*, 15(1), 5–22.

Pettigrew, A.M. (1977). Strategy formulation as a political process. *International Studies of Management and Organization*, 7(2), 78–87.

Porter, M. (1980). *Competitive Strategy: Techniques for Analyzing Industries and Competitors*. New York: Free Press.

Porter, M. (1985). *Competitive Advantage*. New York: Free Press.

Roethlisberger, F. (1977). *The Elusive Phenomena: An Autobiographical Account of My Work in the Field of Organizational Behavior at the Harvard Business School*. Boston, MA: Harvard Business School Press.

Roethlisberger, F. & Dickson, R. (1939). *Management and the Worker*. Cambridge, MA: Harvard University Press.

Sanchez, R. & Mahoney, T. (1996). Modularity, flexibility, and knowledge management in product and organizational design. *Strategic Management Journal*, 17(winter special issue), 63–76.

Shah, P. (2000). Network destruction: The structural implications of downsizing. *Academy of Management Journal*, 43(1), 101–112.

Teece, D.J., Pisano, G. & Shuen, A. (1997). Dynamic capabilities and strategic management. *Strategic Management Journal*, 18(3), 509–533.

Tushman, M.L. (1979). Work characteristics and subunit communication structure: A contingency analysis. *Administrative Science Quarterly*, 24(1), 82–98.

Tushman, M.L. & O'Reilly, C.A. (1997). *Winning Through Innovation*. Cambridge, MA: Harvard Business School Press.

Vangen, S. & Huxham, C. (2003). Nurturing collaborative relations, building trust in inter-organizational collaboration. *The Journal of Applied Behavioral Science*, 39(1), 5–31.

Wasserman, S. & Faust, K. (1994). *Social Network Analysis: Methods and Applications*. New York: Cambridge University Press.

Watts, J. (2003). *Six Degrees: The Science of a Connected Age*. New York: W.W. Norton and Company.

Watts, J. & Strogatz, S. (1998). Collective dynamics of "small-world" networks. *Nature*, 393(4), 440–442.

Weick, K.E. (1979). *The Social Psychology of Organizing* (2nd ed.). Reading, MA: Addison-Wesley.

Wenger, E.C. (2000). Communities of practice: The organizational frontier. *Harvard Business Review*, 78(1), 139–145.

Wernerfelt, B. (1984). A resource-based view of the firm. *Strategic Management Journal*, 5, 171–180.

White, D. & Houseman, M. (2003). The navigability of strong ties: Small worlds, tie strength, and network topology. *Complexity*, 8(1), 82–86.

Whittington, R. (1996). Strategy as Practice. *Long Range Planning*, 29(5), 731–735.

Whittington, R. (2003). The work of strategizing and organizing for a practice perspective. *Strategic Organization*, 1(1), 117–125.

Zwass, V. & Veroy, B. (1988). Capacity expansion for information flow distribution in multipath computer communication networks. *Journal of Management Information Systems*, 5(2), 57–70.

10 Conclusions and Issues for Future Research

Mitsuru Kodama

This chapter provides a conclusion to the book and describes a number of future research issues. Firstly, in regards to the knowledge integration model (knowledge integration firms) discussed theoretically in Chapters 1 and 2, this chapter organizes the main managerial factors (five items) that promote the configurations of new ecosystems through collaborative innovation, and the insights extracted from a number of case studies and existing research. This chapter then presents these five managerial factors wholly assembled as "the knowledge integration model (knowledge integration firm)." Finally, the chapter discusses implications and future research issues.

10.1 COLLABORATIVE INNOVATION AS A FRAMEWORK FOR NEW ECOSYSTEMS

Behind the achievement of new products, services and business models accompanying the fusion of different technologies, the development of ICT is the technical and industrial phenomenon of "convergence." Convergence of the ICT industry in particular with different industries, such as the medical, welfare and healthcare industries, has brought about the new business models known as "health support innovations," such as remote treatment, remote care and remote health management. Therefore, the "collaborative innovation" that links up different businesses and transcends the more simplistic approach to business as competition among different industries has become an increasingly important issue for companies.

The business ecosystems configured in medical institutions through collaborative innovation with other medical institutions, medical equipment and pharmaceutical manufacturers, and the ICT industry have brought improvements to the quality of healthcare and customer service by promoting the development of new treatment methods and raising the levels of various types of healthcare support. As discussed, this book arrives at five managerial factors through detailed case studies and the existing research into the management reform process at medical institutions through collaborative innovation and how ecosystems are brought about through

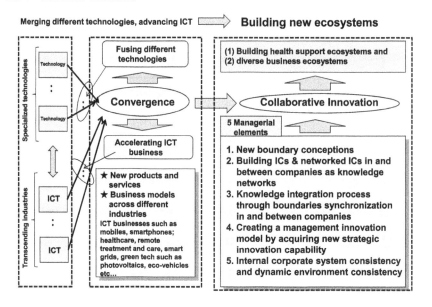

Figure 10.1   A New Framework for Ecosystems through Collaborative Innovation

collaborative innovation across organizations in different industries and businesses, not only within the ICT industry, but also between the ICT, medical, welfare and healthcare industries, as well as local governments and so forth (See Figure 10.1).

This section describes the main managerial elements (five items) needed to drive the configurations of ecosystems, and describes their relationships to the insights cited in this book (in Chapters 1, 2 and 9) (See Table 10.1).

10.1.1 New Boundary Conceptions

The first of these managerial factors, which is described in Chapter 1, is the "boundary conceptions" or "architecture thinking" in a business model that is needed to configure an ecosystem. One of these concepts is the "creativity view," which encompasses the concept of flexibility, and the "capacity to inspire," which can be seen as the organizational capability and strategic action of a company used to bring about new knowledge integration (creation) flexibly, creatively and autonomously.

The creativity view is a factor that drives corporate vertical integration (including virtual systems). Leading global manufacturers use the creativity view to raise the performance not only of path-dependent knowledge, but also of breakthrough knowledge through vertical integration by configuring their internal knowledge networks. At the same time, they accelerate the integration of company knowledge with new knowledge absorbed through collaborative innovation enabled by configuring external knowledge networks

Table 10.1 The Five Managerial Factors of the Knowledge Integration Model

Five Managerial elements	New Insights
1. New boundary conceptions	[Insight 1] The value chain model arising from collaborative innovation promotes the creation of competitive new products and services, as well as innovative business models. [Insight 2] The co-evolution model, through collaborative innovation spanning various industries, promotes the creation of win-win business models.
2. Building ICs and networked ICs in and between companies as knowledge networks	[Insight 4] The dynamic formation of innovation communities as business networks built around leader and major follower companies lies at the core of the formation of business ecosystems. [Insight 9] Small-world networks enable leader and follower companies to integrate the knowledge necessary for creating, developing and growing an ecosystem. [Insight 10] Scale-free networks enable leader and follower companies to integrate the knowledge necessary for creating, developing and growing an ecosystem.
3. The knowledge integration process through boundaries synchronization in and between companies	[Insight 11] Boundaries synchronization as context synchronization and the synchronization of practice integrates the knowledge necessary for creating, developing and growing a business ecosystem.
4. Creating a management innovation model by acquiring new strategic innovation capability	[Insight 3] The process of spiraling the execution of exploration and exploitation centered on leader companies (or organizations) creates, grows and develops business ecosystems. [Insight 7] The integration (asynchronous and synchronous) of dynamic adaptation and dynamic innovation capabilities brings about the strategic innovation capabilities of the companies that execute both environmental adaptation and environmental creation strategies. [Insight 8] Dynamic strategic management involving strategic innovation capability embedded in a corporate management innovation model achieves the creation, growth and development of ecosystems.

(*Continued*)

Table 10.1 (Continued)

Five Managerial elements	New Insights
5. Internal corporate system consistency and dynamic environment consistency	[Insight 5] The dynamic consistency of the boundaries between environments and corporate systems, and the boundaries between the individual business elements within corporate systems builds ecosystems and achieves sustainable corporate development and growth. [Insight 6] Consistency both within and outside of corporate systems ((1) strategy, (2) organizations, (3) technologies, (4) operations and (5) leadership) brings about the dynamic adaptation and dynamic innovation capabilities.

with partner companies and certain customers. In this way, the creativity view serves to set down corporate (organizational) boundaries, while the value chain model enabled through collaborative innovation is a core concept that drives the creation of new competitive products and services or breakthrough business models [Insight 1].

Secondly is the concept of the "dialectic view," which enables the co-evolution model enabled by collaborative innovation across different industries and businesses to bring about new products, services and business models and the expansion of horizontal boundaries. A source of creation of new business models with the co-evolution model, which entails coexistence and co-prosperity between stakeholders, is the "dialectic view" as a strategic action. The dialectic view is a core concept that enables companies (or organizations) to set down boundaries, and create win-win co-evolution models through collaboration across different industries [Insight 2].

10.1.2 Configuring ICs and Networked ICs as Transcendent Internal and External Corporate Knowledge Networks

Chapter 9 discussed the dynamic knowledge integration processes through the formation of "innovation communities" as community systems in companies and organizations that lay behind the success of collaborative innovation responding to convergence. The basic concept of these knowledge integration processes is the formation by practitioners of dynamic knowledge networks (human networks) that span formal organizations.

Innovation communities (ICs) are formed by practitioners cross-functionally between different organizations and companies, and are "small-world structures." As these ICs change dynamically in response to context, they also dynamically change the overall form of the networked ICs that comprise these network formations.

ICs are dynamically rebuilt as a result of practitioners' day-to-day practical activities. Practitioners participate in more than one IC to share information, context and knowledge with other practitioners, which they transfer to their other ICs. The networking of ICs in this way forms a "group interlock network" (see Chapter 9). Within the framework of this group interlock network, ICs can be seen as corresponding to nodes and hubs.

The practitioners belonging to the hub and node ICs within and outside of the company dynamically bridge multiple and dissimilar ICs and create or consolidate networks of ICs. As a result of this integration, ICs create new contexts and knowledge. Practitioners deliberately create networks of multiple ICs and closely link them among the various organizations within and outside of their companies to develop new products and services and to build new business processes.

In the real business world, dynamic ICs and networked ICs enable the knowledge integration process in business networks that are centered on leader companies and main follower companies by integrating the knowledge required to create, grow and develop an ecosystem. Thus, as described by Insights 4, 9 and 10, the critical small-world and scale-free network factors in particular have a major impact on the creation, growth and development of ecosystems in the formation of knowledge networks as ICs and networked ICs.

10.1.3 The Knowledge Integration Process through Boundaries Synchronization Across and Between Companies

In the management innovation models and new business developments in the healthcare field discussed in the case studies and in Chapter 9, and in the research done by the authors into the birth of the iPhone, i-mode and PlayStation business models, practitioners engaged in new practices through collaborative innovation between the leader company (ies) and follower company (ies) in the "small-world" structures configured inside and between companies.

Behind this practice is the occurrence of boundaries synchronization among a range of factors in the small worlds between companies (including customer companies), which are the clusters that play the central roles as hubs for new business models. Boundaries synchronization consists of the two elements of "context synchronization" and "synchronization of practice." Boundaries synchronization promotes collaborative innovation and integrates the knowledge needed to create, grow and develop an ecosystem [Insight 11].

10.1.4 Acquiring New Strategic Innovation Capability to Create a Management Innovation Model

As discussed in detail in Chapter 2, the consistency of the individual managerial factors at the core of corporate systems, such as strategy, organizations, technologies, operations and leadership, and with corporate systems and the environment achieves an optimal management innovation model and the strategic innovation capability required for corporate growth, and thus brings about the competitiveness required to create, grow and develop an ecosystem.

However, as described by Section 2.3.4 in Chapter 2, the management innovation model is also perceived as constantly changing over time and dynamically advancing through configuration and reconfiguration. In other words, the management innovation model is never fixed, but is always changing to achieve consistency with changing environments. The process of altering this management innovation model enables companies to bring about new corporate competitiveness and achieve a sustainable strategic innovation capability (See Figure 2.7 in Chapter 2).

As detailed by [Insight 7] in Chapter 2, the strategic innovation capability is the integration (both asynchronous and synchronous) of the adaption dynamic capability (exploitation) with the innovation dynamic capability (exploration). It is the combination of these that is required to execute both the environment adaptive and environment creation strategies.

Thus, as described by [Insight 3], strategic innovation capabilities that execute a spiral of exploration and exploitation centered on leader companies (or organizations) achieve the creation, growth and development of business ecosystems. Therefore, a corporate management innovation model with the strategic innovation capability embedded in it and that enables dynamic strategic management will achieve the creation, growth and development of an ecosystem [Insight 8].

Dynamic strategic management enables the continuous and sustainable creation of value, and is a dynamic process that leads to the sustainable competitiveness needed to create, grow and develop an ecosystem through the evolution of this management innovation model.

10.1.5 Internal Corporate System Consistency and Dynamic Environment Consistency

To achieve the strategic innovation capability necessary to drive the creation, growth and development of ecosystems, there must be a dynamic consistency of boundaries both within and outside of corporate systems, as discussed in detail in Chapter 2. To achieve this, optimized organizational models must be configured through collaborative innovation among leader and follower companies. As described by [Insight 4], the formation of innovation communities as knowledge networks is key to configuring an ecosystem. In other words, it requires building dynamic community systems through collaboration among stakeholders.

Thus, this means dynamic community systems that sustainably achieve the strategic innovation capability to simultaneously bring about the adaption dynamic capability and the innovation dynamic capability through a management innovation model as an optimized corporate system to develop dynamic consistency in the boundaries of environments and corporate systems, and in the boundaries between the individual business elements within corporate systems [Insight 6]. That therefore enables the configuration of an ecosystem and of sustainable corporate growth and development [Insight 5].

10.2 THE KNOWLEDGE INTEGRATION MODEL (KNOWLEDGE INTEGRATION FIRM)

The case studies in this book have analyzed and considered the factors of the knowledge integration process through convergence within companies (organizations), between companies (organizations), between companies and customers and between industries to build wide-ranging business ecosystems, including the health support ecosystems in the medical, welfare and healthcare fields. One of the important factors of achieving these health support innovations is the configuration of management innovation models through collaborative innovation, in which innovation communities are required as organizational platforms, described as community systems (ICs and networked ICs).

As described by many case studies, collaborative innovation is an innovation process between different specialties, business classes and types, enterprises and industries that include customers, and that operates within and between companies, organizations and industries. Thus, companies

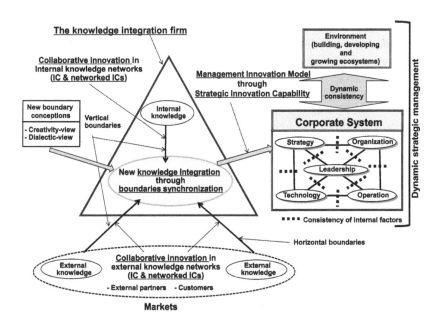

Figure 10.2 The Knowledge Integration Model (Knowledge Integration Firm)

use their new boundaries conceptions (the creativity and dialectic views) to integrate wide-ranging internal and external knowledge in knowledge networks (performed internally and externally) that are configured within and between companies and that include customers. To achieve this knowledge integration process, boundaries synchronization (context synchronization and synchronization of practice) by practitioners is an important requisite in ICs and networked ICs as knowledge networks.

Thus, corporations (organizations) must demonstrate the strategic innovation capability to achieve the knowledge integration process through collaborative innovation as a factor of organizational capability that is optimized to deal with convergence. Not only does the strategic innovation capability bring about consistency between business elements (strategy, organizations, technologies, operations and leadership) within corporate systems, but also enables the configurations of management innovation models to dynamically achieve consistency with environments (ecosystems). In this way, the dynamic strategic management mechanisms in the knowledge integration model (knowledge integration firm) have achieved sustainable corporate growth and development not only with health support ecosystems, but also across a wide range of other business ecosystems (See Figure 10.2).

10.3 IMPLICATIONS AND FUTURE RESEARCH ISSUES

As discussed in Chapter 1, in the modern world, networks are being increasingly configured to share medical, welfare and healthcare-related information using mobile terminals such as smartphones and tablet PCs. In particular, in the developed Western countries, there is an increasing amount of information exchange and social networking in communities (including doctors, caregivers, helpers, volunteers and the able-bodied) to communicate about care advice and offer counseling and medical and healthcare consultation to local citizens.

Thus, expanded health support services such as e-healthcare are gaining a lot of attention in different academic specializations, such as medical, welfare, healthcare, ICT, innovation and management. To seek out a business model that will provide successful c-healthcare, knowledge is required from the academic research into medical informatics, medicine, pharmacy, ICT, innovation theory, business studies and economics.

ICT usage has been discussed in the case studies described in this book, and its applications are rapidly expanding to cover many areas, including communication support, support for creating purpose in life, social participation support, assistance for the physically impaired, and business support in the healthcare, nursing and medical fields. In particular, mobile terminal and cloud computing technologies have become critical ICT platforms that are smoothly driving these medical, welfare and healthcare support ecosystems (health support ecosystems, see Figure 1.3 in Chapter 1) that are indispensable to humans, such as home care, nursing and welfare, support for a wide range of social activities, fitness and increasing levels of public health through health promotions, etc.

This book has presented theoretical research and case studies relating to the management innovation model enabled by the collaborative innovation across wide-ranging organizations, companies and industries and customers needed to configure a health support ecosystem. However, there is little interdisciplinary research in the academic fields of medical informatics, medicine, pharmacy, welfare healthcare, ICT, innovation and business.

With the aim of opening new interdisciplinary research, this book has presented the creation and configurations of health support ecosystems based on the three main pillars of remote diagnosis systems, nursing and welfare systems and health support systems (See Figure 1.3 in Chapter 1). This book has presented case studies and a theoretical framework of a management innovation model and the strategic innovation capability enabled through collaborative innovation in and between companies and organizations to achieve new knowledge integration as new services.

Also, as described by Table 10.1, this book has extracted the 11 insights and five managerial factors required for creating, growing and developing business ecosystems, including health support ecosystems. Of particular practical importance is the configuration of community systems across different industries such as the medical, welfare, healthcare and ICT industries.

In the future, whether countries, companies or organizations aiming to set up and configure health support ecosystems are successful will depend on how they build community systems as knowledge networks across different industries.

Moving forward, empirical studies and theoretical frameworks on the management innovation model will be required from the micro perspective regarding overall medical, welfare and healthcare services, including health support services, based on this accumulated research.

Modern healthcare services are often passively or intermittently delivered, and focus on disease. In contrast, new healthcare services must also engage more proactively in prevention and focus on quality of life and well being, because modern medicine has been centered on hospitals and doctors. This model must be transformed to a patient-centered approach, so that patients can receive wide-ranging care while at home. Therefore, these services must include widened social networks, with households and local societies acting as important contributors to the health and well being of individuals.

In short, healthcare must be tailored to meet the different needs and circumstances of individuals. Therefore, in dealing with factors that contribute to health, illness and recovery from illness, patients must be allowed to contribute as partners.

The existing research describes a range of new healthcare business models, such as the P4 model (participatory, predictive, personalized and preventative) (Hood and Friend, 2011), ubiquitously disseminated patient care (e.g., Chang et al., 2010; OECD, 2013), mobile health (e.g., Free et al., 2013), telemedicine (remote medicine) (e.g., Kodama, 2000, 2005, 2013) and telehealthcare (remote healthcare) (Lin et al., 2010).

In the healthcare service field, there is a great deal of interest in ways of improving the quality of services and welfare through e-healthcare that focuses on the receivers of services (in particular, the patients), and their effectiveness. In the ICT field, many effects on e-healthcare technical solutions (e.g., Kodama, 2001, 2002, 2008) and healthcare in general have been reported as being due to ICT (e.g., Celler, Lovell, and Basilakis, 2003; Yang and Hsiao, 2009). There has also been much research reporting on e-healthcare policy, and the organizational and systematic aspects of it (e.g., Liu et al., 2011; OECD, 2013). There are also innovation theories and social science-related knowledge on the e-healthcare available (e.g., Lin et al., 2010; Omachonu and Einspruch, 2010). However, despite the fact that the existing research commonly handles e-healthcare as related to health support, there still remain large boundaries between different research fields.

An important future research question involves the form that e-healthcare should take to create high-quality customer value (in both its hard and soft aspects). To achieve these ends, how should industrial policy and healthcare systems be configured? What are the factors of success of an e-healthcare business model? In finding the answers to these questions, there must be more thorough research at the scholarly level into the impacts (advantages and disadvantages) brought about by e-healthcare services on all stakeholders, which include customers as the recipients of services (both patients and the healthy), service providers (medical institutions, etc.), ICT companies (providers of technology) and government bodies.

E-healthcare is not just a simple issue of medical or technical development, but in the wider sense, entails a requirement for intention and commitment, both at the local and global levels, among wide-ranging stakeholders (patients and the healthy as customers, medical institutions as service providers, ICT businesses as technical providers and the government bodies involved with policy and systems) who are connected by social networks to improve local and global health support using ICT. Therefore, this field requires further and more thorough research. However, there is hardly any academic research with a scholarly and comprehensive perspective available at the global level.

Taking the discussions in this book as a starting point, there is a necessity for empirical and theoretical research at the micro level into the achievement of health support ecosystems through a model of consistency among stakeholders, such as customers (patients and healthy people), service providers (medical institutions, etc.), ICT companies (technical providers) and governments (involved with policies and social systems).

As specific research questions, the authors believe more detailed research is required into such issues as creating stakeholder value regarding health support services, the clarification of the processes that generate health support service innovations, and the factors of success of the health support ecosystem business models.

REFERENCES

Celler, B.G., Lovell, N.H. & Basilakis, J. (2003).Using information technology to improve the management of chronic disease. *Medical Journal of Australia*, 179(5), 242–246.

Chang, H., Shaw, M., La, F., Ko, W., Ho, Y., Chen, H. & Shu, C. (2010). U-Health: An example of a high-quality individualized healthcare service. *Journal of Future Medicine*, 7(6), 677–687.

Free, C., Phillips, G., Watson, L., Galli, L., Felix, L., Edwards, P., . . . Haines, A. (2013). The effectiveness of mobile-health technologies to improve health care service delivery processes: A systematic review and meta-analysis. *PLoS Medicine*, 10(1). http://journals.plos.org/plosmedicine/article?id=10.1371/journal. pmed.1001363.

Hood, L. & Friend, S.H. (2011). Predictive, personalized, preventive, participatory (P4) cancer medicine. *Nature Reviews Clinical Oncology*, 8(3), 184–187.

Kodama, M. (2000). New multimedia services in the education, medical and welfare sectors. *Technovation*, 20(6), 321–331.

Kodama, M. (2001). New regional community creation, medical and educational applications through video-based information networks. *Systems Research and Behavioral Science*, 18(3), 225–240.

Kodama, M. (2002). Strategic partnership with innovative customers: A Japanese case study. *Information Systems Management*, 19(2), 31–52.

Kodama, M. (2005). New knowledge creation through leadership-based strategic community—a case of new product development in IT and multimedia business fields. *Technovation*, 25(8), 895–908.

Kodama, M. (2008). *New Knowledge Creation Through ICT Dynamic Capability Creating Knowledge Communities Using Broadband*. Charlotte, NC: Information Age Publishing.

Kodama, M. (2013). *Competing Through ICT Capability*. London: Palgrave Macmillan.

Liu, C.F., Hwang, H.G. & Chang, H.C. (2011). e-Healthcare maturity in Taiwan. *Telemedicine and e-Health*, 17(7), 569–573.

Lin, S., Liu, J., Wei, J., Yin, W., Chen, H. & Chiu, W. (2010). A business model analysis of telecardiology service. *Telemedicine and e-Health*, 16(10), 1067–1073.

OECD. (2013). *ICTs and the Health Sector: Towards Smarter Health and Wellness Model*. Paris: OECD.

Omachonu, V. & Einspruch, N. (2010). Innovation in healthcare delivery systems: A conceptual framework. *The Innovation Journal: The Public Sector Innovation Journal*, 15(1), 1–20.

Yang, H.L. & Hsiao, S.L. (2009). Mechanisms of developing innovative IT-enabled services—a case study of Taiwanese healthcare service. *Technovation*, 29(5), 327–337.

Contributors

Takenori Aoki is an Associate Professor at the College of Commerce at Nihon University. His major research fields are operations research/management science and software development project management. He has published some books in Japanese, such as *Accounting Information System* (as part of the *Management Information System* series, Vol. 4, Nikka-Giren Publishing, 1996), in which he was the author, and *Legal and Taxation Problems of e-Commerce* (Gyousei, 2002) and *Introduction to Management Science* (Zeimu-Keiri-Kyoukai, 2005), as co-author, among others. His articles in English have been published in some international conference/symposiums such as the International Conference on Computers and Industrial Engineering (ICC & IE) and the International Society for Professional Innovation Management (ISPIM), among others.

Mitsuru Kodama is Professor of Innovation and Technology Management at the College of Commerce and the Graduate School of Business Administration at Nihon University. His research has been published in international journals, including *Long Range Planning*, *Organization Studies*, *Journal of Management Studies*, *Technovation* and *Information Systems Management*, among others. He also has published ten books in English, including *Competing through ICT Capability* (Palgrave Macmillan, 2012), *Knowledge Integration Dynamics* (World Scientific, 2011), *Boundary Management* (Springer, 2009) and *Knowledge Innovation* (Edward Elgar, 2007), among others. He is an associate editor of two international academic journals, the *International Journal of Mobile Communications* and the *International Journal of Electronic Business*.

Daisuke Koide is Associate Professor of Clinical Epidemiology and Systems at the Graduate School of Medicine, University of Tokyo. He received his Ph.D. in health science from the University of Tokyo in 1996. His research interests are in medical informatics and pharmacoepidemiology. He is currently a Director of the Drug Safety Research Unit, and of Japanese Society for Pharmacoepidemiology. He is also a counselor and an editor of the Japan Association for Healthcare Balanced Score

Card Studies, and of the Japan Association for Medical Informatics. His research has been published in international journals such as the *International Journal of Medical Informatics* (2000, 2008), *Pharmacoepidemiology and Drug Safety* (2002, 2004), *Progress in Informatics* (2005), *Studies in Health Technology and Informatics* (2006) and the *Electronic Journal of Health Informatics* (2007).

Yoshiaki Kondo is Professor of Healthcare Services Management at the School of Medicine and the Graduate School of Medicine at Nihon University. His research has been published in international journals, including the *Journal of Clinical Investigation*, the *American Journal of Physiology*, the *Journal of the American Society of Nephrology*, the *Lancet*, and *Nature Genetics*. He is a member of a number of international academic societies, such as the International Society of Nephrology (ISN), the International Pediatric Nephrology Association (IPNA) and the American Medical Informatics Association (AMIA). He won his third Oshima Award from the Japanese Society of Nephrology in 1996, and his third IPA award from the Information Technology Promotion Agency of Japan (IPA) in 2007.

Mu-Ho Liu is Associate Professor of Management Accounting at the College of Commerce, Nihon University. His research has been published in several journals, including *Accounting* (Kaikei) and the *Journal of Healthcare Balanced Scorecard Research*. He also has published a book in Japanese, called *Accounting and Market Valuation of Research and Development Costs* (Doubunkan Shuppan, 2005). He is currently an editor of the *Journal of Healthcare Balanced Scorecard Research*.

Makoto Shiragami is Professor of Pharmacy at the College of Pharmacy and the Graduate School of Pharmacy at Nihon University. After completion of the master course for pharmaceutical science at the Graduate School of the University of Tokyo in 1977, Dr. Shiragami joined the Ministry of Health and Welfare. During his service in the Ministry, he engaged in various fields such as new drug review, post-marketing safety issues, drug research and development promotions and health insurance programs. From 1984 to 1985, he was sent to the Western Pacific Regional Office of the World Health Organization and then to its Headquarters as an associate expert for two years. He got a Ph.D. in pharmaceutical science from the University of Tokyo in 1999. In 2001, he left the Ministry and became a professor at the College of Pharmacy, Nihon University. He is the Chairman of the Division of Regulatory Sciences of the Pharmaceutical Society of Japan and of the board members of the Japan Association for Healthcare Balanced Scorecard Studies. His fields of specialization are pharmacoeconomics, regulations regarding pharmaceutical affairs and the system of pharmaceutical affairs.

Toshiro Takahashi is a professor at the Nihon University Graduate School of Business Administration and its College of Commerce. He specializes in hospital management, in particular, in hospital management evaluation, hospital management methods and improvements (Kaizen) and in hospital management using a balanced scorecard. Professor Takahashi also serves as Chairman of the Japan Association for Healthcare Balanced Scorecard Studies, is an executive of the Nippon Academy of Management and the Japan Academy of Management, and is a board member of the Japan Society for Healthcare Administration. Professor Takahashi has edited, authored or co-authored 27 books and 134 articles, and has been an editorial board member and/or a reviewer for a number of journals. He has extensive international experience, serving as a consultant to and/or presenting courses for academic and governmental purposes in Taiwan, Vietnam and Canada.

Nobuyuki Tokoro is Professor of Business Administration at the College of Commerce and the Graduate School of Business Administration at Nihon University. His research has been published in international journals such as *Asian Business and Management*, among others. He also has published several books in Japanese.

Index